A John Brown
Reader

A JOHN BROWN READER

DOVER THRIFT EDITIONS

John Brown,
Frederick Douglass,
W.E.B. Du Bois, and Others

DOVER PUBLICATIONS, INC.
GARDEN CITY, NEW YORK

DOVER THRIFT EDITIONS

GENERAL EDITOR: SUSAN L. RATTINER
EDITOR OF THIS VOLUME: MICHAEL CROLAND

Bibliographical Note

This Dover edition, first published in 2021, is a new selection reprinted from standard texts. Misspellings, minor inconsistencies, and other style vagaries derive from the original texts and have been retained for the sake of authenticity. A new introductory Note has been specially prepared for this edition. Readers should be forewarned that the text contains racial and cultural references of the era in which it was written and may be deemed offensive by today's standards.

Library of Congress Cataloging-in-Publication Data

Names: Brown, John, 1800–1859, author. | Douglass, Frederick, 1818–1895, author. | Du Bois, W.E.B. (William Edward Burghardt), 1868–1963, author.
Title: A John Brown reader / John Brown, Frederick Douglass, W.E.B. Du Bois, and others.
Description: Dover thrift editions. | Garden City, New York : Dover Publications, Inc., 2021. | Series: Dover thrift editions | Summary: "Besides a selection of letters by the abolitionist himself, this original collection includes an excerpt from W.E.B. Du Bois's biography, John Brown; addresses by Frederick Douglass and Ralph Waldo Emerson; and poetry by Louisa May Alcott"—Provided by publisher.
Identifiers: LCCN 2020030833 | ISBN 9780486845623 (trade paperback)
Subjects: LCSH: Brown, John, 1800–1859. | Brown, John, 1800–1859—Correspondence.
Classification: LCC E451 .D732 2021 | DDC 973.7/116092—dc23
LC record available at https://lccn.loc.gov/2020030833

Manufactured in the United States by LSC Communications
84562101
www.doverpublications.com

2 4 6 8 10 9 7 5 3 1

2020

Note

John Brown was born in 1800 in Connecticut, and he spent most of his childhood in Ohio. His father was a firm opponent of slavery, and the family's home was a safe house for fugitive slaves via the Underground Railroad. At age twelve, Brown saw the beating of an enslaved African American boy, and the experience informed his worldview.

After being ordained as a Congregational minister, Brown worked as a tanner, a sheep drover, a wool merchant, a farmer, and a land speculator, struggling to support his large family.

Brown got involved in the abolitionist movement after Presbyterian minister and antislavery activist Elijah P. Lovejoy was murdered in 1837. Brown declared, "I consecrate my life to the destruction of slavery!"

In 1849, Brown and his family moved to an African American community in Upstate New York, which was funded by abolitionist Gerrit Smith. Brown bought a farm and advised local African American communities.

Whereas many abolitionists were pacifists, Brown became passionate about taking aggressive actions to achieve emancipation and justice for enslaved African Americans.

In 1855, he followed five of his sons to the Kansas Territory in support of antislavery forces. As part of the conflict known as Bleeding Kansas, Brown led antislavery guerillas. After slavery sympathizers plundered Lawrence, Kansas, in 1856, Brown felt that he was on a divine mission for vengeance. He led the Pottawatomie Massacre, in which five proslavery men were killed.

In 1858, Brown worked to establish a stronghold for fugitive slaves in the mountains of Maryland and Virginia. He gained financial backing from Smith and other prominent abolitionists.

In October 1859, Brown led twenty-one abolitionists in a raid on an armory in Harpers Ferry, Virginia (now West Virginia). They took hostages and battled against a militia before surrendering to troops led by Col. Robert E. Lee. Brown hoped that escaped slaves would join his "army of emancipation." Although a slave revolt did not come to fruition, he inspired opponents of slavery, and historians view the incident as a dress rehearsal for the Civil War.

Brown was wounded in the raid, and ten of his followers were killed. He was tried for murder, slave insurrection, and treason. On December 2, 1859, he was hanged.

This volume collects definitive documents by and about Brown. Part 1 includes his letters, essays, and speeches, ranging from 1832 to the day of his execution in 1859. Part 2 presents the literary heritage he inspired, with prose and poetry by Victor Hugo, Louisa May Alcott, Herman Melville, Ralph Waldo Emerson, Henry David Thoreau, Frederick Douglass, Carl Sandburg, and Stephen Vincent Benet, beginning with a letter to the editor from Brown's death date. Part 3 features several chapters from *John Brown*, the 1909 biography by W.E.B. Du Bois, an African American civil rights activist, scholar, and author of seventeen books.

Contents

Part 1

In His Own Words

Red Rock, Iowa, 15th, July, 1857.

Mr Henry L Stearns   My Dear Young Friend

I have not forgotten my promise to write you; but my constant care, & anxiety: have obliged me [to] put it off a long time. I do not flatter myself that I *can* write anything that will very much interest you: but have concluded to send you a short story of a certain boy of my acquaintance: & for convenience & shortness of name, I will call him John. This story will be mainly a naration of follies & errors; which it is to be hoped *you may avoid*; but there is one thing connected with it, which will be calculated to encourage any young person to perse-vereing effort: & that is the degree of success *in accomplishing his objects* which to a great extent marked the course of this boy throughout my entire acquaintance with him; notwithstanding his moderate capacity; & still more moderate acquirements.

John was born May 9th 1800, at Torrington, Litchfield Co. Connecticut; of poor but respectable parents: a decendant on the side of his Father of one of the company of the Mayflower who landed at Plymouth 1620. His Mother was decended from a man who came at an early period to New England from Amsterdam, in Holland. Both his Fathers and his Mothers Fathers served in the war of the revolution: His Fathers Father; died in a barn at New York while in the service, in 1776.

I cannot tell you of anything in the first Four years of Johns life worth mentioning save that at that *early age* he was tempted by Three Large Brass Pins belonging to a girl who lived in the fam-ily & *stole them*. In this he was detected by his Mother; & after having a full day to think of the wrong: received from her a thorough whipping. When he was Five years old his Father moved to Ohio; then a wilderness filled with wild beasts, & Indians. During the long journey which was performed in part or mostly with an *Ox team*; he was called on by turns to assist a boy Five years older (who had been adopted by his Father & Mother) & learned to think he could accomplish *smart things* in driving the Cows; & riding the horses. Sometimes he met with Rattle Snakes which were very large; & which some of the company generally managed to kill. After getting to Ohio in 1805 he was for some time rather afraid of the Indians, & of their Rifles; but this soon wore off: & he used to hang about them quite as much as was consistent with good manners; & learned a trifle of their talk. His Father learned to dress Deer Skins & at 6 years old John was installed

3

a young Buck Skin. He was perhaps rather observing as he ever after remembered the entire process of Deer Skin *dressing*; so that he could at any time dress his own leather such as Squirel, Raccoon, Cat, Wolf, or Dog Skins: & also learned to make Whip Lashes: which brought him some change at times; & was of considerable service in many ways. At Six years old John began to be quite a rambler in the wild new country finding birds and Squirels, & sometimes a wild Turkeys nest. But about this period he was placed in the School of *adversity*: which my young friend was a most necessary part of his early training. You may *laugh* when you come to read about it; but these were *sore trials* to John: whose earthly treasures were very few, & *small*. These were the beginning of a severe but *much needed course* of dicipline which he afterward was to pass through; & which it is to be hoped has learned him before this time that the Heavenly Father sees it best to take all the little things out of his hands which he has ever placed in them. When John was in his Sixth year a poor *Indian boy* gave him a Yellow Marble the first he had ever seen. This he thought a great deal of; & kept it a good while; but at last *he lost it* beyound recovery. *It took years to heal the wound*; & I *think* he cried at times about it. About Five months after this he caught a young Squirel tearing off his tail in doing it and getting severely bitten at the same time himself. He however held on *to the little bob tail Squirrel*; & finally got him perfectly tamed, so that he almost idolized his pet. *This too he lost*; by its wandering away; or by getting killed: & for a year or Two John was *in mourning*; & looking at all Squirrels he could see to try & discover Bob tail, *if possible*. I must not neglect to tell you of a verry *bad & foolish* habbit to which John was somewhat addicted. I mean *telling lies*: generally to screen himself from blame; or from punishment. He could not well endure to be reproached; & I now think had he been oftener encouraged to be entirely frank; by making *frankness a kind of atonement* for some of his faults; he would not have been so often guilty of this fault; nor have been obliged to struggle *so long* in after life with *so mean* a habit.

John was *never quarrelsome*; but was *excessively* fond of the *hardest & roughest* kind of plays; & could *never get enough* [*of*] them. Indeed when for a short time he was sometimes sent to School the opportunity it afforded to wrestle, & Snow ball, & run, & jump, & knock off old seedy Wool hats; offered to him almost the only compensation for the confinement, & restraints of school. I need not tell you that with such feeling & but little chance of going to school *at all*: he did not become much of a schollar. He would always choose to stay at home & work hard rather than be sent to school; & during the warm season might generally be seen *barefooted, & bare-headed*: with Buckskin Breeches suspended often with one leather strap over his shoulder but sometimes with Two. To be sent off through the wilderness alone to very considerable distances was particularly his delight; & in this he was often indulged so that by the time he was Twelve years old he was sent off more than a Hundred Miles with companies of cattle; & he would have thought his character much injured had he been obliged to be helped in any such job. This was a boyish kind of feeling but characteristic however.

At Eight years old John was left a Motherless boy which loss was complete & permanent for not withstanding his Father again married to a sensible, inteligent, & on many accounts a very estimable woman: *yet he never addopted her in feeling*: but continued to pine after his own Mother for years. This opperated very unfavourably uppon him; as he was both naturally fond of females; & withall extremely diffident; & deprived him of a suitable conne[c]ting link between the different sexes; the want of which might under some circumstances have proved his ruin.

When the war broke out *with England*; his Father soon commenced furnishing the troops with beef cattle, the collecting & driving of which afforded him some opportunity for the chase (on foot) of wild steers, & other cattle through the woods. During this war he had some chance to form his own boyish judgment of *men & measures*: & to become somewhat familiarly acquainted with some who have figured before the country since that time. The effect of what he saw during the war was to so far disgust him with Military affairs that he would neither train, *or drill*; but paid fines; & got along like a Quaker untill his age finally has cleared him of Military duty.

During the war with England a circumstance occurred that in the end made him a most *determined Abolitionist*: & led him to declare, or *Swear: Eternal war* with slavery. He was staying for short time with a very gentlemanly landlord since a United States Marshall who held a slave boy near his own age very active, inteligent, & good feeling; & to whom John was under considerable obligation for numerous little acts of kindness. *The Master* made a great pet of John: brought him to table with his first company; & friends; called their attention to every little smart thing he *said or did*: & to the fact of his being more than a hundred miles from home with a company of cattle alone; while the *negro boy* (who was fully if not more than his equal) was badly clothed, poorly fed; & *lodged in cold weather.* & beaten before his eyes with Iron Shovels or any other thing that came first to hand. This brought John to reflect on the wretched, hopeless condition, of *Fatherless & Motherless* slave *children*: for such children have neither Fathers or Mothers to protect, & provide for them. He sometimes would raise the question: *is God their Father?*

At the age of Ten years, an old friend induced him to read a little history; & offered him the free use of a good library by; which he acquired some taste for reading: which formed the principle part of his early education: & diverted him in a great measure from bad company. He by this means grew to be very fond of the company, & conversation of old & inteligent persons. He never attempted to dance in his life; nor did he ever learn to know *one* of a pack of *Cards,* from *another.* He learned nothing of Grammer; nor did he get at school so much knowledge of comm[on] Arithmetic as the Four ground rules. This will give you some general idea of the first Fifteen years of his life: during which time he became very strong & large of his age & ambitious to perform the full labour of a man; at almost any kind of hard work. By reading the lives of great, wise, & good men their sayings, & writings; he grew to a dislike of vain & frivolous *conversation, & persons*; & was often greatly obliged by the kind manner in which older, & more inteligent persons treated him at their houses; & in conversation; which was a great relief on account of his extreme bashfulness.

He very early in life became ambitious to excel in doing anything he undertook to perform. This kind of feeling I would reccommend to all young persons both *male & female*: as it will certainly tend to secure admission to the company of the more inteligent; & better portion of every community. By all means endeavour to excel in some laudable pursuit.

I had like to have forgotten to tell you of one of Johns misfortunes which set rather hard on him while a young boy. He had by some means *perhaps* by gift of his Father become the owner of a little Ewe Lamb which did finely till it was about Two Thirds grown; & then sickened & died. This brought another protracted *mourning season*: not that he felt the pecuniary loss so heavily: for that was never his disposition: but so strong & earnest were his atachments.

John had been taught from earliest childhood to "fear God & keep his commandments;" & though quite skeptical he had always by turns felt much serious doubt as to his future well being; & about this time became to some extent a convert to Christianity & ever after a firm believer in the divine authenticity of the Bible. With this book he became very familiar: & possessed a most unusual memory of it[s] entire contents.

Now some of the things I have been *telling of*; were just such as I would reccommend to you: & I would like to know that you had selected those out; & adopted them as part of your own plan of life; & I wish you to have some *deffinite plan*. Many seem to have none: & others never stick to any that do they form. This was not the case with John. He followed up with *tenacity* whatever he set about so long as it answered his general purpose: & hence he rarely failed in some good degree to effect the things he undertook. This was so much the case that he *habitually expected to succeed* in his undertakings. With this feeling *should be coupled*; the consciousness that our plans are right in themselves.

During the period I have named John had acquired a kind of ownership to certain animals of some little value but as he had come to understand that the *title* of *minors* might be a little imperfect; he had recourse to various means in order to secure a more *independant*; & *perfect* right of property. One of those means was to exchange with his Father for something of far less value. Another was by trading with other persons for something his Father had never owned. Older persons have sometimes found difficulty with *titles*:

From Fifteen to Twenty years old, he spent most of his time working at the Tanner & Curriers trade keeping Bachelors hall; & he officiateing as Cook; & for most of the time as foreman of the establishment under his Father. During this period he found much trouble with some of the bad habits I have mentioned & with some that I have not told you of: His con[s]cience urging him forward with great power in this matter: but his close attention to *business*; & success in its management: together with the way he got along with a company of men, & boys; made him quite a favorite with the serious & more inteligent portion of older persons. This was so much the case; & secured for him so many little notices from those he esteemed; that his vanity was very much fed by it; & he came forward to manhood quite full of self conceit; & self confident: notwithstanding his *extreme* bashfulness. A younger brother used sometimes to remind him of this: & to repeat to him *this expression* which you may somewhere find; "A King against whom there is no rising up." The habit so early formed of being obeyed rendered him in after life too much disposed to speak in an imperious or dictating way. From Fifteen years & upward he felt a good deal of anxiety to learn; but could only read, & studdy a little; both for want of time; & on account of inflamation of the eyes. He however managed by the help of books to make himse[lf] tolerably well acquainted with common Arithmetic; & Surveying; which he practiced more or less after he was Twenty years old.

At a little past Twenty years led by his own inclination & *prompted also* by his Father he married a *remarkably plain*; but neat industrious & economical girl; of excellent character; earnest piety; & good practical common sence; about one year younger than himself. This woman by her mild, frank, & *more than all else*: by her very consistent conduct; acquired; & ever while she lived maintained a most powerful; and good influence over him. Her plain but kind admonitions generally had the right effect; without arousing his haughty obstinate temper. John began early in life to discover a great liking to fine Cattle, Horses, Sheep; & Swine; & as soon as circumstances would enable him he began to be a practical *Shepherd*: *it being* a calling for which *in early life* he had a kind of *enthusiastic longing*: together with the idea that as a business it bid fair to afford him the means of carrying out his greatest or principle object. I have now given you a kind of general idea of the early life of this boy; & if I believed it would be worth the trouble; or afford much interest to any good feeling person; I might be tempted to tell you something of his course in after life; or manhood. I do not say that I *will do it*.

You will discover that in using up my *half* sheets to *save paper*; I have written Two pages, so that one does not follow the other as it should. I have no time to write it over; & but for unavoidable hindrances in travelling I can hardly say when I should have written what I have. With an honest desire for your best good I subscribe myself   Your Friend

J Brown

P S I had like to have forgotten to acknowledge your contribution in aid of the cause in which I serve. God Allmighty *bless you*; my Son:

J B

Randolph, Pa., August 11, 1832

Dear Father:

We are again smarting under the rod of our Heavenly Father. Last night about eleven o'clock my affectionate, dutiful and faithful Dianthe (to use her own words) bade 'farewell to Earth.' My own health is so poor that I have barely strength to give you a short history of what passed since I wrote you last. Her health, I think mentioned in my last letter, was very poor, partly owing to her pregnancy but more perhaps to a difficulty about her heart. She however kept about a little . . . [The doctor] advised her situation was critical, but this information did not depress her spirits. She made answer 'I thought I might go to rest on God's Sabbath.' At her request the children were brought to her and she with heavenly composure gave faithful advice to each.

Our hopes were quite revived for the first twenty-four hours for her recovery. About that time her difficulty of the heart palpitation became so great that we thought her dying for some hours. She however revived but not to gain much strength after. Her reason was unimpaired and her mind composed with the Peace of God. Tomorrow she is to lay beside our little son.

From your sorrowing son

John Brown

Randolph, Nov. 21, 1834.

Dear Brother,—As I have had only one letter from Hudson since you left here, and that some weeks since, I begin to get uneasy and apprehensive that all is not well. I had satisfied my mind about it for some time, in expectation of seeing father here, but I begin to give that up for the present. Since you left me I have been trying to devise some means whereby I might do something in a practical way for my poor fellow-men who are in bondage, and having fully consulted the feelings of my wife and my three boys, we have agreed to get at least one negro boy or youth, and bring him up as we do our own,— viz., give him a good English education, learn him what we can about the history of the world, about business, about general subjects, and, above all, try to teach him the fear of God. We think of three ways to obtain one: First, to try to get some Christian slave-holder to release one to us. Second, to get a free one if no one will let us have one that is a slave. Third, if that does not succeed, we have all agreed to submit to considerable privation in order to buy one. This we are now using means in order to effect, in the confident expectation that God is about to bring them all out of the house of bondage.

I will just mention that when this subject was first introduced, Jason had gone to bed; but no sooner did he hear the thing hinted, than his warm heart kindled, and he turned out to have a part in the discussion of a subject of such exceeding interest. I have for years been trying to devise some way to get a school a-going here for blacks, and I think that on many accounts it would be a most favorable location. Children here would have no intercourse with vicious people of their own kind, nor with openly vicious persons of any kind. There would be no powerful opposition influence against such a thing; and should there be any, I believe the settlement might be so effected in future as to have almost the whole influence of the place in favor of such a school. Write me how you would like to join me, and try to get on from Hudson and thereabouts some first-rate abolitionist families with you. I do honestly believe that our united exertions alone might soon, with the good hand of our God upon us, effect it all.

This has been with me a favorite theme of reflection for years. I think that a place which might be in some measure settled with a view to such an object would be much more favorable to such an undertaking than would any such place as Hudson, with all its conflicting interests and feelings; and I do think such advantages ought to be afforded the young blacks, whether they are all to be immediately set free or not. Perhaps we might, under God, in that way do more towards breaking their yoke effectually than in any other. If the young blacks of our country could once become enlightened, it would most assuredly operate on slavery like firing powder confined in rock, and all slaveholders know it well. Witness their heaven-daring laws against teaching blacks. If once the Christians in the free States would set to work in earnest in teaching the blacks, the people of the slaveholding States would find themselves constitutionally driven to set about the work of emancipation immediately. The laws of this State are now such that the inhabitants of any township may raise by a tax in aid of the State school-fund any amount of money they may choose by a vote, for the purpose of common schools, which any child may have access to by application. If you will join me in this undertaking, I will make with you any arrangement of our temporal concerns that shall be fair. Our health is good, and our prospects about business rather brightening.

Affectionately yours,
John Brown

New York 5th Decem 1838

Dear Wife and Children

A kind & merciful God has kept me hitherto. I arrived here four days ago, but shall probably leave soon. I have not had the pleasure of hearing from you since I left or yet, hope I may before I leave. I have not yet succeeded in my business, but think the prospect such that I do not by any means despair of final success. As to that, may Gods holy will be done. My unceasing and anxious care for the present and everlasting welfare of evry [member] of my family seems to be threefold as I get seperated farther and farther from them. Forgive the many faults & foibles you have seen in me, and try to proffit by anything good in either my example, or my council; Try and not any of you get weary of well doing. Should the older boys read and coppy my old letters as I proposed to them, I want to have them all preserved with care. The time of my return is verry uncertain, but will be soon as is in any way consistent I will write you again, when I have opportunity. I know of no place where I shall be so likely to hear from you as at this place at present and God Allmighty bless and keep you all

your affectionate Husband and Father
John Brown

New Hartford, 12th June 1839

My dear wife and children;

I write to let you know that I am in comfortable health, and that I expect to be on my way home in the course of a week, should nothing befal me. If I am longer detained, I will write you again. The cattle business has succeeded about as I expected, but I am now somewhat in fear that I shall fail of getting the money I expected on the loan. Should that be the will of Providence, I know of no other way but we must consider ourselves very poor; for our debts must be paid, if paid at a sacrifice. Should that happen (though it may not) I hope God, who is rich in mercy, will grant us grace to conform to our circumstances with cheerfulness and true resignation. I want to see each of my dear family very much, but must wait God's time. Try all of you to do the best you can, and do not one of you be discouraged; tomorrow may be a much brighter day. Cease not to ask God's blessing on yourselves and me. Keep this letter wholly to yourselves, excepting that I expect to start for home soon, and that I did not write confidently about my success, should any one inquire. Edward is well, and Oliver Mills. You may show this to my father, but to no one else. I am not without great hopes of getting relief, I would not [now] have you understand, but things have looked more unfavorable for a few days. I think I shall write again before I start. Earnestly commending you every one to God and to his mercy, which endureth forever, I remain

Your affectionate husband and father
John Brown

The friends here I believe are all well

J. B.

Winchester, Ct. 19th June 1839.

My Dear Wife and Children;

Through the great goodness of God, I am once more on my way home, and should nothing befall me, I hope to see you all by about the 1st of July. I expect to return by way of our place in Pa.

I have left no stone unturned to place my affairs in a more settled and comfortable shape, and now should I, after all my sacrifice of body and mind be compelled to return, a very poor man, how would my family receive me? I do not say that such will be the fact, but such may be the fact. I expect at any rate to bring all of you that can read, a book that has afforded me great support and comfort during my long absence.

I have got the book for John that he wanted me to get for him and mean to get the truss at Albany for Jason.

Should nothing hinder me on the road, perhaps you may not hear from me till I return.

Your affectionate husband and father,
John Brown

Franklin Mills, 27th Aug 1839

George Kellogg, Esqr

Dear Sir:

Yours of the 2nd was received in season, & I have no excuse for not answering it promptly, except that I have found it hard to take up my pen to record, & to publish, my own shame, & abuse of the confidence of those whom I esteem, & who have treated me as a friend, & as a brother. I flattered myself till now, with the hope that I might be able to render a more favorable account of myself, but the truth, & the whole truth, shall be told. When I saw you at Vernon, I was in dayly expectation of receiving a number of thousands of dollars from Boston, something over five of which I owed for money I had used belonging to our cattle company, (viz Wadsworth, Wells & myself). On the day I was to set out for home, as I was disappointed of the money I expected, I found no alternative but to go to jail, or to pledge the money the money [sic] you had confided to my trust, & in my extremity I did so with the most of it, pledging it for thirty days, believing that in less than that time I could certainly redeem it, as I expected a large amount from a source I did believe I could depend uppon. Though I have been waiting in painful anxiety I have been disappointed still, & as the best course I could take, I have made an assignment of all my real & personal property for the benefit of my creditors generally, as our laws forbid any preference. I think my property much more than sufficient to satisfy all demands, & that I shall not have to subject you to anything worse in the end than disappointment & delay. I am determined that shall be all, if I & my family work out by the month, & by the day, to make up a full return. I have yet hopes of relief from Boston, & should that be, it will set matters in measure to right again. I have disposed of about 40 yards of your cloth, & find it would go well if my affairs had stood as I expected. Wool has sold at much higher prices here than was expected, & higher than I should have dared to pay had your money been in my possession when I got home.

Unworthily yours

John Brown

Tyler Co Va 27th April 1840

My Dear Wife & Children

I arived on the 17th at this place. Have been well ever since I lef[t] you & every where kindly used. Have made some progress in my business; but do not now expect to get through before the 8 or 9 of May. I like the country as well as I expected, & its inhabitants rather better I think we can find a place in it that will answer all the purposes for which we kneed this world, & have seen the spot where if it be the will of Providence, I hope one day to live with my family. I do not find the season so forward as I expected compared with our Ohio country but to enable you to compare a little I would say that some have planted their Corn more than a week since. Onion tops are pretty well grown, & I saw Potatoes out of the ground more than a week ago on the river. Apples are about the size of large Peas & other things about in the same proportion Were the inhabitants as resolute and industrious, as the northern people, & did they understand how to manage as well, they would become rich, but they are not generally so. They seem to have no Idea of improvement in their Cattle Sheep, or Hogs nor to know the use of enclosed pasture fields for their stock, but spend a large portion of their time in hunting for their Cattle, Sheep & Horses, & the same habit continues from Father to Son. They have so little idea of moveing off any thing they have to sell, or of going away for any thing they kneed to buy, that their Merchants extort uppon them prodigiously. By compareing them with the people of other parts of the Country, & world, I can see new and abundant proof that knowledge is power. I think we might be verry useful to them on many accounts, were we so disposed. May God in mercy keep us all, & enable us to get wisdom, and with all our getting or looseing to get understanding

Affectionately yours
John Brown

I intended to have left word to have some one go to Dazlys for Upper leather so that Jason might have a pair of boots made, but forgot it
Yours J B

Hudson 18th Jany 1841

Dear Son John

Since I parted with you at Hudson some thoughts have passed through my mind which my intence anxiety for your welfare prom[p]ts me to communicate by writing. I think the situation in which you have been placed by Providence at this early period of your life will afford to yourself and others some little test of the sway you may be expected to exert over mind in after life, & I am glad on the whole to have you brought in some measure to the test in your youth. If you cannot now go into a disordered country school and gain its confidence, & esteem, & reduce it to good order, & waken up the energies & the verry soul of every rational being in it yes of every mean ill behaved, ill governed, snotty, boy & girl that compose it; & secure the good will of the parents, then how how how are you to stimulate Asses to attempt a passage of the Alps. If you run with footmen & they should we[a]ry you how should you contend with horses. If in the land of peace they have wearied you, then how how how will you do in the swelling of Jordan. Shall I answer the question myself. If any man lack wisdom let him ask of God who giveth liberally unto all and upbraideth not. Let me say to you again love them all & commend them, & yourself to the God to whom Solomon sought in his youth & he shall bring it to pass. You have heard me tell of dividing a school into two great spelling classes & of its effects if you should think best & can remember the process you can try it. Let the grand reason that one course is right, & another wrong be kept continueally before your own mind & before your school

From your affectionate father

John Brown

Richfield, Oct. 17, 1842

Whereas I, John Brown, on or about the 15th day of June, A.D. 1839, received of the New England Company (through their agent, George Kellogg, Esq.), the sum of twenty-eight hundred dollars for the purchase of wool for said company, and imprudently pledged the same for my own benefit, and could not redeem it; and whereas I have been legally discharged from my obligations by the laws of the United States,—I hereby agree (in consideration of the great kindness and tenderness of said Company toward me in my calamity, and more particularly of the moral obligation I am under to render to all their due), to pay the same and the interest thereon, from time to time, as Divine Providence shall enable me to do. Witness my hand and seal

John Brown

Richfield, Summit County, Ohio, Oct. 17, 1842

George Kellogg, Esq.

Dear Sir,—I have just received information of my final discharge as a bankrupt in the District Court, and I ought to be grateful that no one of my creditors has made any opposition to such discharge being given. I shall now, if my life is continued, have an opportunity of proving the sincerity of my past professions, when legally free to act as I choose. I am sorry to say that in consequence of the unforeseen expense of getting the discharge, the loss of an ox, and the destitute condition in which a new surrender of my effects has placed me, with my numerous family, I fear this year must pass without my effecting in the way of payment what I have encouraged you to expect (notwithstanding I have been generally prosperous in my business for the season).

Respectfully your unworthy friend,
John Brown

                                    Richfield 29th Oct 1842
Whereas Heman Oviatt of this place on or about 17th September
AD 1839 paid on my account the sum of $5667.96 and costs of
Court, and whereas I have since been discharged from all legal
obligations by a decree of the United States Court I hereby (in consideration of numerous favors received of said Oviatt, but more
particularly on account of the ever binding moral obligation I am
under to render to all their due) agree to pay the same and the interest thereon from time to time (together with all other equitable claims
of said Oviatt against me) as Divine Providence shall hereafter enable
me to do.

               Witness my hand and Seal
                          John Brown   Seal

                                    Richfield 25th Sept 1843
Dear Son
   God has seen fit to visit us with the pestilence since you left us,
and Four of our number sleep in the dust, and Four of us that are
still living have been more or less unwell but appear to be nearly
recovered. On the 4th Sept Charles was taken with the Dysentery
and died on the 11th, about the time that Charles died Sarah, Peter, &
Austin were taken with the same complaint. Austin died on the 21st,
Peter on the 22d & Sarah on the 23d and were all buried together
in one grave. This has been to us all a bitter cup indeed, and we have
drunk deeply, but still the Lord reigneth and blessed be his great and
holy name forever. In our sore affliction there is still some comfort.
Sarah (like your own Mother) during her sickness discovered great
composure of mind, and patience, together with strong assureance
at times of meeting God in Paradise. She seemed to have no idea of
recovering from the first, nor did she ever express the least desire
that she might, but rather the reverse. We fondly hope that she is
not disappointed. They were all children towards whom perhaps we
might have felt a little partial but they all now lie in a little row
together. Jason wants to add a few lines & I shall be short. I am yet
feeble from the same disorder which may account for some of my
blunders. We hope to see you when your term is out, it perhaps will
not be best before. May you be enabled to cleanse your way
                        [signature cut out]

Dear Brother

These days are days of rebuke and severe trial with us. A few days ago you parted with us all in good health and cheerfulness, but now how different. Little did any of us think that that parting would be final with four of our number. I will not be lengthy, let us not murmur, The Judge of all the Earth, has done, and will do right. But let us give glory and honor and power and thanks unto him that sitteth on the throne forever and ever.

Your Brother
Jason Brown

Agreement—John Brown & Simon Perkins

The undersigned, Simon Perkins, Jr. and John Brown have this day agreed as follows viz. They agree to place the flocks of sheep which they each now have in a joint concern at their value, and to share equally the gain or loss yearly, commencing on the 15th day of April of each year.

Said Perkins agrees to furnish all the food and shelter that shall be necessary for the good of the flock from the 1st of December of each year to the 15th of April of each year.

Said Brown agrees on his part to furnish throughout the year all the care and attention of every description which the good of the flock may require, wash the sheep, shear the wool, sack and ship the same for market in the neatest and best manner, an equal set-off against the food &c. necessary for the wintering of the flock.

The said parties agree to share equally the pasturing, and all other expenses of said flock yearly, and to improve and increase the same from time to time as the business will justify, and they may agree.

Said Perkins agrees to let said Brown the frame dwelling-house on his farm (south of the house in which he now lives) door-yards, garden grounds, and the privilege of getting wood for fuel, for the rent of thirty-dollars a year commencing on the First of April next. Said Brown agrees to pay that amount yearly, so long as he may continue to occupy said house, from his share of the proceeds of said flock.

Said Brown agrees to harvest the turnips and potatoes which said Perkins may raise yearly for the use of said flock.

This agreement to remain in force for full years until the parties shall think proper to alter or dissolve it.

Witness our names this ninth day of January 1844

[Signed] Simon Perkins, Junior
John Brown

Richfield 11th Jany. 1844

Dear Son

Your Letter dated 21st Dec was received some days ago but I have purposely delayed till now in order to comply the better with your request that I should write you about every thing. We are all in health; amongst the number is a new sister about three weeks old. I know of no one of our friends that is not comfortably well. I have just met with Father he was with us a few days since & all were then well in that quarter. Our flock is well and we seem to be overtakeing our business in the tanery. Divine Providence seems to smile on our works at this time, I hope we shall not prove unthankful for any favour, nor forget the giver. I have gone to sleep a great many times while writing the above. The boys and Ruth are trying to improve some this winter & are effecting a little I think I have lately entered into a copartnership with Simon Perkins Jr of Akron with a view to carry on the Sheep business extensively He is to furnish all the feed, & shelters for wintering as a set off against our taking all the care of the flock. All other expences we are to share equally, & to divide the proffits equally This arangement will reduce our cash rents at least $250, yearly & save our hireing help in Haying. We expect to keep the Capt Oviatt farm for pasturing, but my family will go into a verry good House belonging to Mr Perkins say from half a mile, to a mile, out of Akron. I think this is the most comfortable and the most favourable arangement of my worldly concerns that I ever had, and calculated to afford us more leisure for improvement, by day, & by Night, than any other I do hope that God has enabled us to make it in mercy to us, & not that he should send leanness into our soul. Our time will all be at our own command except the care of the flock. We have nothing to do with providing for them in the winter excepting harvesting Rootabaga and Potatoes. This I think will be considered no mean alliance for our family & I most earnestly hope they they [sic] will have wisdom given to make the most of it. It is certainly endorseing the poor Bankrupt & his family three of whom were but recently in Akron jail in a manner quite unexpected, & proves that notwithstanding we have been a company of Belted Knights, our industrious & steady endeavours to maintain our integrity & our character have not been wholly overlooked. Mr P[erkins] is perfectly advised of our poverty, & the times that have passed over us. Perhaps you may think best to have some connection with this business: I do not know of ANY person in (Richfield) that you would be likely to be fond of hearing from in particular excepting one at

(Cleaveland) and if hearing from ANY person prove to be (a verry up stream) business I would advise not to worry at present. Will you let me know how it stands between you & all parties concerned.

Your Father John Brown

I will try to send at least $1, the next time I write you. Do not pay the Postage on what you write me

JB

Akron 23d May 1845

Dear Son John

Yours of the 28th April we did not get verry seasonably as we have been verry busy, & not at the P office often. We are all obliged for your letter & I hope thankful for any comforts or success that may attend you. If the days of mourning have in deed & in truth *ceased*; then I trust all is well, all is well, as it should be, & I have known fair days to follow after verry foul wether. The great trouble is we are apt to get too damp in a wet foggy spell. We are all well but little Anne who is afflicted with a singular eruption of the skin: & is withall quite unwell. We get along in our business as well as we ever have done I think. We loose some sheep but not as many as for two seasons past. Matters seem to go well betwixt us, & our friend Perkins, & for any thing that I know our worldly prospects are as good as we can bear. I hope that entire leanness of soul may not attend any little success in business. I do not know as we have yet any new plans. When we have we will let you hear. We are nearly through another yeaning time, & have lost but verry few. Have not yet counted Tails: Think there may be about Four Hundred. Never had a finer, or more thrifty lot. Expect to begin washing next week. Have received our medals, & Diploma. They are splendid toys, & appear to be knock down arguments among the sheep folk who have seen them. All were well at Hudson a few days since. Father was here, & had just moved into the Humiston house out west. You did not say in your letter whether you ever conversed with him in regard to his plans for his old age, as was talked of when you were here, & was helping pick sheep. Should like to know if you did, &c. Cannot tell you much more now, except it be that we all appear to think a great deal more about this world than about the next which proves that we are still verry foolish. I leave room for some others of the family to write if they will. Affectionately Yours

John Brown

Springfield Mass 23d July 1846

Friend Perkins
    Dear Sir

Yours of the 10th is received for which we are much obliged & we now are anxiously looking for another. I did not write you last week as I intended in consequence of the extreme press of business. Your kind hint about coppying the letters we write on business is exactly right and will be accepted, & I hope you will continue to give any hints you may think of. We had however commenced doing so on the first day after our arrival here, & I have never found our coppies worth more even now than they have cost. We have received so much wool that our freight bills have given us a good deal of anxiety, & trouble, but have got over that for the present by the sale of our wool yesterday (I mean) our own clip. We sold for 69 cents all round, & are to get 70 cents if the new Tarriff bill does not pass. This is as well as we could do while the bill is pending, & makes the whole business *drag*, & we were badly cramped. We have bargained off some 20 odd thousand lbs to be taken as fast as we can class it. Our experiment will work finely, but we have been a little lame for want of the whole building we occupy only in part, & for want of some 10 to 20 thousand Dollars to deal out in safe advances on wool as received here. Had we been fixed right in these two things our most sanguine expectations would have been exceeded. Our business would yet be vastly increased could we make advances. Please say whether you would think it worth while to undertake it, or whether you would advise to have me affect some arrangement of that kind here. I have no doubt I could find abundance of partners here that would find the means if that were *best,* but I have never named the thing to any one, & do not intend to till you may advise to such steps. I might perhaps arrange with one of the banks here, *if that were best*. However would it suit one of your brothers to come on here, & take hold with us in such an operation. There is no mistake about doing a vast business, & perfectly safe. I have got a standing insurance on $15,000 worth of wool for three months. Cost $23. I intended most of what I have said above for your own ear *exclusively*. The immediate want of some money, & the fear of delay is what will take away perhaps 3/4 of the customers we should otherwise get this year. Persons being so much in a hurry is the principal objection any one raises to the measure. As it now is, it is not bad. It might not do any harm to let it be publicly known what our wool has sold at, with all the panic that now exists in the wool market on account of the

Tarriff. The prospects of good & brisk sales is very different from what it was before the Dough faces passed the bill through the house. If you are not more pressed for time than we are, please let me hear all about matters at home &c &c on receipt of this. We shall neglect to coppy this into our book. If wool sells low we shall feel it more in our own clip than in business here.

Respectfully Yours
John Brown

P S We shall find no difficulty in selling the inferior grades of wool here at some price, & we get the same for it as for selling fine. Can not yet say what Col Dodger wool is worth. Will write again soon.

Yours
JB

Springfield 8th Nov 1846

Sabbath evening

MY DEAR AFFLICTED WIFE & CHILDREN

I yesterday at night returned after an absence of several days from this place & am uterly unable to give any expression of my feelings on hearing of the dreadful news contained in Owens letter of the 30th & Mr. Perkins of the 31st Oct. I seem to be struck almost dumb.

One more dear little feeble child I am to meet no more till the dead small & great shall stand before God. This is a bitter cup indeed, but blessed be God: a brighter day shall dawn; & let us not sorrow as those that have no hope. Oh that we that remain, had wisdom wisely to consider; & to keep in view our latter end. Divine Providence seems to lay a heavy burden; & responsibility on you *my dear Mary*; but I trust you will be enabled to bear it in some measure as you ought. I exceedingly regret that I am unable to return, & be *present* to share your trials with you: but anxious as I am to be once more at home I do not feel at liberty to return yet. I hope to be able to get away before verry long; but cannot say when. I trust that none of you will feel disposed to cast an unreasonable blame on my dear Ruth on account of the dreadful trial we are called [to] suffer; for if the want of proper care in each, & all of us has not been attended with fatal consequenses it is no thanks to us. If I had a right sence of my habitual neglect of my familys Eternal interests; I should probably go crazy. I humbly hope this dreadful afflictive Providence will lead us all more properly to appreciate the amazeing, unforseen, untold, consequences; that hang upon the right or wrong doing of things seemingly of trifling account. Who can tell or comprehend the vast results for good, or for evil; that are to follow the saying of one little word. Evrything worthy of being done *at all*; is worthy of being done in *good earnest,* & in the best possible manner. We are in midling health & expect to write some of you again soon. Our warmest thanks to our kind friends Mr. & Mrs. Perkins & family. From your affectionate husband, & father

John Brown

Springfield 29th Nov 1846

Dear Mary

It is once more Sabbath evening, & kneed I say that with its return
my mind is more than ever filled with the thoughts of home, of my
wife, & my children. In immagination I seem to be present with you;
to share with you the sorrows, or joys you experience. Your letter
dated the 20th was received last night, & afforded one *a real* though
a mournful satisfaction. That you had received; or were to receive a
letter from either John, or Jason, I was in perfect ignorance of; till
you informed me; & I am glad to learn that wholly uninfluenced by
me; they have shown a disposition to afford you all the comfort in
your *deep affliction* which the nature of the case would admit of.
Nothing is scarsely equ[a]l with *me*; to the satisfaction of seeing that
one portion of my *remaining* family are not disposed to exclude from
their sympathies, & their warm affections, another portion. I accept
it as one of the most grateful returns that can be made to me; for any
care or exertions on my part to promote either their present or their
future well being; & while I am able to discover such a feeling, I feel
assured that notwithstanding God has chastised us *often, & sore*; yet
he has not *himself* entirely withdrawn from us, nor forsaken us *utterly*.
The sudden, & dreadful manner in which he has seen fit to call *our
dear little Kitty* to take her leave of us, is I kneed not tell you how
much on mind; but before *Him*; *I* will bow my head in submission, &
hold my peace. I suppose Jason is with you before this can reach
you, & I trust that nothing on his part, or on the part of *any one* of
my older children will be wanting to render your situation as comfortable as may be. Of the motives that lead one into such business as
will, or does deprive me of the society of my family I will say nothing,
but any ideas that *to me* the separation is not a painful one are wholly
mistaken ones. I have sailed over a somewhat stormy sea for nearly half
a century, & have experienced enough to teach me thoroughly that
I may most reasonabl[y] buckle up & be prepared for the tempest.
Mary let us try to maintain a cheerful self command while we are
tossing up & down, & let our motto still be Action, Action; as we
have but one life to live. How long I shall yet feel constrained to stay
here, I am not yet able to foresee, sometimes the prospect seems quite
disheartening, & at other times it brightens. Since Jason left things
look a little more encourageing than at that time. When the day *comes*
that will afford me an opportunity to return I shall be awake to greet
the earliest dawn; if not its *midnight birth.* I want to have you write
me oftener; & as there is another man belonging in Springfield of the

same name as myself, & son, who sometimes opens my letters; you might direct to care of Perkins & Brown. I want to hear how Jason got home, (as he appeared lately to be in rather a poor state of health) & whether you have received the cloth, fish & Tea I had tried to send you or not. Mr. Perkins has done us a great kindness in writing us so often; & has manifested the kindest feeling in all that he has written, & in being midling particular about things at home. I hope he will not get tired of it. I mean to write him again shortly. I neither forget him, nor Mrs. P, or any of their family.

Affectionately Yours
John Brown

I think Ruth promised to write me again

Springfield Mass 5th Jany 1847

Dear Daughter Ruth

Your dated 20th & Jasons dated 16th Decem were both received in season, & were verry grateful to our feelings; as we are anxious to hear from home often; & had become verry uneasy before we got word from Jason. We are midling well & verry much pressed with our work, accounts, & correspondence. We expect now to go home if our lives, & health are spared next month, & we feel rejoiced that the time is so near when we hope to meet you all once more. Sometimes my immagination follows those of my family who have passed behind the scenes, & I would almost rejoice to receive permision to make them a personal visit. I have outlived nearly half of all my numerous family, & I ought to realize that in any event a large proportion of my journey is traveled over. You say you would like verry much to have a letter from me; with as much good advice as I will give.

Well what do you suppose I feel most anxious for; in regard to yourself, & all at home? Would you believe that I ever had any such care on my mind about them, as we read that Job had about his family? (Not that I would ever think to compare myself with Job.) Would you believe that the long story would be that ye *sin* not; that you form no foolish atachment; & that you be not a companion of Fools

Your Affectionate Father
John Brown

Springfield, Mass 7th March 1844 [1847]

My Dear Mary

It is once more Sabbath evening & nothing so much accords with my feelings as to spend a portion of it converseing with the partner of my own choice, & the sharer of my poverty, trials, discredit, & sore afflictions; as well as what of comfort, & seeming prosperity has fallen to my lot; for quite a number of years. I would you should realise that notwithstanding I am absent in boddy I am verry much of the time present in spirit. I do not forget the firm attachment of her who has remained my fast, & faithful affectionate friend, when others said of me (now that he lieth he shall rise up no more.) When I reflect on these things together with the verry considerable difference in our age, as well as all the follies, & faults with which I am justly chargeable, I really admire at your constancy; & I really feel notwith-standing I sometimes chide you severely that you ar[e] *really* my better half. I now feel encouraged to believe that my absence will not be verry long. After being so much away, it seems as if I knew pretty well how to appreciate the quiet of home. There is a peculiar music in the world which a half years absence in a distant country would enable you to understand. Millions there are who have no such thing to lay claim to. I feel considerable regret by turns that I have lived so many years, & have in reality done so verry little to increase the amount of human happiness. I often regret that my manner is no more kind & affectionate to those I really love, & esteem; but I trust my friends will overlook my harsh rough ways when I cease to be in their way; as an occasion of pain, & unhappi-ness. In immagination I often see you in your room with Little Chick; & that strange Anna. You must say to her that Father means to come home before long, & kiss someboddy. I will close for this time by saying what is my growing resolution to endeavour to pro-mote my *own* happiness by doing what I can to render those around me more so. If the large boys do wrong call them alone into your room, & expostulate with them kindly, & see if you cannot reach them by a kind but powerful appeal to their honor. I do not claim that such a theory accords verry much with *my practice*. *I frankly confess it does not*; but I want *your face* to shine even if my own should be dark, & cloudy. You can let the family read this letter, & perhaps you may not feel it a great burden to answer it & let hear me [sic] all about how you get along.

Affectionately Yours
John Brown

Springfield Mass 2d April 1847

Dear Father

Your verry kind as well as rational letter I received last evening. I trust I do in some small measure realize that only a few, *verry few* years will of necessity bring to me a literal accomplishment of the sayings of the Preacher. I am quite sensible of the truth of your remark that my family are quite as well off as though we possessed millions. I hope we may not be left to a feeling of ingratitude or greediness of gain, & I feel unconcious of a desire to become rich. I hope my motive for exerting myself is higher. I feel no inclination to move my family to Springfield on account of any change that I am itching for; & think it verry doubtful whether I ever conclude on it as the last course. My only motive would be to have them with me, if I continue in my present business; *which I am by no means atached too*. I seem to get along midling well, & hope to return in short time. Wrote Jeremiah some days since. I shall pay ten cents verry cheerfully to hear that you are alive, & well at any time; & should not grudge to pay more for such kind & ever seasonable pointing me to the absolute vanity of this worlds treasures; as well as the sollemn picture, which is before me. It affords me great satisfaction to get a letter from you at this period of your life, so handsomely written, so well worded, & so exactly in point both as to manner, & (what is much more) and matter. I intend to preserve it carefully

Your Affectionate Son
John Brown

Sambos Mistakes

Chapter 1st.

For the Rams Horn

Mess Editors Notwithstanding I may have committed a few mistakes in the course of a long life like others of my colored brethren yet you will perceive at a glance that I have always been remarkable for a seasonable discovery of my errors & quick perception of the true course. I propose to give you a few illustrations in this & the following chapters. For instance when I was a boy I learned to read but instead of giving my attention to sacred & profane history by which I might have become acquainted with the true character of God & of man learned the true course for individuals, societies, & nations to pursue stored my mind with an endless variety of rational and practical ideas, profited by the experience of millions of others of all ages, fitted myself for the most important stations in life & fortified my mind with the best & wisest resolutions, & noblest sentiments, & motives, I have spent my whole life devouring silly novels & other miserable trash such as most of newspapers of the day & other popular writings are filled with, thereby unfitting myself for the realities of life & acquiring a taste for nonsense & low wit, so that I have no rellish for sober truth, useful knowledge or practical wisdom. By this means I have passed through life without proffit to myself or others, a mere blank on which nothing worth peruseing is written. But I can see in a twink where I missed it. Another error into [which] I fell in early life was the notion that chewing & smoking tobacco would make a man of me but little inferior to some of the whites. The money I spent in this way would with the interest of it have enabled me to have relieved a great many sufferers supplyed me with a well selected interesting library, & pa[i]d for a good farm for the support & comfort of my old age; whereas I have now neith[er] books, clothing, the satisfaction of having benefited others, nor where to

33

lay my hoary head. But I can see in a moment where I missed it. Another of the few errors of my life is that I have joined the Free Masons Odd Fellows Sons of Temperance, & a score of other secret societies instead of seeking the company of inteligent wise & good men from whom I might have learned much that would be interesting, instructive, & useful & have in that way squandered a great amount of most precious time; & money enough sometime in [a] single year which if I had then put the same out on interest & kept it so would have kept me always above board given me character, & influence amongst men or have enabled me to pursue some respectable calling so that I might employ others to their benefit & improvement, but as it is I have always been poor, in debt, & now obliged to travel about in search of employment as a hostler shoe black & fidler. But I retain all my quickness of perception I can see readily where I missed it.

Chapter 2d

Another error of my riper years has been that when any meeting of colored people has been called in order to consider of any important matter of general interest I have been so eager to display my spouting talents & so tenacious of some trifling theory or other that I have adopted that I have generally lost all sight of the business in hand consumed the time disputing about things of no moment & thereby defeated entirely many important measures calculated to promote the general welfare; but I am happy to say I can see in a minute where I missed it. Another small error of my life (for I never committed great blunders) has been that I never would (for the sake of union in the furtherance of the most vital interests of our race) yield any minor point of difference. In this way I have always had to act with but a few, or more frequently alone & could accomplish nothing worth living for, but I have one comfort, I can see in a minute where I missed it. Another little fault which I have committed is that if in anything another man has failed of coming up to my standard that notwithstanding he might possess many of the most valuable traits & be most admirably adapted to fill some one important post, I would reject him entirely, injure his influence, oppose his measures, & even glory in his defeats while his intentions were good, & his plans well laid. But I have the great satisfaction of being able to say without fear of contradiction that I can see *verry quick* where I missed it.

Chapter 3d

Another small mistake which I have made is that I could never bring myself to practice any present self denial although my theories have been excellent. For instance I have bought expensive gay clothing nice Canes, Watches, Safety Chains, Finger rings, Breast Pins, & many other things of a like nature, thinking I might by that means distinguish myself from the vulgar as some of the better class of whites do. I have always been of the foremost in getting up expensive parties, & running after fashionable amusements, have indulged my appetite freely whenever I had the means (& even with borro[w]ed means) have patronized the dealers in Nuts, Candy, &c freely & have sometimes bought good suppers & was always a regular customer at Livery stables. By these & many other means I have been unable to benefit my suffering Brethren, & am now but poorly able to keep my own Soul & boddy together; but do not think me thoughtless or dull of appre[he]ntion for I can see at once where I missed it.

Another trifling error of my life has been that I have always expected to secure the favour of the whites by tamely submitting to every species of indignity contempt & wrong insted of nobly resisting their brutal aggressions from principle & taking my place as a man & assuming the responsibilities of a man a citizen, a husband, a father, a brother, a neighbour, a friend as God requires of every one (if his neighbour will allow him to do it:) but I find that I get for all my submission about the same reward that the Southern Slaveocrats render to the Dough faced Statesmen of the North for being bribed & browbeat, & fooled & cheated, as the Whigs & Democrats love to be. & think themselves highly honored if they may be allowed to lick up the spittle of a Southerner. I say I get the same reward. But I am uncomm[only] quick sighted I can see in a minute where I missed it. Another little blunder which I made *is,* that while I have always been a most zealous Abolitionist I have been constantly at war with my friends about certain religious tenets. I was first a Presbyterian but I could never think of acting with my Quaker friends for they were the rankest heretiks & the Baptists would be in the water, & the Methodists denied the doctrine of

Election. & of later years since becoming enlightened by Garrison Abby Kelley & other really benevolent persons I have been spending all my force on my friends who love the Sabbath & have felt that all was at stake on that point just as it has proved to be of late in France in the abolition of Slavery in their colonies. Now I cannot doubt Mess Editors notwithstanding I have been unsuccessful that you will allow me full credit for my *peculiar* quick sightedness. I can see in one second where I missed it.

Springfield, Mass., 16th Jan., 1848.

Dear Father,—It is Sabbath evening; and as I have waited now a long time expecting a letter from you, I have concluded to wait no longer for you to write to me. I received the Hudson paper giving an account of the death of *another* of our family. I expected to get a letter from you, and so have been waiting ever since getting the paper. I never seemed to possess a faculty to console and comfort my friends in their grief; I am inclined, like the poor comforters of Job, to sit down in silence, lest in my miserable way I should only add to their grief. Another feeling that I have in your case, is an entire consciousness that I can bring before your mind no new source of consolation, nor mention any which, I trust, you have not long since made full proof of. I need not say that I know how to sympathize with you; for that you equally well understand. I will only utter one word of humble confidence,—"Though He slay me, yet will I trust in Him, and bless His name forever." We are all in health here, but have just been taking another lesson on the uncertainty of all we hold here. One week ago yesterday, Oliver found some root of the plant called hemlock, that he supposed was carrot, and eat some of it. In a few minutes he was taken with vomiting and dreadful convulsions, and soon became senseless. However, by resorting to the most powerful emetics he was recovered from it, like one raised from the dead, almost.

The country in this direction has been suffering one of the severest money pressures known for many years. The consequence to us has been, that some of those who have contracted for wool of us are as yet unable to pay for and take the wool as they agreed, and we are on that account unable to close our business. This, with some trouble and perplexity, is the greatest injury we have suffered by it. We have had no winter as yet scarcely, the weather to-day being almost as warm as summer. We want to hear how you all are very much, and all about how you get along. I hope to visit you in the spring. Farewell.

Your affectionate, unworthy son,
John Brown

Springfield, Mass 22d June 1848.

Hon. J. R. Giddings.

Dear Sir

I have at my command a fund of One Thousand Dollars & some thing over to be expended in premiums of from Three to Ten Eagles each on the best cases of American Woolen goods manufactured from American grown wools *exclusively*. I wish to manage the business in such a way as to benefit the abolition cause to which I am most thoroughly devoted; whilst at the same time I wish to encourage American tallent, & industry. I have thought that were this fund or these premiums to be offered by you in some way as an encouragement to American Tallent, & industry, it might do a two fold good by showing that you are an *American* to the *core*; as well as an abolitionist. It seems to me that it might be so used at this time as to secure favour to the cause of humanity which you have *nobly* defended often. I know perfectly well that I am not the man to offer them but I feel so deeply interested in having the thing done *right* that I will go to Washington if need be to consult about it. Now sir you will see at once that some of the strong interests of the country are to be both *flattered, & benefited,* by the encouragement these premiums offer. All the controll I wish over the matter is to advise as to the kinds of goods that may compete, & who are to be the Judges to award the premiums; & at what time the exhibition shall come off.

Now Dear Sir will you think this matter over & write *me* on the subject directing your letter to care of Perkins & Brown, Springfield Mass *without* putting on your *Frank* as I wish the whole matter to be kept a most *profound secret.*————The premiums will be of a much more liberal character than any heretofore offered in the United States. Perhaps you may think of something that will be of service in carrying out my plan. I do not wish to impose any burden on you that you would not cheerfully bear, & will at any time you *wish* explain to you my reasons for wishing myself to be kept *wholly & absolutely out of sight*. The fund may be increased if best

Verry Respectfully Yours
John Brown of the
Firm of Perkins & Brown

Mr. H. Clay has been called an *American*. *Why* may not Abolitionists?

Springfield Mass 7th Sept 1848

Hon. Joshua R. Giddings

Dear Sir

I have by no means given up the measure I proposed to you at Springfield, but ill health prevented my going to Washington to see you as I intended. Please say to me at what time or times I may find you at home, or at any other points nearer to this place. I wrote you by Telegraph at Washington after I recovered, but it seems that you had then left.

Verry Respectfully Yours
John Brown

Please direct to care of Perkins & Brown as before
Yours in truth
JB

Springfield Mass 10th Jany 1849

Dear Father

Your verry kind & excellent letter of the 1st inst is received & as you say you never loved letters so well as you do now, I will send you one, even though it be a verry poor one. We have had considerable poor health this winter, arising from hard colds mostly. Our youngest child is verry much out of order in the lungs so that we have a good deal of fear that she will not be able to hold out till warm weather. Owens arm is (we think a little) better. We feel a good deal of spirit about the oppressions, & cruelties that are done in the land, but in regard to other verry important interests we are quite too indifferent. I suppose it may well be questioned whether any one duty can be *acceptably* performed; while most others are, neglected. I was on some of the Gerrit Smith lands lying opposite Burlington Vt last fall that he has given away to the blacks & found no objection to them but the high Northern Lattitude in which they lie. They are indeed rather inviting on many accounts. There are a number of good colored families on the ground; most of whom I visited. I can think of no place where I think I would sooner go; *all things considered* than to live with those poor despised Africans to try, & encourage them; & show them a little so far as I am capable how to manage. You kneed not be surprised if at some future day I should do so. Our business is prosperous; to all appearance. Money is becoming more easy. Write us often; the oftener the better. Dr. Humphrey has called twise.

From your Affectionate but unworthy Son   John Brown

Springfield, Mass. 24th May 1849

Friend Perkins
    Dear Sir

Your favour of the 12th inst received, & will now proceed to answer your questions (without repeating) them, in the order in which they come. Those who send wool pay all expenses. The Exchange will cover all expenses of Insurance, Freight, Commission &c &c less by about 2 per cent as near as we can get at it, from Proforma Bills of Sale sent us by two first rate English Houses recommended to us by the Banks in New York. The prospect now is that wool will nett in England full our 1847 prices. Prices have been there about those rates within the last three months. I do not think the present moment as favourable as though they were in a more settled state. Still I think a good sale may be effected, & valuable acquaintances formed even under present circumstances. At any rate we *must do so,* or put the wool under the hammer, the very thing the manufacturers have boasted they would drive us to. All business at Springfield will be closed except the selling of some graded wool for a few who decline sending it to Europe. I do not think of starting until after I see you, which will be (I think) in about three weeks or thereabouts. I should expect to be gone Eight or Nine weeks, & to close up the sales there before returning. Have corresponded with the greater part of those who have sent us fine wool, & as a general thing they say "send off the fine wool & get what you can for it." *I shall pay off all our indebtedness* before leaving by advances of about 50 per cent on the value of the wool here; made by the English Houses to whom we ship. Have begun to ship already. Have hired a farm in Essex Co N. Y. at $50 a year, bought me some cows & an ox team, & started my family on to it for a home until I can close up the wool business here. The small Pox is raging in Springfield. We mean to embrace every opportunity of selling out here & to send for none to Europe who do not fully approve of the measure. I believe however that nineteen out of twenty will choose to have their wool go out of the country under all the circumstances.

                                        Yours Truly

                                                John Brown

Boston 15th Aug 1849

Simon Perkins Esqr

Dear Sir

I write you as follows viz Sail today by Steamer Cambria for Liverpool. Have settled up wool business so far as it could be done at present. Have left matters so at Springfield that I think you will have no trouble with them except it be with Fowler of Westfield. He has been calculating to get a lawyers job out of the business for a good while; & I know of no way to prevent him as we have offered to pay those men either here or in Ohio, unless by your making to them at Medina a specie tendery of the nett proceeds of their wool. John will write you whether they will accept payment here or not; & the amount due each. We have given Fowler from the first candid, & true statements, & such as would satisfy any body *but a little trifling Pettifogger* but he represents things so to those men at Medina that that [sic] they accuse us of fraud. Explanation with them is to no purpose while he contradicts what we say, & they are determined to give him a job. Perhaps were you to see them, & show them my letters to you it might have some good effect. Have reduced our indebtedness at this time to about $13000, all told. Due in Sept with opportunity to renew for 60 days in order to close up some more accounts this indebtedness may have for a time to be some increased. This is provided for should it be needed. Most persons do not expect their accounts closed till we get returns from England. . . .

Your Friend

John Brown

London, Aug. 29, 1849.

Dear Son John,—I reached Liverpool on Sabbath day, the 26th inst., and this place the 27th at evening,—a debtor to Grace for health and for a very pleasant and quick passage. Have called on the Messrs. Pickersgill, and find they have neither sold any wool nor offered any. They think that no time has been lost, and that a good sale can yet be expected. It is now the calculation to offer some of it at the monthly sale, September next, commencing a little before the middle of the month. I have had no time to examine any wools as yet, and can therefore express no opinion of my own in the matter. England is a fine country, so far as I have seen; but nothing so very wonderful has yet appeared to me. Their farming and stone-masonry are very good; cattle, generally more than middling good. Horses, as seen at Liverpool and London, and through the fine country betwixt these places, will bear no comparison with those of our Northern States, as they average. I am here told that I must go to the Park to see the fine horses of England, and I suppose I must; for the streets of London and Liverpool do not exhibit half the display of fine horses as do those of our cities. But what I judge from more than anything is the numerous breeding mares and colts among the growers. Their hogs are generally good, and mutton-sheep are almost everywhere as fat as pork. Tell my friend Middleton and wife that England affords me plenty of roast beef and mutton of the first water, and done up in a style not to be exceeded. As I intend to write you very often I shall not be lengthy; shall probably add more to this sheet before I seal it. Since writing the above, I find that it will be my best way to set out at once for the Continent, and I expect to leave for Paris this evening. So farewell for this time,—now about four o'clock P.M.

Your affectionate father,

John Brown.

London Oct 1849

Simon Perkins Esqr

Dear Sir

I expect to get through with the sale of wool today, & was in hopes of doing it so as to get on my way homeward by steamer tomorrow, but find it cannot be brought about. I find that with all the prejudices that exist against American wools that have come to this country for the most part, that a good sale is out of the question. Many manufacturers that have lately paid from $.74 to more than One Dollar per lb I cannot persuade even to take a single bag to try at $.50. Some are less fearful, & particularly the French & belgians who I expect will probably take it all. I know they want to get it, but they want it as they get the Colonial wools here. I expect to get from about $.30 to a little over $.50 & to let it slide. However much I may be blamed for doing poorly with the wool, I believe the wool business in the country (U S) will be permanently helped by the means; & at any rate I have done every thing in my power. I do not expect to write again before I leave for home. Am in good health.

Respectfully Yours

John Brown

Burgettstown, Penn., April 12, 1850.

Dear son John and Wife,—When at New York, on my way here, I called at Messrs. Fowler & Wells's office, but you were absent. Mr. Perkins has made me a visit here, and left for home yesterday. All well at Essex when I left; all well at Akron when he left, one week since. Our meeting together was one of the most cordial and pleasant I ever experienced. He met a full history of our difficulties and probable losses without a frown on his countenance, or one syllable of reflection; but, on the contrary, with words of comfort and encouragement. He is wholly averse to any separation of our business or interest, and gave me the fullest assurance of his undiminished confidence and personal regard. He expresses strong desire to have our flock of sheep remain undivided, to become the joint possession of our families when we have gone off the stage. Such a meeting I had not dared to expect, and I most heartily wish each of my family could have shared in the comfort of it. Mr. Perkins has in the whole business, from first to last, set an example worthy of a philosopher, or of a Christian. I am meeting with a good deal of trouble from those to whom we have over-advanced, but feel nerved to face any difficulty while God continues me such a partner. Expect to be in New York within three or four weeks.

Your affectionate father,
John Brown

Springfield, Mass. 28th Nov. 1850

Dear Wife;

As I cannot yet say how soon I can return, or what the prospect is of our moving at all this winter, I write to let you hear from me, as you said. I have been well, and have effected a sale of our wool at about 60¢ per lb. Since leaving home I have thought that under all the circumstances of doubt attending the time of our removal; and the possibility that we may not remove at all that I had perhaps encouraged the boys to feed out the potatoes too freely. I now wish them to stop when they have fed out the small ones, as, should anything prevent our moving longer than we have expected, or prevent it entirely I do not wish to be obliged to buy. When the small potatoes are fed out, the boys can mess the cows that give milk with cleaned vats. I want to have them very careful to have no hay or straw wasted, but I would have them use enough straw for bedding the cattle to keep them from lying in the mire. I heard from Ohio a few days since; all were then well. It now seems that the fugitive slave law was to be the means of making more abolitionists than all the lectures we have had for years. It really looks as if God had his hand in this wickedness also. I of course keep encouraging my friends to "trust in God and keep their powder dry" I did so today at thanksgiving meeting publicly. I may get ready to go home the middle of next month, but am wholly in the dark about it yet: do not mean that idleness shall prevent me. While here, and at almost all places where I stop, I am treated with all kindness and attention, but it all does not make home. I feel lonely and restless, no matter how neat and comfortable my room and bed, nor how richly loaded may be the table; they have very few charms for me. Away from home, I can look back to our log cabin at the centre of Richfield with a supper of Porridge and Johnny-cake as to a place of far more interest to me than the Massasoit of Springfield. But, "there's mercy in every place, and mercy, encouraging thought." I shall endeavor when I come home to bring the things that Owen and others of the family stood in need of. I told Mr. Cutting of Westport he might have either of the yearling heifers for thirty dollars. I want Owen to get the largest bull in order, if he can do it by any means. May God in very deed bless and keep all my family is the continued prayer of

Your affectionate husband

John Brown

Will any of them write me here? I should think they might afford to, some one of them.

Springfield Mass 4th Decem 1850

Dear Sons John, Jason, & Frederick, & daughters

I this moment received the Letter of John, & Jason, of the 29th Nov, & feel grateful not only to learn that you are all alive, & well, but also for almost every thing your letters communicate. *I am much pleased* with the reflection that you are all three once more together, & all engaged in the same calling that the old Patriarchs followed, & will say but one word more on that score, & that is taken from their history. "See that ye fall not out by the way" & all will be exactly right in the end. I should think matters were brightening a little in this direction in regard to our claims but I have not yet been able to get any of them to a final isue. I think too that the prospect for the fine wool business rather improves. What burdens me *most of all is*; the apprehension that Mr Perkins expects of me in the way of bringing matters to a close what no living man can possibly bring *about*; in a short time, & that he is getting out of patience, & becoming distrustfull. If I could be with him in all I do, or could possibly attend to all my cares, & give him full explanations by letter of all my movements I should be greatly relieved. He is a most noble spirited man, to whom I feel most deeply indebted, & no amount of money would attone to my feelings for the loss, of a feeling of confidence, & cordiality on his part. If my sons who are so near him conduct wisely, & faithfully, & kindly, in what they have undertaken, they will beyond the possibility of a doubt secure to themselves a full reward if they should not be the means of entirely relieveing a Father of his burdens. I will once more repeat an idea I have often mentioned in regard to business of life in general. A world of pleasure, & of success is the sure, & constant attendant upon *early rising*. It makes all the business of the day go off with a peculiar cheerfulness, while the effects of the contrary course are a great, & constant draught upon ones "vitality" & good temper. When last at home in Essex I spent every day but the first afternoon Surveying, or in tracing out old lost boundaries about which I was very successful; working early, & late at $2,00 per day. This was of the utmost service to both boddy and mind; It exercised me to the full extent, & for the time being almost entirely diverted my mind from its burdens so that I returned to my task verry greatly refreshed, & invigorated. John asks me about Essex. I will say that the family there were living upon the Bread, Milk, Butter, Pork, Chickens, Potatoes, Turnips, Carrots &c of their own raising; & *the most of them* abundant in quantity, & of superior quality. I have no where seen such Potatoes. Essex Co so abounds in Hay, Grain, Potatoes, Rutabaga, &c that I find unexpected difficulty in selling for cash Oats, & some other things we have to spare. Last year it was exactly the reverse. The weather was charming up to the 15th Nov when I left, & never before did the country seem to hold out so many things to entice me to stay on its soil. *Nothing* but the strong sence of duty, obligation, & propriety, would keep me from laying my bones to rest there; but I shall cheerfully endeavour to make that sense my guide; God always helping. It is a source of the utmost comfort to feel that I retain a warm place in the sympathies, affections, & confidence of my own most familiar acquaintance, *my family*; & allow me to say that a man can hardly get into difficulties too big to be surmounted if he has a firm foothold at home. *Remember that*. . . . I am sorry for Johns trouble in his throat, & hope he will get relieved of that. I have some doubt about the Cold Water practice in cases of that kind, but do not suppose a resort to medicines of much account. Regular out of Door labour I believe to be one of the best medicines of all that God has as yet provided. As to Essex I have no question at all. For stock growing, & dairy business considering its healthiness, cheapness of price, & nearness to the two best markets in the Union (New York, & Boston,) I do not know where one could go to do better. I am much refreshed by your letters, & untill you hear from me to the contrary, shall be glad to have you write me here often. Last night I was up till after midnight writing to Mr Perkins, & perhaps used some expressions in my rather *cloudy* state of feeling, that I had better not have used. I mentioned to him that Jason understood he disliked his management of the flock somewhat, & was worried about that, & about the poor Hay he would have to feed out during the Winter. I did not mean to write him any thing offensive, & hope he will so understand me. There is now a fine Plank Road completed from Westport to Elisabethtown. We have no hired person about the family in Essex. Henry Thompson is clearing up a piece of ground that the "colored Brethren" choped for me. he boards with the family, & by the way he gets Ruth out of bed so as [to] have Breakfast before light mornings. It is again getting late at night, & I close by wishing every present as well as future good.

[Signature cut out]

PS   I want to have you *save or secure* the first real prompt, fine looking, Black, Shepherd Puppy whose Ears stand erect that you can get. I do not care about his training at all further than to have him learned to come to you when bid, to set down & lie down, when told; or something in the way of play. Mess Cleaveland, & Titus our Lawyers in New York are verry anxious to get one for a play thing & I am well satisfied that should I give them one as a matter of friendship it would be more appreciated by them, & do more to secure their best services in our suit with Pickersgill than would a hundred Dollars paid them in the way of fees. I want to have Jason obtain from Mr Perkinses or any where he can get them Two good Junk Bottles have them thoroughly cleaned & filled with the Cherry Wine being verry careful not to rile it up before filling the Bottles providing good Corks & filling them perfectly full. These I want him to pack safely in a verry small strong Box he can make: direct them to Perkins & Brown Springfield Mass & send them by Express. We can effect something to purpose by producing unadulterated Domestic Wines. They will command great prices.

JB

Words of Advice

Branch of the United States League of Gileadites.
Adopted Jan. 15, 1851, as Written and Recommended
by John Brown.

"Union Is Strength"

Nothing so charms the American people as personal bravery. Witness the case of Cinques, of everlasting memory, on board the "Amistad." The trial for life of one bold and to some extent successful man, for defending his rights in good earnest, would arouse more sympathy throughout the nation than the accumulated wrongs and sufferings of more than three millions of our submissive colored population. We need not mention the Greeks struggling against the oppressive Turks, the Poles against Russia, nor the Hungarians against Austria and Russia combined, to prove this. *No jury can be found in the Northern States that would convict a man for defending his rights to the last extremity. This is well understood by Southern Congressmen, who insisted that the right of trial by jury should not be granted to the fugitive.* Colored people have ten times the number of fast friends among the whites than they suppose, and would have ten times the number they now have were they but half as much in earnest to secure their dearest rights as they are to ape the follies and extravagances of their white neighbors, and to indulge in idle show, in ease, and in luxury. Just think of the money expended by individuals in your behalf in the past twenty years! Think of the number who have been mobbed and imprisoned on your account! Have any of you seen the Branded Hand? Do you remember the names of Lovejoy and Torrey?

Should one of your number be arrested, you must collect together as quickly as possible, so as to outnumber your adversaries who are taking an active part against you. Let no able-bodied man appear on the ground unequipped, or with his weapons exposed to view: let that be understood beforehand. Your plans must be known only to yourself, and with the understanding that all traitors must die, wherever caught and proven to be guilty. "Whosoever is fearful or afraid, let him return and part early from Mount Gilead" (Judges, vii. 3; Deut. xx. 8). Give all cowards an opportunity to show it on condition of holding their peace. *Do not delay one moment after you are ready; you will lose all your resolution if you do. Let the first blow be the signal for all to engage; and when engaged do not do your work by halves, but make clean work with your enemies,—and be sure you meddle not with any others.* By going about your business quietly, you will get the job disposed of before the number that an uproar would bring together can collect; and you will have the advantage of those who come out against you, for they will be wholly unprepared with either equipments or matured plans; all with them will be confusion and terror. Your enemies will be slow to attack you after you have done up the work nicely; and if they should, they will have to encounter your white friends as well as you; for you may safely calculate on a division of the whites, and may by that means get to an honorable parley.

Be firm, determined, and cool; but let it be understood that you are not to be driven to desperation without making it an awful dear job to others as well as to you. Give them to know distinctly that those who live in wooden houses should not throw fire, and that you are just as able to suffer as your white neighbors. *After effecting a rescue, if you are assailed, go into the houses of your most prominent and influential white friends with your wives; and that will effectually fasten upon them the suspicion of being connected with you, and will compel them to make a common cause with you, whether they would otherwise live up to their profession or not. This would leave them no choice in the matter.* Some would doubtless prove themselves true of their own choice; others would flinch. That would be taking them at their own words. You may make a tumult in the court-room where a trial is going on, by burning gunpowder freely in paper packages, if you cannot think of any better way to create a momentary alarm, and might possibly give one or more of your enemies a hoist. But in such case the prisoner will need to take the hint at once, and bestir himself; and so should his friends improve the opportunity for a general rush.

A lasso might possibly be applied to a slave-catcher for once with good effect. Hold on to your weapons, and never be persuaded to leave them, part with them, or have them far away from you. *Stand by one another and by your friends, while a drop of blood remains; and be hanged, if you must, but tell no tales out of school. Make no confession.*

Union is strength. Without some well-digested arrangements nothing to any good purpose is likely to be done, let the demand be never so great. Witness the case of Hamlet and Long in New York, when there was no well-defined plan of operations or suitable preparation beforehand.

The desired end may be effectually secured by the means proposed; namely, the enjoyment of our inalienable rights.

Agreement

As citizens of the United States of America, trusting in a just and merciful God, whose spirit and all-powerful aid we humbly implore, *we will ever be true to the flag of our beloved country, always acting under it.* We, whose names are hereunto affixed, do constitute ourselves a branch of the United States League of Gileadites. That we will provide ourselves at once with suitable implements, and will aid those who do not possess the means, if any such are disposed to join us. We invite every colored person whose heart is engaged in the performance of our business, whether male or female, old or young. The duty of the aged, infirm, and young members of the League shall be to give instant notice to all members in case of an attack upon any of our people. We agree to have no officers except a treasurer and secretary *pro tem.,* until after some trial of courage and talent of able-bodied members shall enable us to elect officers from those who shall have rendered the most important services. Nothing but wisdom and undaunted courage, efficiency, and general good conduct shall in any way influence us in electing our officers.

Springfield, Mass., Jan. 17, 1851.

Dear Wife,— . . . Since the sending off to slavery of Long from New York, I have improved my leisure hours quite busily with colored people here, in advising them how to act, and in giving them all the encouragement in my power. They very much need encouragement and advice; and some of them are so alarmed that they tell me they cannot sleep on account of either themselves or their wives and children. I can only say I think I have been enabled to do something to revive their broken spirits. I want all my family to imagine themselves in the same dreadful condition. My only spare time being taken up (often till late hours at night) in the way I speak of, has prevented me from the gloomy homesick feelings which had before so much oppressed me: not that I forget my family at all.

Boston, Mass. 22d Dec. 1851

Dear Mary;

I shall take a few moments to write as prompted by my inclination rather than from feeling that I have any other sufficient reason. My prospects about getting back soon are rather poor at this moment, but still it may be I shall be on my way within a day or two. . . . I wrote to Fred'k Douglas a few days since to send on his paper, which I suppose he has done before this, as he very promptly acknowledged the receipt of my letter. There is an unusual amount of very interesting things happening in this and other countries at present, and no one can foresee what is yet to follow. The great excitement produced by the coming of Kossuth, and the last news of a new revolution in France, with the prospect that all Europe will soon again be in blaze seem to have taken all by surprise. I have only to say in regard to these things that I rejoice in them from the full belief that God is carrying out his eternal purpose in them all. . . . I know of nothing unfavorable in our prospects except the slow progress we make and the great expense attending it.

Your affectionate husband
John Brown

Troy N Y 23 Jany 1852

Dear Children

I returned here on the evening of the 19th inst & left Akron on the 14th the date of your letters to John. I was very glad to hear from you again in that way, not having received any thing from you while at home. I left all in usual health & as comfortable as could be expected; but am afflicted *with you* on account of your little Boy. Hope to hear by return mail that you are all well. As in this trouble you are only tasteing of a Cup I have had to drink of deeply, & very often; I need not tell how fully I can sympathize with you in your anxiety. My atachments to this world have been very strong, & Divine Providence has been cutting me loose one Cord after another, up to the present time, but notwithstanding I have so much to remind me that all ties must *soon* be severed; I am still clinging like those who have hardly taken a single lesson. I really hope some of my family may understand that this world is not the *Home* of man; & act in accordance. *Why* may I not hope this of you? When I look forward as regards the religious prospects of my numerous family (the most of them) I am forced to say, & to feel too; that I have *little, very little* to cheer. That this should be so, is I perfectly well understand the legitimate fruit of my own planting; and that only increases my punishment. Some Ten or Twelve years *ago,* I was cheered with the belief that my elder children had chosen the *Lord,* to be their *God*; & I valued much on their influence & example in attoning for my deficiency, & bad example with the younger children. But; *where are we now?* Several have gone to where neither a good or bad example from me will better their condition or prospects or make them the worse. The younger part of my children seem to be far less thoughtful, & disposed to reflection than were my older children at their age. I will not dwell longer on this distressing subject but only say that so far as I *have* gone; it is from no disposition to reflect on any one but myself. I think I can clearly discover where I wandered from the Road. How to now get on it with my family is beyond my ability to *see*; or my courage to *hope.* God grant you *thorough* conversion from sin, & full purpose of heart to continue steadfast in his ways through the *very short* season of trial you will have to pass.

How long we shall continue here is beyound our ability to foresee, but think it very probable that if you write us by return mail we shall get your letter. Something may *possibly* happen that may enable us, (or one of us) to go & see you but do not look for us. I should feel it a great privilege if I could. We seem to be getting along well with our business *so far*; but progress miserably slow. My journeys back & forth this Winter have been very tedious. If you find it difficult for you to pay for Douglas paper, I wish you would let me know *as I know I took* some *liberty* in ordering it continued. You have been very Kind in helping me, & I do not mean to make myself a burden

Your Affectionate Father

John Brown

Akron, Ohio, June 30, 1853.

Dear Children,—Your very welcome letters were received last night. In regard to a house, I did not prefer a log one, only in view of the expense; and I would wish Henry to act according to his own best judgment in regard to it. If he builds a better house than I can pay for, we must so divide the land as to have him keep it. I would like to have a house to go into next spring, if it can be brought about comfortably. I ought to have expressed it more distinctly in better season, but forgot to do so. We are in comfortable health, so far as I know, except father, Jason, and Ellen, all of whom have had a run of ague. Father, when I saw him last, was very feeble; and I fear that in consequence of his great age he will never get strong again. It is some days since I went to see him. We are not through sheep-shearing or hoeing, and our grass is needing to be cut now. We have lately had very dry weather. . . . I am much rejoiced at the news of a religious kind in Ruth's letter; and would be still more rejoiced to learn that all the sects who bear the Christian name would have no more to do with that mother of all abominations—man-stealing. I hope, unfit and unworthy as I am, to be allowed a membership in your little church before long; and I pray God to claim it as his own, and that he will most abundantly bless all in your place who love him in truth. "If any man love not his brother whom he *hath* seen, *how* can he love God whom he *hath not* seen?" I feel but little force about me for writing or any kind of business, but will try to write you more before long. Our State fair commences at Dayton the 20th of September, and will be held open four days.

Your affectionate father,

John Brown

Akron, Ohio, Aug. 26, 1853.

Dear Son John,—Your letter of the 21st instant was received yesterday, and as I may be somewhat more lengthy than usual I begin my answer at once. The family have enjoyed as good health as usual since I wrote before, but my own health has been poor since in May. Father has had a short turn of fever and ague; Jason and Ellen have had a good deal of it, and were not very stout on Sunday last. The wheat crop has been rather light in this quarter; first crop of grass light; oats very poor; corn and potatoes promise well, and frequent rains have given the late grass a fine start. There has been some very fatal sickness about, but the season so far has been middling healthy. Our sheep and cattle have done well; have raised five hundred and fifty lambs, and expect about eighty cents per pound for our wool. We shall be glad to have a visit from you about the time of our county fair, but I do not yet know at what time it comes. Got a letter from Henry dated the 16th of August; all there well. Grain crops there very good. We are preparing (in our minds, at least) to go back next spring. Mrs. Perkins was confined yesterday with another boy, it being her eleventh child. The understanding between the two families continues much as formerly, so far as I know.

In Talmadge there has been for some time an unusual seriousness and attention to future interests. In your letter you appear rather disposed to sermonize; and how will it operate on you and Wealthy if I should pattern after you a little, and also quote some from the Bible? In choosing my texts, and in quoting from the Bible, I perhaps select the very portions which "another portion" of my family hold are not to be wholly received as *true*. I forgot to say that my younger sons (as is common in this "progressive age") appear to be a *little in advance* of my older, and have thrown off the *old shackles* entirely; after THOROUGH AND CANDID investigation they have discovered the Bible to be ALL a fiction! Shall I add, that a letter received from *you* some time since gave me little else than pain and sorrow? "The righteous shall hold on his way;" "By and by he is offended."

My object at this time is to recall your particular attention to the fact that the earliest, as well as all other, writers of the Bible seem to have been impressed with such ideas of the character of the religion they taught, as led them to apprehend a want of steadfastness among those who might profess to adhere to it (no matter what may have been the motives of the different writers). Accordingly we find the writer of the first five books putting into the mouth of his Moses expressions like the following,—and they all appear to dwell much on the idea of two distinct classes among their reputed disciples; namely, a genuine and a spurious class:—

"Lest there should be among you man, or woman, or family, or tribe, whose heart turneth away this day from the Lord our God, to serve the gods of these nations; lest there should be among you a root that beareth gall and wormwood." "Then men shall say, because they have forsaken the covenant of the Lord God of their fathers." "But if thine heart turn away so that thou wilt not hear, but shalt be *drawn away,* and worship other gods, and serve them." . . . .

The writer here makes his *Moses* to dwell on this point with a most remarkable solicitude, a most heart-moving earnestness. The writer of the next book makes his *Joshua* to plead with Israel with the same earnestness. "Choose you this day whom you will serve." "Ye are witnesses against yourselves that ye have chosen you the Lord, to serve him." The writer of the book called Judges uses strong language in regard to the same disposition in Israel to backslide: "And it came to pass when the judge was dead, that they returned and corrupted themselves more than their fathers; they ceased not from their own doings, nor from their stubborn way." The writer of the book Ruth makes Naomi say to Orpah, "Thy sister-in-law is gone back unto her people and unto her gods." The writer of the books called Samuel represents Saul as one of the same spurious class. Samuel is made to say to him, "Behold, to obey is better than sacrifice; and to hearken, than the fat of rams,"—clearly intimating that all service that did not flow from an obedient spirit and an honest heart would be of no avail. He makes his Saul turn out faithless and treacherous in the end, and finally consult a woman "having a familiar spirit," near the close of his sad career. The same writer introduces Ahitophel as one whose counsel "was as if a man had inquired at the oracle of God;" a writer of the Psalms makes David say of him, "We took sweet counsel together, and walked to the house of God in company;" but he is left advising the son of David to incest publicly, and soon after hangs himself. The spot of those men seems not to be genuine.

Akron, Ohio, Sept. 13, 1853.

Dear Children,—It is now nearly a month since I began on another page. Since writing before, father has seemed quite well, but Jason, Ellen, Owen, and Frederick have all had more or less of the ague. They were as well as usual, for them, yesterday. Others of the family are in usual health. . . .

I hope that through the infinite grace and mercy of God you may be brought to see the error of your ways, and be in earnest to turn many to righteousness, instead of leading astray; and then you might prove a great blessing to Essex County, or to any place where your lot may fall. I do not feel "estranged from my children," but I cannot flatter them, nor "cry peace when there is *no* peace." My wife and Oliver expect to set out for Pennsylvania before long, and will probably call on you; but probably not until after the fair. We have a nice lot of chickens fattening for you, when you come.

Your affectionate father,
John Brown

Akron, O., Jan. 9, 1854.

F. Douglass, Esqr., Dear Sir:-I have thought much of late of the extreme wickedness of persons who use their influence to bring law and order and good government, and courts of justice into disrespect and contempt of mankind, and to do what in their power lies to destroy confidence in legislative bodies, and to bring magistrates, justices, and other officers of the law into disrespect amongst men. Such persons, whoever they may be, would break down all that opposes the passions of fallen men; and could they fully carry out their measures, would give to the world a constant succession of murder, revenge, robbery, fire and famine; or, first, of anarchy in all its horrid forms; and then of the most bloody despotisms, to be again succeeded by anarchy, and that again to terminate in a despotism. What punishment ever inflicted by man or even threatened of God, can be too severe for those whose influence is a thousand times more malignant than the atmosphere of the deadly Upas—for those who hate the right and the Most High.

I will now enquire who are such malignant spirits—such fiends clothed in human form? Among the first are men who, neglecting honorable and useful labor to seek office and electioneer, have come to be a majority in our national Legislature, and in most of our State Legislatures, and who there pass unjust and wicked enactments, and call them laws. Another set are from the same description of men, and who fill the offices of Chief Magistrate of the United States, and of different States, and affix the official signature to such enactments. Next comes another set from the same horde, who fill the offices of judge, justices, commissioners, &c, who follow that which is altogether unjust. Next comes a set of Capt. Rynders men—marshals, sheriffs, constables and policemen—brave cat paws of the last named, ever prompt to execute their decisions. Another set are such as sometimes succeed in getting *nominated* for some office, and are very loud at hotels, in cars, on steam-boats, and in stages, urging upon others the duty of fulfilling all our solemn engagements, and "last but not least" comes the devil's drummers and fifers—such fellows as in *black cloth* get in the "sacred desk" there to publish the Gospel, (no doubt): for numbers of them are Doctors of Divinity. But what Gospel do they preach? Is it the Gospel of God, or the Son of God? God commands "That which is altogether just shall thou follow," and every man's conscience says Amen! God commanded "That thou shalt not deliver unto his master the servant which is escaped from his master unto thee. He shall dwell with thee, even among you in that place which he shall choose, in one of thy gates where it liketh him best. *Thou shalt not oppress him.*" Every man's conscience says Amen to that command. The Son of God said- "Therefore all things whatsoever ye would that men should do to you, do ye even so to them; for this is the law and the Prophets." The conscience of every man that ever heard or read that command says Amen! But what say these so-called Divines? You must obey the enactments of the United States Congress, even to the violation of conscience, and the trampling under foot of the laws of our final Judge. "Remember them, O my God, because they have defiled the priesthood."

There is one other set of the same throngers of the "broad way" which I have not mentioned. (Would to God I had already done!) I mean Editors of, and writers in the pro-slavery newspapers and periodicals. These seem to vie with each other in urging men on to greater and still greater lengths in stifling conscience, and insulting God. What, I ask, could possibly tend so to destroy all possible respect for legislators, presidents, judges, or other magistrates or officers—or to root out all confidence in the integrity of civil rulers and courts, as well as legislative bodies, as the passing of enactments which it is self-evident are most abominably wicked and unjust, dignifying them with the name of laws, and then employing the public purse and sword to execute them? But I have done. I am too destitute of words to express the tithe of what I feel, and utterly incapable of doing the subject any possible degree of justice, in my own estimation. My only encouragement to begin, was the earnest wish that if I might express, so that it may be understood to all, an important fact, that you or some friend of God and the right, will take it up and clothe it in the suitable language to be noticed and felt. I want to have the enquiry everywhere raised—Who are the men that are undermining our truly republican and democratic institutions at their very foundations? I forgot to head my remarks "Law and Order."

Yours in Truth

John Brown

Akron, August 21,1854

If you or any of my family are disposed to go to Kansas or Nebraska, with a view to help defeat *Satan* and his legions in that direction, I have not a word to say; *but I feel committed to operate in another part of the field.* If I were not so committed, I would be on my way this fall. Mr. Adair [who married Brown's half sister Florilla] is fixing to go, and wants to find "good men and true" to go along. I would be glad If Jason would give away his Rock and go. Owen is fixing for some move; I can hardly say what.

Akron, Ohio, 30th Sept 1854

Dear Children

After being hard pressed to go with my family to Kansas as more likely to benefit the colored people *on the whole* than to return with them to North Elba; I have consented to ask for your *advice & feeling* in the matter; & also to ask you to learn from Mr. Epps & all the colored people (so far as you can) how they would wish, & advise me to act in the case, all things considered. As I volunteered in their service; (or the service of the colored people); they have a right to vote, as to course I take. I have just written Gerrit Smith, Fredk Douglas, & Dr McCune Smith, for their advice. We have a new daughter now Five days old. Mother & child, are both doing well to appearance. Other friends well so far as I know. John & Wealthy are still with us. Will you write as soon as you can? Have not received your reply to my other questions.

Your Affectionate Father
John Brown

Akron, Nov 2, 1854

Dear Children,—I feel still pretty much determined to go back to North Elba; but expect Owen and Frederick will set out for Kansas on Monday next, with cattle belonging to John, Jason, and themselves, intending to winter somewhere in Illinois. . . . Gerrit Smith wishes me to go back to North Elba; from Douglass and Dr. McCune Smith I have not yet heard. . . .

Your affectionate father,
John Brown

Brownsville Kansas Territory 19th Oct 1855

Dear Father

We arrived here Two Weeks ago Tomorrow Evening; & finding but Two well persons in all the number, with no Houses to shelter them; nor any crop of Hay, Corn, Beans, or Potatoes, secured for Winter; I have felt driven to neglect writing almost entirely; & have only written One Letter before this (this one to my Wife) since I got on. I might have written before day Mornings but had no place with the cold chilling Winds shut out where I could improve such Hours. I felt very much disappointed at finding all my children here in such very uncomfortable circumstances. We are doing all we can to help them; & that is not much as Henry Thompson, & Oliver have both had something of the Ague since we got on. I was at Mr. Adairs over Sunday last; & found them all more or less sick; but all able to be up, & about a little. I think all here are on the gain slowly; Frederick however has it on him now while I am writing. Mr. Adairs family are much more comfortable situated. I think much of the sickness in my family out here is from most unreasonable exposure; but from what we learn the sickness has been quite general over the more Eastern country. We hear that you have been sick and not expected to live but that you had got about a little. We shall be looking anxiously to hear from you again. We had a slow tedious journey out on account of our heavy load and our Horse having the distemper. He has got well. We used all the money we had, & all you sent in getting on but Sixty cents. Think I can soon sell something Horse, or Waggon, so as to replace what we used. We came by the place where Austin was buried, & took him up; & brought him on with us; which seems to have had a good effect on Jason, & Ellen. We reached in time to be at the *Free State* election & hearing that trouble was expected we turned out powerfully armed; but no enemy appeared. From what we can learn not only Missouri but other Slave States are getting quite discouraged about Kansas; & I think there is no doubt of a favourable result, if Free State folks will hold on patiently. The country is much like the upland portion of Illinois where you have been; but I have seen no wet or Marchy lands as yet, & I may say on the whole is just about as good as I expected, & better timbered. I do not think this is the only desirable spot on Earth I have seen but believe that in the end it will be a good country; & generally healthy. I should think a majority of the settlers were of the poorer class, & will have to submit to some privations for some little time. Jason thinks the prospect for a sale of fruit Trees will not be very good for some time yet. I think there is no doubt that stock growing & dairy business will do well here for those who take hold of them right in connection with corn growing. We are all anxious to hear from you; & we know that you will write if you are able. My advantages for writing at present are so very poor that I hope this letter will answer for as many of the friends as is consistent; & that you will accept it as in some measure from all here. I hope the afflictions of Jason & Wife will not be wholly lost on them. Wishing you & all our Ohio friends the full blessing; & the peace of God; I remain

Your Affectionate but unworthy Son
John Brown

Osawatomie, Kansas Territory,
20th December, 1855.

Editor of Summit *Beacon*:

My Dear Sir:—You will greatly oblige me by allowing me the use of your columns in order to give a little account of my movements to my numerous friends in Akron and vicinity, who, as well as yourself, contributed towards supplying arms and ammunition to the Free State men of Kansas. It would afford me the utmost pleasure were it in my power to write each a letter individually, to show my strong regard for all those numerous friends; but I *must beg* them to accept this as a substitute.

Soon after leaving Chicago with the arms and ammunition, in company with a son-in-law and son, one of our company was taken sick. This rendered our journey through Illinois, Iowa and Missouri so slow, that, when we finally reached their neighborhood, October 5th, we had between us all but sixty cents. We got the most valuable part of the arms and ammunition through safe, and just in time to have them on hand at the Free State Election, at Pottawatomie, October 8th, where difficulty was expected; but no disturbance occurred.

When we reached the territory there was not, among the five sons I had already there, one well person; and they had not been able to provide themselves comfortable houses, or to secure their crops. Since then, for much of the time, I have been the only well man out of eight. Since the cold weather commenced four of the young men have become middling strong, and the other three have improved. The care of my friends has prevented my being as active among the emigrants generally as I intended.

You have doubtless learned of the late invasion of Kansas, and something of its results; but I will give you a little of my version of the affair. Free State men here, as all well know, had openly avowed their determination to disregard the enactments of the Bogus Legislature, and to resist their enforcement; and, as *reports say,* it was contrived in what they call the Blue *Lodge* in Missouri (in the White House it is likely), to have some three or four Free State men killed in Kansas, in order to have an opportunity of showing before the country and the world that those enactments *could and would be enforced*—just before the sitting of Congress. Be that as it may, about four weeks since, news came around that a Free State man named Dow, had been deliberately murdered by a Missourian, who had given himself up to Governor Shannon; that the only Free State witness of the murder had been arrested, under a warrant issued by a justice of bogus origin, on complaint of pro-slavery men swearing that they were afraid he would take their lives, etc.; that such excessive bail had been required as he could not give; that he had been started for jail by a bogus sheriff named Jones, with a party of fifteen armed men, taking a circuitous route through Lawrence, on purpose to let the people of that place see that the bogus laws would be enforced; that some eight men with Sharp's rifles, had met their company and rescued the man; that Governor Shannon had ordered out the pro-slavery men of Kansas; called on the Government for troops, and on Missouri to help him: that a force of about two thousand had collected under Governor Shannon, near Lawrence; that the Free State men had collected in nearly equal numbers; that it was supposed a battle had been or would be fought immediately. This news proved in the main to be correct. The numbers were overstated; but Coleman, the murderer, was made a leader in the Governor's camp. When this news came I was here, a distance of ten miles from where my boys are located. I left immediately, intending to set out next morning for Lawrence to learn the facts; but as J. Brown, jun. was acquainted with the road and the people of Lawrence he was started on horseback: but before going many rods he was met with news by a runner, asking for help immediately. We at once set about preparing bread, meat, blankets and horsefeed, running bullets, loading all the guns and pistols and packing them in a one-horse wagon. All of us who were able to walk, five in all, set off on foot the same afternoon. Our guns, ammunition, baggage, &c, made a fair load for our horse. We walked that afternoon and all the following night, except for a short time spent in cooking our supper and resting our horse. We reached Lawrence the next forenoon, having traveled in a dark night (for the most part) a distance of from 35 to 40 miles.

On our way an accident occurred at a bridge about three miles from Lawrence, which will serve a little, in connection with other circumstances, to show the real character of those *dreadful Missourians,* who have invaded Kansas in time past. We had to pass the bridge (so far as we had information of the road) and it was guarded, as differently reported, by from 15 to 25 of the enemy, armed, and in a log house at the end of the bridge next to us. We had no means of counting them, part being in the log house and part at the door. On our approach a small boy ran ahead, and gave the men notice. We each carried a good gun, two large revolvers in a belt, and one small revolver in our pockets, all loaded. We were prepared to give from 95 to 100 shots without reloading, and were certainly well equipped. As we moved directly on the bridge without making any halt, they silently suffered us to pass *with the free will offerings* of our dear friends at Akron and elsewhere, without any interruption save that of looking very earnestly at us. In a few hours after, five more of a volunteer company to which we belonged passed the same bridge and received similar respectful treatment. They, however, stopped a boy of 15 or 16 years, and carefully examined him the same day; but the evening before some 15 or 20 of them, armed, attacked three or four men (mostly without arms) and killed a Mr. Barber from Ohio, who had no arms. From these and numerous other circumstances, I am led to conclude that *even Missourians* are amused with trinkets, or with those who wear them.

We learned on our arrival in Lawrence that numerous demands had been sent in from the Governor's camp, viz: that the rescued man, and those who rescued him, should be given up: that the people should allow some forty or fifty warrants to be served; that the Sharp's rifles should be surrendered; that certain buildings and fortifications should be destroyed by the inhabitants; the printing presses should be demolished and thrown into the river, and that the inhabitants generally should swear to support the enactments of the so-called Kansas Legislature. Some of these demands were officially made, the others, however, emanating from his camp. We were told that Governor Shannon had signified to the inhabitants repeatedly that if they had any business to transact with him, to come to his camp and attend to it; and that word had so often been returned, that if he had business with any person in Lawrence, to come in and see to it.

After thus parleying for some days, Governor Shannon sent word that he wished to visit town, and an escort was sent from Lawrence, which conducted him in. During this time eleven companies of Free State Volunteers had collected in Lawrence, who were employed, (with the inhabitants) night and day, under the direction of Colonel Lane, in the construction of embankments and earthworks, and which they had in a good degree completed. After Governor Shannon had met some of the principal inhabitants, they very soon 'found him out'; and taking advantage of his weakness, frailties and fear of the result of an engagement, together with some resort on their part to Yankee ingenuity, and his own consciousness of the awkward fix he had got himself into, and a most *horrible* supply of *Brandy,* they got him quite elated, and succeeded in making just about such a treaty with him as they desired. Among the conditions agreed to on his part, was the ordering home of the pro-slavery force he had called out; the issuing of a proclamation, requiring the foreign invaders to quit the Territory immediately, with a promise from him no more to call for such aid. In short, he abandoned his entire ground; recognized the volunteers, as the militia of Kansas, and empowered the officers in command to call them out at their discretion, for the protection of Lawrence and the Territory. Governor Shannon in return, got a promise from two individuals, for the people of Lawrence and the Territory, that they would assist him in the execution of the laws of the Territory.

How much of truthfulness or sincerity characterized these negotiations, I will not say. The invaders soon left, covered over with glory, after suffering great expenses, hardships and privations; not having fulfilled any of their threatenings, or fought any battles, or accomplished anything for which they set out, save the commission of certain robberies, and a few acts of violence on the defenceless inhabitants in the neighborhood of their camps, and the killing of one unarmed man, leaving the Territory entirely in the power of the Free State men, with an organized militia, armed, equipped, and in full force for its protection; but the result is not yet fully known. What now remains for the Free State men of Kansas, and their friends in the State, and the world to do, is to *hold* the ground they now possess, *and Kansas is free*.

A great part of the volunteers were strong, hardy farmers and mechanics, who had left their work and their homes (on hearing of the invasion) without even waiting to change their clothes; and were, as a whole, the most intelligent, sober and orderly set of men I have ever seen collected, in equal number, except at religious worship. They were sober, earnest thinking men, betraying no anxiety as to the result of what they had undertaken, as composed and quiet as though they had been collected from some first rate country neighborhood, to raise a house or barn. Here were developed such a set of determined men as I had no idea this Territory could boast of, in any such numbers. They now know their own members, and their condition for self-government and self-defence. They have now become acquainted, and in their feelings, strongly knit together, the result of having shared together some of the conditions of war in actual service. Many of those volunteers were sterling Free State men from several of the Slave States. They have my warmest blessing.

We are exceedingly anxious to learn how matters go off in the States and in Congress this winter. We are very much shut away from news. Please acknowledge this by sending one number of the *Beacon,* for which I would subscribe had I the means.

Yours truly,   John Brown

Osawatomie Kansas Territory 1st Feby 1856
Dear Wife & Children every One

Your & Watsons Letter to the Boys, & Myself of Decem 30th &
Jany 1st were received by last Mail. We are all very glad to hear again
of your welfare; & I am particularly grateful when I am noticed by
a Letter from *you*. I have just taken out Two Letters for Henry One
of which I suppose is from Ruth. Salmon & myself are so far on our
way home from Missouri; & only reached Mr Adairs last night. They
are all well & we know of nothing but all are well at the Boys Shantees.
The weather continues very severe: & it is now nearly Six Weeks
that the Snow has been almost constantly driven (like dry Sand)
by the fierce Winds of Kansas. Mr. Adair has been collecting Ice of
late from the Osage River; which is 9½ Inches thick, of perfect clean
sollid Ice, formed under the Snow. By means of the sale of our
Horse & Waggon: our present wants are tolerably well met; so that
if health is continued to us we shall not probably suffer much. The
idea of again visiting those of my dear family at North Elba; is so
calculated to unMan me that I seldom allow my thoughts to dwell
uppon it: & I do not think best to write much about it. "Suffise it
to Say"; that God is *abundantly* able to keep both us, & you: & *in him
let us all trust*. We have just learned of some *new*; & shocking outrages
at Leavenworth: & that the Free State people there have fled to
Lawrence: which place is again threatened with an attack. *Should* that
take place we may soon again be called uppon to "buckle on our
Armor"; which by the help of God we will do: when I suppose
Henry, & Oliver will have a chance. *My judgement is*; that we shall
have no more general disturbance until warmer weather. I have more
to say; but not time now to say it. So farewell for this time. *Write*

Your Affectionate Husband & Father
John Brown

Near Brown's Station, K. T., June, 1856.

DEAR WIFE AND CHILDREN, EVERY ONE,—It is now about five weeks since I have seen a line from North Elba, or had any chance of writing you. During that period we here have passed through an almost constant series of very trying events. We were called to the relief of Lawrence, May 22, and every man (eight in all), except Orson turned out; he staying with the women and children, and to take care of the cattle. John was captain of a company to which Jason belonged; the other six were a little company by ourselves. On our way to Lawrence we learned that it had been already destroyed, and we encamped with John's company overnight. Next day our little company left, and during the day we stopped and searched three men.

Lawrence was destroyed in this way: Their leading men had (as I think) decided, in a very *cowardly* manner, not to resist any process having any Government official to serve it, notwithstanding the process might be wholly a bogus affair. The consequence was that a man called a United States marshal came on with a horde of ruffians which he called his posse, and after arresting a few persons turned the ruffians loose on the defenceless people. They robbed the inhabitants of their money and other property, and even women of their ornaments, and burned considerable of the town.

On the second day and evening after we left John's men we encountered quite a number of proslavery men, and took quite a number prisoners. Our prisoners we let go; but we kept some four or five horses. We were immediately after this accused of murdering five men at Pottawatomie, and great efforts have since been made by the Missourians and their ruffian allies to capture us. John's company soon afterwards disbanded, and also the Osawatomie men.

Jason started to go and place himself under the protection of the Government troops; but on his way he was taken prisoner by the Bogus men, and is yet a prisoner, I suppose. John tried to hide for several days; but from feelings of the ungrateful conduct of those who ought to have stood by him, excessive fatigue, anxiety, and constant loss of sleep, he became quite insane, and in that situation gave up, or as we are told, was betrayed at Osawatomie into the hands of the Bogus men. We do not know all the truth about this affair. He has since, we are told, been kept in irons, and brought to a trial before a bogus court, the result of which we have not yet learned. We have great anxiety both for him and Jason, and numerous other prisoners with the enemy (who have all the while had the

Government troops to sustain them). We can only commend them to God.

The cowardly mean conduct of Osawatomie and vicinity did not save them; for the ruffians came on them, made numerous prisoners, fired their buildings, and robbed them. After this a picked party of the Bogus men went to Brown's Station, burned John's and Jason's houses, and their contents to ashes; in which burning we have all suffered more or less. Orson and boy have been prisoners, but were soon set at liberty. They are well, and have not been seriously injured. Owen and I have just come here for the first time to look at the ruins. All looks desolate and forsaken,—the grass and weeds fast covering up the signs that these places were lately the abodes of quiet families. After burning the houses, this self-same party of picked men, some forty in number, set out as they supposed, and as was the fact, on the track of my little company, boasting, with awful profanity, that they would have our scalps. They however passed the place where we were hid, and robbed a little town some four or five miles beyond our camp in the timber. I had omitted to say that some murders had been committed at the time Lawrence was sacked.

On learning that this party were in pursuit of us, my little company, now increased to ten in all, started after them in company of a Captain Shore, with eighteen men, he included (June 1). We were all mounted as we travelled. We did not meet them on that day, but took five prisoners, four of whom were of their scouts, and well armed. We were out all night, but could find nothing of them until about six o'clock next morning, when we prepared to attack them at once, on foot, leaving Frederick and one of Captain Shore's men to guard the horses. As I was much older than Captain Shore, the principal direction of the fight devolved on me. We got to within about a mile of their camp before being discovered by their scouts, and then moved at a brisk pace, Captain Shore and men forming our left, and my company the right. When within about sixty rods of the enemy, Captain Shore's men halted by mistake in a very exposed situation, and continued the fire, both his men and the enemy being armed with Sharpe's rifles. My company had no long-shooters. We (my company) did not fire a gun until we gained the rear of a bank, about fifteen or twenty rods to the right of the enemy, where we commenced, and soon compelled them to hide in a ravine. Captain Shore, after getting one man wounded, and exhausting his ammunition, came with part of his men to the right of my position, much discouraged. The balance of his men, including the one wounded, had left the ground. Five of Captain Shore's men came boldly down and joined my company, and all but one man, wounded, helped to maintain the fight until it was over. I was obliged to give my consent that he should go after more help, when all his men left but eight, four of whom I persuaded to remain in a secure position, and there busied one of them in shooting the horses and mules of the enemy, which served for a show of fight. After the firing had continued for some two to three hours, Captain Pate with twenty-three men, two badly wounded, laid down their arms to nine men, myself included,—four of Captain Shore's men and four of my own. One of my men (Henry Thompson) was badly wounded, and after continuing his fire for an hour longer was obliged to quit the ground. Three others of my company (but not of my family) had gone off. Salmon was dreadfully wounded by accident, soon after the fight; but both he and Henry are fast recovering.

A day or two after the fight, Colonel Sumner of the United States army came suddenly upon us, while fortifying our camp and guarding our prisoners (which, by the way, it had been agreed mutually should be exchanged for as many Free-State men, John and Jason included), and compelled us to let go our prisoners without being exchanged, and to give up their horses and arms. They did not go more than two or three miles before they began to rob and injure Free-State people. We consider this as in good keeping with the cruel and unjust course of the Administration and its tools throughout this whole Kansas difficulty. Colonel Sumner also compelled us to disband; and we, being only a handful, were obliged to submit.

Since then we have, like David of old, had our dwelling with the serpents of the rocks and wild beasts of the wilderness; being obliged to hide away from our enemies. We are not disheartened, though nearly destitute of food, clothing, and money. God, who has not given us over to the will of our enemies, but has moreover delivered them into our hand, will, we humbly trust, still keep and deliver us. We feel assured that He who sees not as men see, does not lay the guilt of innocent blood to our charge.

I ought to have said that Captain Shore and his men stood their ground nobly in their unfortunate but mistaken position during the early part of the fight. I ought to say further that a Captain Abbott, being some miles distant with a company, came onward promptly to sustain us, but could not reach us till the fight was over. After the fight, numerous Free-State men who could not be got out before were on hand; and some of them, I am ashamed to add, were very busy not only with the plunder of our enemies, but with our private effects, leaving us, while guarding our prisoners and providing in regard to them, much poorer than before the battle.

If, under God, this letter reaches you so that it can be read, I wish it at once carefully copied, and a copy of it sent to Gerrit Smith. I know of no other way to get these facts and our situation before the world, nor when I can write again.

Owen has the ague to-day. Our camp is some miles off. Have heard that letters are in for some of us, but have not seen them. Do continue writing. We heard last mail brought only three letters, and all these for proslavery men. It is said that both the Lawrence and Osawatomie men, when the ruffians came on them, either hid or gave up their arms, and that their leading men counselled them to take such a course.

May God bless and keep you all!

Your affectionate husband and father,
John Brown

P. S. Ellen and Wealthy are staying at Osawatomie.

The above is a true account of the first regular battle fought between Free-State and proslavery men in Kansas. May God still gird our loins and hold our right hands, and to him may we give the glory! I ought in justice to say, that, after the sacking and burning of several towns, the Government troops appeared for their protection and drove off some of the enemy.

J. B.

June 26. Jason is set at liberty, and we have hopes for John. Owen, Salmon, and Oliver are down with fever (since inserted); Henry doing well.

Topeka, Kansas Ter, 4th July, 1856

Dear Wife & Children every one

I have again through the mercy of God opportunity to write you a few words. Wrote you in pencil somewhat at length a few days ago: but have no assurance that anything I send will ever meet your eyes. Have seen nothing that came from you since some time in May last. Since I wrote you last we have had more of quiet; but in the mean time Salmon, Owen, Fred^k & Oliver have all been sick; Owen *very* sick & was still so, when Oliver & I left our camp about four or Five days since. We are very anxious about him, Henry & Salmon are both much better of their wounds. We came here with Free State men collected to attend the convening of the Free State Legislature who were threatened with general arrest if they met again. A large number of US troops are on the ground to enforce Bogus Legislation; & to scatter the Free State men, who are also on the ground in considerable force. Today will probably decide whether the Free State Legislature is to be broken up or not. *If they are*: It will be done by the *government troops*; as I have no idea of the Bogus men fighting us at all without them. A dreadful state of things exists here but I have no doubt but that in the end *Right* will triumph. We are near where John is held prisner by US troops, but no Free State friends are allowed to visit him for some days past. None of us have seen him since he was taken. Jason has been set at liberty I here stop hoping to report further before I close.

July 5th 1856

Yesterday Col Sumner of the US army with his men took possession of the Hall or rooms to be occupied by the Free State Legislature; then called in the members, & in the name of Franklin Pierce, & as he said by his direction commanded the Legislature to disperse to which they submitted. There was no fighting. We leave today for our camp. Are in hopes John will soon now be liberated. May God Keep & bless You all

                    Your Affectionate Husband & Father   John Brown

Lawrence K T 7th Sept 1856

Dear Wife & Children every one

I have one moment to write you to say that I am yet alive that Jason & family were well yesterday John; & family I hear are well; (he being yet a prisoner. On the morning of the 30th Aug an attack was made by the ruffians on Osawatomie numbering some 400 by whose scouts our dear Fred^k was shot dead without warning he supposing them to be Free State men as near as we can learn. One other man a Cousin of Mr Adair was murdered by them about the same time that Fred^k was killed & one badly wounded at the same time. At this time I was about 3 miles off where I had some 14 or 15 men over night that I had just enlisted to serve under me as regulars. There I collected as well as I could with some 12 or 15 more & in about 3/4 of an Hour attacked them from a wood with thick undergroth., with this force we threw them into confusion for about 15 or 20 Minuets during which time we killed & wounded from 70 to 80 of the enemy *as they say* & then we escaped as well as we could with one killed while escaping; Two or Three wounded; & as many more missing. Four or Five Free State men were butchered during the day in all. Jason fought bravely by my side during the fight & escaped with me he being unhurt. I was struck by a partly spent, Grape, Canister, or Rifle shot which bruised me some but did not injure me seriously. "Hitherto the Lord hath helped me" notwithstanding my afflictions. Things now seem rather quiet just now; but what another Hour will bring I cannot say - I have seen Three or four letters from Ruth & One from Watson of July or Aug which are all I have seen since in June. I was very glad to hear once more from you & hope you will continue to write to some of the friends so that I may hear from you. I am utterly unable to write you for most of the time. May the God of of [sic] our Fathers bless & save you all

Your Affectionate Husband & Father
John Brown

Monday Morning 8th Sept/56
Jason has just come in. Left all well as usual Johns trial is to come off or commence today

Yours ever

John Brown

Speech in Lawrence, Kansas, September 13, 1856

"GENTLEMEN,—It is said there are twenty-five hundred Missourians down at Franklin, and that they will be here in two hours. You can see for yourselves the smoke they are making by setting fire to the houses in that town. Now is probably the last opportunity you will have of seeing a fight, so that you had better do your best. If they should come up and attack us, don't yell and make a great noise, but remain perfectly silent and still. Wait till they get within twenty-five yards of you; get a good object; be sure you see the hind sight of your gun,—then fire. A great deal of powder and lead and very precious time is wasted by shooting too high. You had better aim at their legs than at their heads. In either case, be sure of the hind sights of your guns. It is from the neglect of this that I myself have so many times escaped; for if all the bullets that have ever been aimed at me had hit, I should have been as full of holes as a riddle."

Tabor, Iowa, 11th Oct 1856

Dear Wife & Children every one

I am *through Infinite grace,* once more in a Free State; & on my way to make you a visit. I left Kansas a day or Two since by a waggon in which I had a bed; as I was so unwell that I had to lie down. I first had the Dysentary, & then Chill Fever. Am now rapidly improveing. Wealthy & Ellen with their little boys started for home by way of the River about Ten day since. John, Jason, & Owen; all came out with me. John & Jason have gone on towards Chicago with a horse but *expects* to meet me next week on the Rail Road on the East line of the State. *I expect* to go by stage. *Owen* thinks of wintering here. *Mr Adair and family* were all midling well Two Weeks ago. Mr. Day and *Family have* been sick but were better. When we left there seemed to be a little calm *for the present* in Kansas; Cannot say how long it will last. You need not be anxious about me if I am some time on the road as I have to stop at several places; & go some out of my way; having left partly on business expecting to return if the troubles continue in Kansas; & my health will admit. Now that I am where I can write you, I may do it midling often. May God bless & Keep you all. Your Affectionate Husband & Father—

John Brown

P S Ruths letter to John of 16th Sept was received

Yours

JB

Speech in Connecticut, 1857

"I am trying to raise from twenty to twenty-five thousand dollars in the free States, to enable me to continue my efforts in the cause of freedom. Will the people of Connecticut, *my native State,* afford me some aid in this undertaking? Will the gentlemen and ladies of Hartford, where I make my first appeal in this State, set the example of an earnest effort? Will some gentleman or lady take hold and try what can be done by small contributions from counties, cities, towns, societies, or churches, or in some other way? I think the little beggar-children in the streets are sufficiently interested to warrant their contributing, if there was any need of it, to secure the object. I was told that the newspapers in a certain city were dressed in mourning on hearing that I was killed and scalped in Kansas, but I did not know of it until I reached the place. Much good it did me. In the same place I met a more cool reception than in any other place where I have stopped. If my friends will hold up my hands while I live, I will freely absolve them from any expense over me when I am dead. I do not ask for pay, but shall be most grateful for all the assistance I can get."

To the Friends of Freedom

The undersigned, whose individual means were exceedingly limited when he first engaged in the struggle for Liberty in Kansas, being now still more destitute and no less anxious than in time past to continue his efforts to sustain that cause, is induced to make this earnest appeal to the friends of Freedom throughout the United States, in the firm belief that his call will not go unheeded. I ask all honest lovers of *Liberty and Human Rights, both male and female,* to hold up my hands by contributions of pecuniary aid, either as counties, cities, towns, villages, societies, churches or individuals.

I will endeavor to make a judicious and faithful application of all such means as I may be supplied with. Contributions may be sent in drafts to W. H. D. Callender, Cashier State Bank, Hartford, Ct. It is my intention to visit as many places *as I can* during my stay in the States, provided I am first informed of the disposition of the inhabitants to aid me *in my efforts,* as well as to receive my visit. Information may be communicated to me (care of Massasoit House) at Springfield, Mass. Will editors of newspapers friendly to the cause kindly second the measure, and also give this some half dozen insertions? Will either gentlemen or ladies, or both, who love the cause, volunteer to take up the business? It is with *no little sacrifice of personal feeling* that I appear in this manner before the public.

John Brown

New York, March, 1857.

Springfield, Mass, 31st March, 1857.

Dear Wife

Your letter of the 21st inst is just received. I have only to say as regards the resolution of the boys to "learn, & practice war no more"; that it was not at my solicitation that they engaged in it at the first: & that while I may *perhaps* feel no more love of the business than they do; still I think there may be *possibly* in their day that which is more to be dreaded: if such things *do not now exist.* I have all along intended to make the best provision I may be capable of; for all my family. What I may hereafter be able *to effect*; I cannot now say. I now enclose a Draft on New York for $30, Thirty Dollars payable to the order of Watson. I have wholly forgotten how much I had of his sheep money; but I think I made an account of it in my book. If I do not send enough; perhaps Henry will spare him a little for a few days, until I get back again; if he has it on hand. I cannot well send any more just now; & get the articles that have been sent for since I left home. I expect more soon. I have just got a long letter from Mr. Adair. All midling well March 11th; but had fears of further trouble after a while. Your Affectionate Husband

John Brown

This Bible, presented to my dearly beloved daughter Ellen Brown, is not intended for common use, but to be carefully preserved *for her* and *by her,* in remembrance of her father (of whose care and attentions she was deprived in her infancy), he being absent in the territory of Kansas from the summer of 1855.

May the Holy Spirit of God incline your heart, *in earliest childhood,* "to receive the truth in the love of it," and to form your thoughts, words, and actions by its wise and holy precepts, is *my best wish* and *most earnest* prayer to Him in whose care I leave you. Amen.

From your affectionate father,

John Brown

April 2, 1857

Boston, Mass. 3d April, 1857

Wm Barnes Esqr
   Albany, N. Y.

My Dear Sir

I expect soon to return West; & to [go] back without securing even an outfit. I go with a *sad heart* having failed to secure even the means of equiping; to say nothing of feeding men. I had when I returned no more that I could peril; & could make no further sacrifice, except to go about in the attitude of a beggar; & that I have done, humiliating as it is. You once in conversation mentioned the propriety of my taking a claim in Kansas, but I have no means of securing a claim; & shall be obliged to leave my Wife & Three little Girls dependent on the charities of friends to a great extent. If persons in your place are disposed to encourage me so far as to enable me to secure a claim in Kansas; it may enable me to avail myself of some State appropriations for actual Settlers. *I am prepared to expect nothing but bad faith* from the National Kansas Committee at Chicago, as I will show you hereafter. *This* is for the present *confidential.*

Very respectfully Yours
John Brown

P. S. Shall be glad to hear from you at Springfield, Mass., care of Massasoit House.

Yours   J B

West Newton, Mass, 15th April 1857

Dear Son John

I received your welcome letter of the 6th inst. last night, at Boston; & am very glad of all the information it gives. I have had no letters from home for several days; but when I last heard from N, E, all were well. I am much gratifyed to learn of Mr. Giddings full redemption from Slavery. I am also very glad at the kind feeling expressed by your "Bail" towards you; & have no doubt of the correctness of your ideas about *not going back* to stand trial. That would never do. If any of us are hereafter to be tried in Kansas; I would much rather it should be with Irons *in* rather than *uppon* our hands. The old Monument (perhaps I forgot to say) is an old fashioned Granite, Grave Stone; with a short old style account of Capt John Brown who died at New York (*almost to a day*) Eighty years from the death of his *Great, Grand, Son, Fred^k Brown*; in Kansas. I value the old relic, much the more for its *age, & homeliness*; & it is of sufficient size to contain more *brief* inscriptions. One Hundred years from 1856 should it then be in the possession of the same posterity: it will be a great curiosity. Your remarks about the value & importance of dicipline, I fully appreciate; & I had been making arangements to secure the assistance, & instruction; of a distinguished Scotch officer; & *author* quite popular *in this country*. I am quite sanguine of my success in the matter. My collections I may safely put down at $13000, & I think I have got matters in such a train that it will soon reach $30,000, I have had a good deal of discouragement; & *have often* felt quite depressed; *but "hither to God hath helped me."* About the *last* of last Week, I gave vent to those feelings in a short piece (which you may yet see in the prints,) headed Old Browns, Farewell: to the Plymouth Rocks; Bunker Hill, Monuments; Charter Oaks; & Uncle Toms Cabbins. The effect on a Boston Merchant who saw the manuscript was that he immediately sent me a letter authorizing me to draw on him at sight for $7000, & others were also moved to be in earnest: *Wendell Phillips*; & *Theodore Parker* (who though sick) said of the merchant (above named) that his "*name* had been written in the Lambs Book of life." A. A. Lawrence & Brother have started a Subscription to provide for my Wife, & little Girls in my *absence; & in case I never return to them. About these things I do not wish any remarks made.* Jason wrote me that Charly had been sick "unto death;" but appeared better & that one of "U.S. Hounds" had been at Cleveland going East *after me*. I have been hideing about a week for my track to get cold; & the papers gave it out last Week that I had left en Route for Kansas. I think I shall not "be delivered into the hands of the wicked"; & feel quite easy; but mean to make it very difficult to follow me. I mean if I can to call on you. Jeremiah wrote me that Abi was very sick. Hope to hear soon of her recovery. Write me through *Henry*. May God abundantly bless you all. Train up the Wolf hunter "in the way he *should go*.

Your Affectionate Father
John Brown

Old Brown's Farewell to
The Plymouth Rocks, Bunker Hill Monuments,
Charter Oaks, and Uncle Thoms Cabbins.

He has left for Kansas. Has been trying since he came out of the territory to secure an outfit or in other words; the means of arming and thoroughly equipping his regular Minuet men, who are mixed up *with the people of Kansas,* and *he leaves* the States, *with a feeling of deepest sadness;* that after having exhausted *his own small means* and with his *family and his brave men;* suffered hunger, cold, nakedness, *and some* of them sickness, wounds, imprisonment *in irons;* with extreme cruel treatment, *and others death:* that after lying on the ground for months in the most sickly, unwholesome, and uncomfortable places; *some of the time with sick and wounded* destitute of any shelter; and hunted like wolves; sustained in part by Indians: that after all this; in order to sustain a cause which every citizen of this *"glorious Republic,"* is under equal moral obligation to do: *and for the neglect of which, he will be held accountable by God:* a cause in which every man, woman, and child; of the *entire human family* has a *deep* and *awful* interest; that when *no wages* are asked; or expected; he cannot secure, amidst all the wealth, luxury, and extravagance of this "Heaven exalted," people; even the necessary supplies of the common soldier. "How are the mighty fallen"?

Boston, April, A. D. 1857.

HUDSON, OHIO, May 27, 1857.

DEAR WIFE AND CHILDREN, EVERY ONE,—. . . I have got Salmon's letter of the 19th instant, and am much obliged for it. There is some prospect that Owen will go on with me. If I should never return, it is my particular request that no other monument be used to keep me in remembrance than the same plain one that records the death of my grandfather and son; and that a short story, like those already on it, be told of John Brown the fifth, under that of grandfather. I think I have several good reasons for this. I would be glad that my posterity should not only remember their parentage, but also the cause they labored in. I do not expect to leave these parts under four or five days, and will try to write again before I go off. I am much confused in mind, and cannot remember what I wish to write. May God abundantly bless you all! . . .

Your affectionate husband and father,

John Brown.

TABOR, FREMONT COUNTY, IOWA, Aug. 13, 1857.

Much as I love to communicate with you, it is still a great burden for me to write when I have nothing of interest to say, and when there is something to be active about. Since I left New England I have had a good deal of ill-health; and having in good measure exhausted my available means toward purchasing such supplies as I should certainly need if again called into active service, and without which I could accomplish next to nothing, I had to begin my journey back with not more than half money at any time to bear my expenses through and pay my freights. This being the case, I was obliged to stop at different points on the way, and to go to others off the route to solicit help. At most places I raised a little; but it consumed my time, and my unavoidable expenses so nearly kept pace with my incomes that I found it exceedingly discouraging. With the help of Gerrit Smith, who supplied me with sixty dollars at Peterboro', and two hundred and fifty dollars at Chicago, and other smaller amounts from others, I was able to pay freights and other expenses to this place; hiring a man to drive one team, and driving another myself; and had about twenty-five dollars on hand, with about one hundred dollars' worth of provisions, when I reached here. Among all the good friends who had promised to go with me, *not one* could I get to stick by me and assist me on my way through. I have picked up, at different times on the way, considerable value in articles (indispensable in active service) which were scattered on the way, and had been provided either by or for the National Committee. On reaching here I found one hundred and ten dollars, sent me by Mr. Whitman, from sale of articles in Kansas, sent there by the National Committee. This is all the money I have got from them on their appropriation at New York. On the road one of my horses hurt himself so badly that I lost about ten days in consequence, not being in condition to go on without him, or to buy or to hire another. I find the arms and ammunition voted me by the Massachusetts State Committee nearly all here, and in middling good order,—some a little rusted. Have overhauled and cleaned up the worst of them, and am now waiting to know what is best to do next, or for a little escort from Kansas, should I and the supplies be needed. I am now at last within a kind of hailing distance of our Free-State friends in Kansas.

On the way from Iowa City I and my third son (the hired man I mentioned), in order to make the little funds we had reach as far as possible, and to avoid notice, lived exclusively on herring, soda crackers, and sweetened water for more than three weeks (sleeping every night in our wagons), except that twice we got a little milk, and a few times some boiled eggs. Early in the season, in consequence of the poor encouragement I met with, and of their own losses and sufferings, my sons declined to return; and my wife wrote me as follows: "The boys have all determined both to practise and learn war no more." This I said nothing about, lest it should prevent my getting any further supplies. After leaving New England I could not get the scratch of a pen to tell whether anything had been deposited at Hartford, from New Haven and other places, for me or not; until, since I came here, a line comes from Mr. Callender, dated 24th July, saying nothing has been deposited, in answer to one I had written June 22, in which he further says he has answered all my letters. The parting with my wife and young uneducated children, without income, supplies of clothing, provisions, or even a comfortable house to live in, or money to provide such things, with at least a fair chance that it was to be a *last and final separation,* had lain heavily on me, and was about as much a matter of self-sacrifice and self-devotion on the part of my wife as on my own, and about as much her act as my own. When Mr. Lawrence, of his own accord, proposed relieving me on that score, it greatly eased a burdened spirit; but I did not rely upon it absolutely, nor make any certain bargain on the strength of it, until after being positively assured by Mr. Stearns, in writing, that it should, and by yourself that it would, certainly be done.

It was the poor condition of my noble-hearted wife and of her young children that made me follow up that encouragement with a tenacity that disgusted him and completely exhausted his patience. But after such repeated assurances from friends I so much respected that I could not suspect they would trifle with my feelings, I made a positive bargain for the farm; and when I found nothing for me at Peterboro', I borrowed one hundred and ten dollars of Mr. Smith for the men who occupied the farm, telling him it would certainly be refunded, and the others that they would get all their money very soon, and even before I left the country. This has brought me only extreme mortification and depression of feeling; for all my letters from home, up to the last, say not a dime has been paid in to Mr. Smith. Friends who never know the lack of a sumptuous dinner little comprehend the value of such trifling matters to persons circumstanced as I am. But, my noble-hearted friend, I am "though faint, yet pursuing." My health has been much better of late. I believe my anxiety and discouragements had something to do with repeated returns of fever and ague I have had, as it tended to deprive me of sleep and to debilitate me. I intend this letter as a kind of report of my progress and success, as much for your committee or my friend Stearns as yourself. I have been joined by a friend since I got here, and get no discouraging news from Kansas.

Your friend,

J. Brown.

ROCHESTER, N. Y., Jan. 30, 1858.

MY DEAR WIFE AND CHILDREN, EVERY ONE,—I am (praised be God!) once more in York State. Whether I shall be permitted to visit you or not this winter or spring, I cannot now say; but it is some relief of mind to feel that I am again so near you. Possibly, if I cannot go to see you, I may be able to devise some way for some one or more of you to meet me somewhere. The anxiety I feel to see my wife and children once more I am unable to describe. I want exceedingly to see my big baby and Ruth's baby, and to see how that little company of sheep look about this time. The cries of my poor sorrow-stricken despairing children, whose "tears on their cheeks" are ever in my eyes, and whose sighs are ever in my ears, may however prevent my enjoying the happiness I so much desire. But, courage, courage, courage!—the great work of my life (the unseen Hand that "guided me, and who has indeed holden my right hand, may hold it still," though I have not known him at all as I ought) I may yet see accomplished (God helping), and be permitted to return and "rest at evening."

O my daughter Ruth! could any plan be devised whereby you could let Henry go "to school" (as you expressed it in your letter to him while in Kansas), I would rather now have him "for another term" than to have a hundred average scholars. I have a particular and very important, but not dangerous, place for him to fill in the "school," and I know of no man living so well adapted to fill it. I am quite confident some way can be devised so that you and your children could be with him, and be quite happy even, and safe; but God forbid me to flatter you into trouble! I did not do it before. My dear child, could you face such music if, on a full explanation, Henry could be satisfied that his family might be safe? I would make a similar inquiry of my own dear wife; but I have kept her tumbling here and there over a stormy and tempestuous sea for so many years that I cannot ask her such a question. The natural ingenuity of Salmon in connection with some experience he and Oliver have both had, would point him out as the next best man I could now select; but I am dumb in his case, as also in the case of Watson and all my other sons. Jason's qualifications are, some of them, like Henry's also.

Do not noise it about that I am in these parts, and direct to N. Hawkins, care of Frederick Douglass, Rochester, N. Y. I want to hear how you are all supplied with winter clothing, boots, etc.

God bless you all!

Your affectionate husband and father,

John Brown.

Rochester, N. Y. 12*th Feb'y,* 1858.

MY DEAR SIR,—I have just read your kind letter of the 8th inst., and will now say that Rail Road business on a *somewhat extended* scale is the *identical* object for which I am trying to get means. I have been connected with that business as *commonly conducted* from my boyhood and *never* let an opportunity slip. I have been opperating to some purpose *the past season*; but I now have a measure on *foot* that I feel *sure* would awaken in you something more than a *common interest* if you could understand it. I have just written my friends G. L. Stearns and F. B. Sanborn asking them to meet me for consultation at Gerrit Smith's, Peterboro' [N. Y.]. I am very anxious to have *you come along; certain as I feel,* that you will never regret having been one of the council. I would most gladly pay your expenses had I the means to spare. *Will you come on?* Please write as before.

Your Friend   John Brown.

Provisional Constitution and Ordinances for the People of the United States

Preamble

Whereas slavery, throughout its entire existence in the United States, is none other than a most barbarous, unprovoked, and unjustifiable war of one portion of its citizens upon another portion—the only conditions of which are perpetual imprisonment and hopeless servitude or absolute extermination—in utter disregard and violation of those eternal and self-evident truths set forth in our Declaration of Independence:

Therefore we, citizens of the United States, and the oppressed people who, by a recent decision of the Supreme Court, are declared to have no rights which the white man is bound to respect, together with all other people degraded by the laws thereof, do, for the time being, ordain and establish for ourselves the following Provisional Constitution and Ordinances, the better to protect our persons, property, lives, and liberties, and to govern our actions:

Article I
Qualifications for Membership

All persons of mature age, whether proscribed, oppressed, and enslaved citizens, or of the proscribed and oppressed races of the United States, who shall agree to sustain and enforce the Provisional Constitution and Ordinances of this organization, together with all minor children of such persons, shall be held to be fully entitled to protection under the same.

Article II
Branches of Government

The provisional government of this organization shall consist of three branches, viz.: legislative, executive, and judicial.

Article III
Legislative

The legislative branch shall be a Congress or House of Representatives, composed of not less than five nor more than ten members, who shall be elected by all citizens of mature age and of sound mind connected with this organization, and who shall remain in office for three years, unless sooner removed for misconduct, inability, or by death. A majority of such members shall constitute a quorum.

Article IV
Executive

The executive branch of this organization shall consist of a President and Vice-President, who shall be chosen by the citizens or members of this organization, and each of whom shall hold his office for three years, unless sooner removed by death or for inability or misconduct.

Article V
Judicial

The judicial branch of this organization shall consist of one Chief Justice of the Supreme Court and of four associate judges of said court, each constituting a circuit court. They shall each be chosen in the same manner as the President, and shall continue in office until their places have been filled in the same manner by election of the citizens. Said court shall have jurisdiction in all civil or criminal causes arising under this constitution, except breaches of the rules of war.

Article VI
Validity of Enactments

All enactments of the legislative branch shall, to become valid during the first three years, have the approbation of the President and of the Commander-in-chief of the army.

Article VII
Commander-in-Chief

A Commander-in-chief of the army shall be chosen by the President, Vice-President, a majority of the Provisional Congress, and of the Supreme Court, and he shall receive his commission from the President, signed by the Vice-President, the Chief Justice of the Supreme Court, and the Secretary of War, and he shall hold his office for three years, unless removed by death or on proof of incapacity or misbehavior. He shall, unless under arrest, (and until his place is actually filled as provided for by this constitution,) direct all movements of the army and advise with any allies. He shall, however, be tried, removed, or punished, on complaint of the President, by at least three general officers, or a majority of the House of Representatives, or of the Supreme Court; which House of Representatives, (the President presiding,) the Vice-President, and the members of the Supreme Court, shall constitute a court-martial for his trial; with power to remove or punish, as the case may require, and to fill his place, as above provided.

Correspondence of The N.Y. Tribune.

Trading Post, Kansas, Jan., 1859.

The editor of The N.Y. Tribune will greatly oblige a humble friend by allowing me the use of his columns while I briefly state two parallels, in my poor way.

Not one year ago, eleven quiet citizens of this neighborhood, viz: Wm. Calfsetzer [Colpetzer], Wm. Robertson, Amos Hall, Austin Hall, John Campbell, Asa Snyder, Thomas Stilwell, William Hairgrove, Asa Hairgrove, Patrick Ross and B. L. Reed were gathered up from their work and their homes, by an armed force under one Hamilton, and, without trial or opportunity to speak in their own defense, were formed into a line, and all but one shot—five killed and five wounded. One fell unharmed, pretending to be dead. All were *left for dead*. The only crime charged against them was that of being Free-State men. Now, I inquire, what action has ever, since the occurrence in May last, been taken by either the President of the United States, the Governor of Missouri, the Governor of Kansas, or any of their tools, or by any Pro-Slavery or Administration man, to ferret out and punish the perpetrators of this crime?

Now for the other parallel. On Sunday, the 19th of December, a negro man named Jim, came over to the Osage settlement, from Missouri, and stated that he, together with his wife, two children and one other negro man, were to be sold within a day or two, and begged for help to get away. On Monday, the following night, two small companies were made up to go to Missouri, and forcibly liberate the five slaves, *together with other slaves*. One of these companies I assumed to direct. We proceeded to the place, surrounded the buildings, liberated the slaves, and also took certain property supposed to belong to the estate. We, however, learned before leaving, that a portion of the articles we had taken belonged to a man living on the plantation as a tenant, and who was supposed to have no interest in the estate. We promptly returned to him *all we had taken*. We then went to another plantation, where we freed five more slaves, took some property, and two white men. We moved slowly away into the Territory, for some distance, and then sent the white men back, telling them to follow us as soon as they chose to do so. The other company freed one female slave, took some property, and, as I am informed, killed one white man (the master), who fought against the liberation.

Now for a comparison. Eleven persons are forcibly restored to their "natural and inalienable rights," with but one man killed, and all "Hell is stirred from beneath." It is currently reported that the Governor of Missouri has made a requisition upon the Governor of Kansas for the delivery of all such as were concerned in the last-named "dreadful outrage." The Marshal of Kansas is said to be collecting a posse of Missouri (not Kansas) men at West Point, in Missouri, a little town about ten miles distant, to "enforce the laws." All Pro-Slavery, conservative Free-State, and doughface men, and Administration tools, are filled with holy horror.

Consider the two cases, and the action of the Administration party.

Respectfully yours,   John Brown.

Boston, Mass, 13th May, 1859.

My Dear Daughter Ellen

I will send you [a] short letter.

I want very much to have you *grow* good every day: to have you learn to mind your mother very quick: & sit very still at the table; & to mind what all older persons say to you; that is right. I hope to see you soon again; & if I should bring some little thing that will please you; it would not be very strange. I want you to be uncommon *good natured*. *God* bless you my child.

Your Affectionate Father
John Brown

Chambersburg, Pa. 8th Sept. 1859

Dear Wife & Children All

I write to say that we are all well: & are getting along as well as we could reasonably expect. It now appears likely that Martha, & Anne: will be on their way home in the course of this month: but they may be detained to a little later period. I do not know what to advise about fattening the old Spotted cow: as much will depend on what you have *to feed her with*; whether your heifers will come in or not; next Spring: also upon her present condition. You must exercise the best judgment you have in the matter: as I know but little about your crops. *I should like* to know more as soon as I can. I am now in hopes of being able to send you something in the way of help before long. May God abundantly bless you all. *Ellen I want you to be very good.*   Your Affectionate husband & Father.

IS

Sept 9th Bells letter of 30th Aug to Watson is received

Sept 20th 1859. All well. Girls will probably start for home soon.

IS

Harper's Ferry, Oct. 19, 1859,

"Old Brown," or "Ossawattomie Brown," as he is often called, the hero of a dozen fights or so with the "border ruffians" of Missouri, in the days of "bleeding Kansas," is the head and front of this offending—the commander of the abolition filibuster army. His wounds, which at first were supposed to be mortal, turn out to be mere flesh wounds and scratches, not at all dangerous in their character. He has been removed, together with Stephens, the other wounded prisoner, from the engine room to the office of the armory, and they now lie on the floor, upon miserable shake-downs, covered with some old bedding.

Brown is fifty-five years of age, rather small sized, with keen and restless gray eyes, and a grizzly beard and hair. He is a wiry, active man, and should the slightest chance for an escape be afforded, there is no doubt that he will yet give his captors much trouble. His hair is matted and tangled, and his face, hands and clothes all smouched and smeared with blood. Colonel Lee stated that he would exclude all visiters from the room if the wounded men were annoyed or pained by them, but Brown said he was by no means annoyed; on the contrary he was glad to be able to make himself and his motives clearly understood. He converses freely, fluently and cheerfully, without the slightest manifestation of fear or uneasiness, evidently weighing well his words, and possessing a good command of language. His manner is courteous and affable, and he appears to make a favorable impression upon his auditory, which, during most of the day yesterday, averaged about ten or a dozen men.

When I arrived in the armory at Harper's Ferry, shortly after two o'clock in the afternoon of October 19, Brown was answering questions put to him by Senator Mason, who had just arrived from his residence at Winchester, thirty miles distant; Colonel Faulkner, member of Congress, who lives but a few miles off; Mr. Vallandigham, member of Congress from Ohio; and several other distinguished gentlemen. The following is a verbatim report of the conversation:—

Brown's Interview with Mason, Vallandigham, and Others

Senator Mason. Can you tell us who furnished money for your expedition?

John Brown. I furnished most of it myself; I cannot implicate others. It is by my own folly that I have been taken. I could easily have saved myself from it, had I exercised my own better judgment rather than yielded to my feelings.

Mason. You mean if you had escaped immediately?

Brown. No. I had the means to make myself secure without any escape; but I allowed myself to be surrounded by a force by being too tardy. I should have gone away; but I had thirty odd prisoners, whose wives and daughters were in tears for their safety, and I felt for them. Besides, I wanted to allay the fears of those who believed we came here to burn and kill. For this reason I allowed the train to cross the bridge, and gave them full liberty to pass on. I did it only to spare the feelings of those passengers and their families, and to allay the apprehensions that you had got here in your vicinity a band of men who had no regard for life and property, nor any feelings of humanity.

Mason. But you killed some people passing along the streets quietly.

Brown. Well, sir, if there was anything of that kind done, it was without my knowledge. Your own citizens who were my prisoners will tell you that every possible means was taken to prevent it. I did not allow my men to fire when there was danger of killing those we regarded as innocent persons, if I could help it. They will tell you that we allowed ourselves to be fired at repeatedly, and did not return it.

A Bystander. That is not so. You killed an unarmed man at the corner of the house over there at the water-tank, and another besides.

Brown. See here, my friend; it is useless to dispute or contradict the report of your own neighbors who were my prisoners.

Mason. If you would tell us who sent you here,—who provided the means,—that would be information of some value.

Brown. I will answer freely and faithfully about what concerns myself,—I will answer anything I can with honor,—but not about others.

Mr. Vallandigham (who had just entered). Mr. Brown, who sent you here?

Brown. No man sent me here; it was my own prompting and that of my Maker, or that of the Devil,—whichever you please to ascribe it to. I acknowledge no master in human form.

Vallandigham. Did you get up the expedition yourself?

Brown. I did.

Vallandigham. Did you get up this document that is called a Constitution?

Brown. I did. They are a constitution and ordinances of my own contriving and getting up.

Vallandigham. How long have you been engaged in this business?

Brown. From the breaking out of the difficulties in Kansas. Four of my sons had gone there to settle, and they induced me to go. I did not go there to settle, but because of the difficulties.

Mason. How many are there engaged with you in this movement?

Brown. Any questions that I can honorably answer I will,—not otherwise. So far as I am myself concerned, I have told everything truthfully. I value my word, sir.

Mason. What was your object in coming?

Brown. We came to free the slaves, and only that.

A Volunteer. How many men, in all, had you?

Brown. I came to Virginia with eighteen men only, besides myself.

Volunteer. What in the world did you suppose you could do here in Virginia with that amount of men?

Brown. Young man, I do not wish to discuss that question here.

Volunteer. You could not do anything.

Brown. Well, perhaps your ideas and mine on military subjects would differ materially.

Mason. How do you justify your acts?

Brown. I think, my friend, you are guilty of a great wrong against God and humanity,—I say it without wishing to be offensive,—and it would be perfectly right for any one to interfere with you so far as to free those you wilfully and wickedly hold in bondage. I do not say this insultingly.

Mason. I understand that.

Brown. I think I did right, and that others will do right who interfere with you at any time and at all times. I hold that the Golden Rule, "Do unto others as ye would that others should do unto you," applies to all who would help others to gain their liberty.

Lieutenant Stuart. But don't you believe in the Bible?

Brown. Certainly I do.

Mason. Did you consider this a military organization in this Constitution? I have not yet read it.

Brown. I did, in some sense. I wish you would give that paper close attention.

Mason. You consider yourself the commander-in-chief of these "provisional" military forces?

Brown. I was chosen, agreeably to the ordinance of a certain document, commander-in-chief of that force.

Mason. What wages did you offer?

Brown. None.

Stuart. "The wages of sin is death."

Brown. I would not have made such a remark to you if you had been a prisoner, and wounded, in my hands.

A Bystander. Did you not promise a negro in Gettysburg twenty dollars a month?

Brown. I did not.

Mason. Does this talking annoy you?

Brown. Not in the least.

Vallandigham. Have you lived long in Ohio?

Brown. I went there in 1805. I lived in Summit County, which was then Portage County. My native place is Connecticut; my father lived there till 1805.

Vallandigham. Have you been in Portage County lately?

Brown. I was there in June last.

Vallandigham. When in Cleveland, did you attend the Fugitive Slave Law Convention there?

Brown. No. I was there about the time of the sitting of the court to try the Oberlin rescuers. I spoke there publicly on that subject; on the Fugitive Slave Law and my own rescue. Of course, so far as I had any influence at all, I was supposed to justify the Oberlin people for rescuing the slave, because I have myself forcibly taken slaves from bondage. I was concerned in taking eleven slaves from Missouri to Canada last winter. I think I spoke in Cleveland before the Convention. I do not know that I had conversation with any of the Oberlin rescuers. I was sick part of the time I was in Ohio with the ague, in Ashtabula County.

Vallandigham. Did you see anything of Joshua R. Giddings there?

Brown. I did meet him.

Vallandigham. Did you converse with him?

Brown. I did. I would not tell you, of course, anything that would implicate Mr. Giddings; but I certainly met with him and had conversations with him.

Vallandigham. About that rescue case?

Brown. Yes; I heard him express his opinions upon it very freely and frankly.

Vallandigham. Justifying it?

Brown. Yes, sir; I do not compromise him, certainly, in saying that.

Vallandigham. Will you answer this: Did you talk with Giddings about your expedition here?

Brown. No, I won't answer that; because a denial of it I would not make, and to make any affirmation of it I should be a great dunce.

Vallandigham. Have you had correspondence with parties at the North on the subject of this movement?

Brown. I have had correspondence.

A Bystander. Do you consider this a religious movement?

Brown. It is, in my opinion, the greatest service man can render to God.

Bystander. Do you consider yourself an instrument in the hands of Providence?

Brown. I do.

Bystander. Upon what principle do you justify your acts?

Brown. Upon the Golden Rule. I pity the poor in bondage that have none to help them: that is why I am here; not to gratify any personal animosity, revenge, or vindictive spirit. It is my sympathy with the oppressed and the wronged, that are as good as you and as precious in the sight of God.

Bystander. Certainly. But why take the slaves against their will?

Brown. I never did.

Bystander. You did in one instance, at least.

(Stephens, the other wounded prisoner, here said, "You are right. In one case I know the negro wanted to go back.")

Bystander. Where did you come from?

Stephens. I lived in Ashtabula County, Ohio.

Vallandigham. How recently did you leave Ashtabula County?

Stephens. Some months ago. I never resided there any length of time; have been through there.

Vallandigham. How far did you live from Jefferson?

Brown. Be cautious, Stephens, about any answers that would commit any friend. I would not answer that.

(Stephens turned partially over with a groan of pain, and was silent.)

Vallandigham. Who are your advisers in this movement?

Brown. I cannot answer that. I have numerous sympathizers throughout the entire North.

Vallandigham. In northern Ohio?

Brown. No more there than anywhere else; in all the free States.

Vallandigham. But you are not personally acquainted in southern Ohio?

Brown. Not very much.

A Bystander. Did you ever live in Washington City?

Brown. I did not. I want you to understand, gentlemen, and (to the reporter of the "Herald") you may report that,—I want you to understand that I respect the rights of the poorest and weakest of colored people, oppressed by the slave system, just as much as I do those of the most wealthy and powerful. This is the idea that has moved me, and that alone. We expected no reward except the satisfaction of endeavoring to do for those in distress and greatly oppressed as we would be done by. The cry of distress of the oppressed is my reason, and the only thing that prompted me to come here.

Bystander. Why did you do it secretly?

Brown. Because I thought that necessary to success; no other reason.

Bystander. Have you read Gerrit Smith's last letter?

Brown. What letter do you mean?

Bystander. The "New York Herald" of yesterday, in speaking of this affair, mentions a letter in this way:—

"Apropos of this exciting news, we recollect a very significant passage in one of Gerrit Smith's letters, published a month or two ago, in which he speaks of the folly of attempting to strike the shackles off the slaves by the force of moral suasion or legal agitation, and predicts that the next movement made in the direction of negro emancipation would be an insurrection in the South."

Brown. I have not seen the "New York Herald" for some days past; but I presume, from your remark about the gist of the letter, that I should concur with it. I agree with Mr. Smith that moral suasion is hopeless. I don't think the people of the slave States will ever consider the subject of slavery in its true light till some other argument is resorted to than moral suasion.

Vallandigham. Did you expect a general rising of the slaves in case of your success?

Brown. No, sir; nor did I wish it. I expected to gather them up from time to time, and set them free.

Vallandigham. Did you expect to hold possession here till then?

Brown. Well, probably I had quite a different idea. I do not know that I ought to reveal my plans. I am here a prisoner and wounded, because I foolishly allowed myself to be so. You overrate your strength in supposing I could have been taken if I had not allowed it. I was too tardy after commencing the open attack—in delaying my movements through Monday night, and up to the time I was attacked by the Government troops. It was all occasioned by my desire to spare the feelings of my prisoners and their families and the community at large. I had no knowledge of the shooting of the negro Heywood.

Vallandigham. What time did you commence your organization in Canada?

Brown. That occurred about two years ago; in 1858.

Vallandigham. Who was the secretary?

Brown. That I would not tell if I recollected; but I do not recollect. I think the officers were elected in May, 1858. I may answer incorrectly, but not intentionally. My head is a little confused by wounds, and my memory obscure on dates, etc.

Dr. Biggs. Were you in the party at Dr. Kennedy's house?

Brown. I was the head of that party. I occupied the house to mature my plans. I have not been in Baltimore to purchase caps.

Dr. Biggs. What was the number of men at Kennedy's?

Brown. I decline to answer that.

Dr. Biggs. Who lanced that woman's neck on the hill?

Brown. I did. I have sometimes practised in surgery when I thought it a matter of humanity and necessity, and there was no one else to do it; but I have not studied surgery.

Dr. Biggs. It was done very well and scientifically. They have been very clever to the neighbors, I have been told, and we had no reason to suspect them, except that we could not understand their movements. They were represented as eight or nine persons; on Friday there were thirteen.

Brown. There were more than that.

Q. Where did you get arms? *A.* I bought them.

Q. In what State? *A.* That I will not state.

Q. How many guns? *A.* Two hundred Sharpe's rifles and two hundred revolvers,—what is called the Massachusetts Arms Company's revolvers, a little under navy size.

Q. Why did you not take that swivel you left in the house? *A.* I had no occasion for it. It was given to me a year or two ago.

Q. In Kansas? *A.* No, I had nothing given to me in Kansas.

Q. By whom, and in what State? *A.* I decline to answer. It is not properly a swivel; it is a very large rifle with a pivot. The ball is larger than a musket ball; it is intended for a slug.

Reporter. I do not wish to annoy you; but if you have anything further you would like to say, I will report it.

Brown. I have nothing to say, only that I claim to be here in carrying out a measure I believe perfectly justifiable, and not to act the part of an incendiary or ruffian, but to aid those suffering great wrong.

I wish to say, furthermore, that you had better—all you people at the South—prepare yourselves for a settlement of this question, that must come up for settlement sooner than you are prepared for it. The sooner you are prepared the better. You may dispose of me very easily,—I am nearly disposed of now; but this question is still to be settled,—this negro question I mean; the end of that is not yet. These wounds were inflicted upon me—both sabre cuts on my head and bayonet stabs in different parts of my body—some minutes after I had ceased fighting and had consented to surrender, for the benefit of others, not for my own. I believe the Major would not have been alive; I could have killed him just as easy as a mosquito when he came in, but I supposed he only came in to receive our surrender. There had been loud and long calls of "surrender" from us,—as loud as men could yell; but in the confusion and excitement I suppose we were not heard. I do not think the Major, or any one, meant to butcher us after we had surrendered.

An Officer. Why did you not surrender before the attack?

Brown. I did not think it was my duty or interest to do so. We assured the prisoners that we did not wish to harm them, and they should be set at liberty. I exercised my best judgment, not believing the people would wantonly sacrifice their own fellow-citizens, when we offered to let them go on condition of being allowed to change our position about a quarter of a mile. The prisoners agreed by a vote among themselves to pass across the bridge with us. We wanted them only as a sort of guarantee of our own safety,—that we should not be fired into. We took them, in the first place, as hostages and to keep them from doing any harm. We did kill some men in defending ourselves, but I saw no one fire except directly in self-defence. Our orders were strict not to harm any one not in arms against us.

Q. Brown, suppose you had every nigger in the United States, what would you do with them? *A.* Set them free.

Q. Your intention was to carry them off and free them? *A.* Not at all.

A Bystander. To set them free would sacrifice the life of every man in this community.

Brown. I do not think so.

Bystander. I know it. I think you are fanatical.

Brown. And I think you are fanatical. "Whom the gods would destroy they first make mad," and you are mad.

Q. Was it your only object to free the negroes? *A.* Absolutely our only object.

Q. But you demanded and took Colonel Washington's silver and watch? *A*. Yes; we intended freely to appropriate the property of slaveholders to carry out our object. It was for that, and only that, and with no design to enrich ourselves with any plunder whatever.

Bystander. Did you know Sherrod in Kansas? I understand you killed him.

Brown. I killed no man except in fair fight. I fought at Black Jack Point and at Osawatomie; and if I killed anybody, it was at one of these places.

John Brown's Last Speech to the Court, November 2, 1859

I have, may it please the Court, a few words to say.

In the first place, I deny everything but what I have all along admitted,—the design on my part to free the slaves. I intended certainly to have made a clean thing of that matter, as I did last winter, when I went into Missouri and there took slaves without the snapping of a gun on either side, moved them through the country, and finally left them in Canada. I designed to have done the same thing again, on a larger scale. That was all I intended. I never did intend murder, or treason, or the destruction of property, or to excite or incite slaves to rebellion, or to make insurrection.

I have another objection; and that is, it is unjust that I should suffer such a penalty. Had I interfered in the manner which I admit, and which I admit has been fairly proved (for I admire the truthfulness and candor of the greater portion of the witnesses who have testified in this case),—had I so interfered in behalf of the rich, the powerful, the intelligent, the so-called great, or in behalf of any of their friends,— either father, mother, brother, sister, wife, or children, or any of that class,—and suffered and sacrificed what I have in this interference, it would have been all right; and every man in this court would have deemed it an act worthy of reward rather than punishment.

This court acknowledges, as I suppose, the validity of the law of God. I see a book kissed here which I suppose to be the Bible, or at least the New Testament. That teaches me that all things whatsoever I would that men should do to me, I should do even so to them. It teaches me, further, to "remember them that are in bonds, as bound with them." I endeavored to act up to that instruction. I say, I am yet too young to understand that God is any respecter of persons. I believe that to have interfered as I have done—as I have always freely admitted I have done—in behalf of His despised poor, was not wrong, but right. Now, if it is deemed necessary that I should forfeit my life for the furtherance of the ends of justice, and mingle my blood further with the blood of my children and with the blood of millions in this slave country whose rights are disregarded by wicked, cruel, and unjust enactments,—I submit; so let it be done!

Let me say one word further.

I feel entirely satisfied with the treatment I have received on my trial. Considering all the circumstances, it has been more generous than I expected. But I feel no consciousness of guilt. I have stated from the first what was my intention, and what was not. I never have had any design against the life of any person, nor any disposition to commit treason, or excite slaves to rebel, or make any general insurrection. I never encouraged any man to do so, but always discouraged any idea of that kind.

Let me say, also, a word in regard to the statements made by some of those connected with me. I hear it has been stated by some of them that I have induced them to join me. But the contrary is true. I do not say this to injure them, but as regretting their weakness. There is not one of them but joined me of his own accord, and the greater part of them at their own expense. A number of them I never saw, and never had a word of conversation with, till the day they came to me; and that was for the purpose I have stated.

Now I have done.

Charlestown Jefferson County Va Oct. 21, 1859
Hon. Thos. Russell

Dear Sir

I am here a prisoner with several sabre cuts in my head, & bayonet stabs in my body. My object in writing to you is to obtain able, & faithful counsel for myself; & fellow prisoners five in all, as we have the faith of Virginia, pledged through her Governor and numerous other prominent citizens, to give us a fair trial. Without we can obtain such counsel from without the slave states: neither the facts in our case can come before the world: nor can *we* have the benefit of such facts (as might be considered mitigating in the view of others) upon our trial. I have money on hand *here* to the amount of $250. and personal property sufficient to pay a most liberal fee to yourself; or to any suitable man who will undertake our defence, if I can be allowed the benefit of said property. Can you or some other good man come in immediately for the sake of the young men prisoners at least? My wounds are doing well. Do not send an ultra Abolitionist.

Very respectfully yours,

John Brown

The trial is set for Wednesday next the 25th inst.

J. W. Campbell
Sheriff Jeff. County

Charlestown, Jefferson Co., Va., 31st. Oct. 1859.
My dear Wife, and Children every one

I suppose you have learned before this by the newspapers that two weeks ago today we were fighting for our lives at Harpers ferry: that during the fight Watson was mortally wounded; Oliver killed, Wm Thompson killed, & Dauphin slightly wounded. That on the following day I was taken prisoner immediately after which I received several Sabre cuts in my head; & Bayonet stabs in my body. As nearly as I can learn Watson died of his wound on Wednesday the 2d or on Thursday the 3d day after I was taken. Dauphin was killed when I was taken; & Anderson I suppose also. I have since been tried, & found guilty of treason, &c; and of murder in the first degree. I have not yet received my sentence. No others of the company with whom you were acquainted were so far as *I can learn* either killed or taken. Under all these terible calamities; I feel quite cheerful in the assurance that God reigns; & will overrule all for his glory; & the best possible good. I feel *no* con[s]ciou[s]ness of *guilt* in the matter: nor even mortifycation on account of my imprisonment; & irons; & I feel perfectly assured that very soon no member of my family will feel any possible disposition to "blush on my account." Already dear friends at a distance with kindest sympathy are cheering me with the assurance that *posterity* at least: will do me justice. I shall commend you all together with my beloved; but bereaved daughters in law to their sympathies which I have no doubt will soon reach you. I also commend you all to him "whose mercy endureth forever": to the God of my *fathers* "whose I am; & whom I serve." "He will never leave you nor forsake you" unless you forsake him. Finally my dearly beloved be of good comfort. Be sure to remember *& to follow my advice* & my example *too*: so far as it has been consistent with the holy religion of Jesus Christ in which I remain a most firm, & humble believer. Never forget the poor nor think any thing you bestow on them to be lost, to you even though they may be as *black* as Ebedmelch, the Ethiopian eunuch who cared for Jeremiah in the pit of the dungeon; or as *black* as the one to whom Phillip preached Christ. Be sure to entertain strangers for thereby some have—"Remember them that are in bonds as bound with them." I am in the charge of a jailor *like* the one who took charge of "Paul & Silas;" & you may rest assured that both *kind hearts* and *kind faces* are more or less about me: whilst thousands are thirsting for my blood. "These *light* afflictions which are but *for a moment* shall work out for us a far *more exceeding & eternal* weight of glory." I hope to be able to write you again. My

wounds are doing well. Copy this & send it to your sorrow stricken brothers, *Ruth*; to comfort them. Write me a few words in regard to the welfare of all. God Allmighty bless you all: & make you "joyful in the midst of all your tribulations." Write to John Brown, Charlestown, Jefferson Co, Va, care of Capt John Avis
Your Affectionate Husband, & Father.

John Brown

Nov. 3d 1859

P. S. Yesterday Nov 2d I was sentenced to be hanged on 2 Decem next. Do not grieve on my account. I am still quite cheerful.
Go[d] bless you all Your Ever

J Brown

Charlestown, Jefferson County, Va., Nov. 1, 1859.

My Dear Friend E. B. of R. I.,—Your most cheering letter of the 27th of October is received; and may the Lord reward you a thousandfold for the kind feeling you express toward me; but more especially for your fidelity to the "poor that cry, and those that have no help." For this I am a prisoner in bonds. It is solely my own fault, in a military point of view, that we met with our disaster. I mean that I mingled with our prisoners and so far sympathized with them and their families that I neglected my duty in other respects. But God's will, not mine, be done.

You know that Christ once armed Peter. So also in my case I think he put a sword into my hand, and there continued it so long as he saw best, and then kindly took it from me. I mean when I first went to Kansas. I wish you could know with what cheerfulness I am now wielding the "sword of the Spirit" on the right hand and on the left. I bless God that it proves "mighty to the pulling down of strongholds." I always loved my Quaker friends, and I commend to their kind regard my poor bereaved widowed wife and my daughters and daughters-in-law, whose husbands fell at my side. One is a mother and the other likely to become so soon. They, as well as my own sorrow-stricken daughters, are left very poor, and have much greater need of sympathy than I, who, through Infinite Grace and the kindness of strangers, am "joyful in all my tribulations."

Dear sister, write them at North Elba, Essex County, N. Y., to comfort their sad hearts. Direct to Mary A. Brown, wife of John Brown. There is also another—a widow, wife of Thompson, who fell with my poor boys in the affair at Harper's Ferry—at the same place.

I do not feel conscious of guilt in taking up arms; and had it been in behalf of the rich and powerful, the intelligent, the great (as men count greatness), or those who form enactments to suit themselves and corrupt others, or some of their friends, that I interfered, suffered, sacrificed, and fell, it would have been doing very well. But enough of this. These light afflictions, which endure for a moment, shall but work for me "a far more exceeding and eternal weight of glory." I would be very grateful for another letter from you. My wounds are healing. Farewell. God will surely attend to his own cause in the best possible way and time, and he will not forget the work of his own hands.

Your friend,
John Brown.

Charlestown, Jefferson Co. Va. 4th. Nov. 1859.
Rev. T. W. Higginson
                    Dear Friend—
    If my Wife were to come here just now it would *only tend* to
distract *her mind, ten fold;* & would *only add* to my affliction; & *cannot
possibly* do me *any good.* It will also use up the scanty means she has
to supply Bread & cheap but comfortable clothing, fuel &C for
herself, and Children *through the Winter.* DO PERSUADE her to remain
at home for a time (*at least*) till she can learn further from me. She will
secure a Thousand times the consolation AT HOME that she can possibly find elsewhere. I have just *written her there & will* write her
CONSTANTLY. Her presence *here* will deepen my affliction a thousand
fold. I beg of her to be *calm, & submissive;* & not to go *wild* on my
account. I lack *for nothing* & was feeling quite cheerful before I learned
she talked of *coming on. I ask her to compose her mind* & to remain *quiet*
till the last of *this month;* out of pity to me. I can certainly judge
better in this matter than *any one else.* My warmest thanks to yourself; & *all other* kind friends. *God bless you all. Please send this line to
my afflicted Wife,* by first possible conveyance.
                                Your friend in truth   John Brown

Charlestown, Jefferson Co. Va. 4th. Nov. 1859

Mrs L Maria Child
    Wayland
       Mass   My Dear friend

(Such you prove to be though an entire stranger) Your most kind letter has reached me; with your kind offer to come here & take care of me. Allow me to express my gratitude for your great sympathy: & at the same time to propose to you a different course; together with my reasons for wishing it. I should certainly be greatly pleased to become personally acquainted with one so gifted; & so kind; but I cannot avoid seeing some objections to it under present circumstances. First I am in charge of a most humane gentleman who with his family have rendered me every possible attention I have desired or that could be of the least advantage: and I am so far recovered from my wounds as no longer to require nursing. Then again it would subject you to great personal inconvenience, & quite a heavy expence; without doing me any good. Now allow me to name to you another channel through which you may reach me with your sympathies much more effectually. I have at home a Wife & three young daughters. The youngest of whom is but a little over Five years old; the oldest is nearly Sixteen. I have also two daughters in law whose Husbands have both fallen near me here. One of these is a Mother & the other like to become so. There is also another Widow a Mrs. Thompson whose Husband also fell here. Whether she is a Mother or not I cannot say. They all (my Wife included) live at North Elba, Essex Co. New York. I have or suppose I have a middle aged Son who has been in some degree a cripple from childhood who would have as much as he could well do to earn a living. He was a most dreadful sufferer in Kansas; & lost all he had laid up: & has not enough to clothe himself for the Winter comfortably. I have *no Son or Son in law living*; who did not suffer terribly in Kansas. Now dear friend would you not as soon contribute Fifty Cents now: & a like sum *yearly* for the relief of those very poor; & deeply afflicted persons to enable them to supply themselves, & Children with Bread: & very plain clothing; & to enable the children to receive a common English education: & also to devote your own energies to induce others to join you in giving a like or other amount to constitute a little fund for the purpose named? I cannot see how your coming here can possibly do me the least good: & I feel quite certain you can do me *immence good* where you are. I am quite cheerful under all my afflicting circumstances; & prospects, having as I humbly trust "the peace of God which passeth all understanding, to rule in my heart." You may make just such use of this as you see fit. Yours *in sincerity; & truth,* (God Allmighty bless; and reward you a thousand fold.)

John Brown

Charlestown, Jefferson County, Va., Nov. 8, 1859.
Dear Wife and Children, Every One,—I will begin by saying that
I have in some degree recovered from my wounds, but that I am
quite weak in my back and sore about my left kidney. My appetite
has been quite good for most of the time since I was hurt. I am
supplied with almost everything I could desire to make me comfortable, and the little I do lack (some articles of clothing which I lost)
I may perhaps soon get again. I am, besides, quite cheerful, having
(as I trust) "the peace of God, which passeth all understanding," to
"rule in my heart," and the testimony (in some degree) of a good
conscience that I have not lived altogether in vain. I can trust God
with both the time and the manner of my death, believing, as I now
do, that for me at this time to seal my testimony for God and humanity with my blood will do vastly more toward advancing the cause
I have earnestly endeavored to promote, than all I have done in my
life before. I beg of you all meekly and quietly to submit to this, not
feeling yourselves in the least *degraded* on that account. Remember,
dear wife and children all, that Jesus of Nazareth suffered a most
excruciating death on the cross as a felon, under the most aggravat-
ing circumstances. Think also of the prophets and apostles and
Christians of former days, who went through greater tribulations
than you or I, and try to be reconciled. May God Almighty comfort
all your hearts, and soon wipe away all tears from your eyes! To him
be endless praise! Think, too, of the crushed millions who "have no
comforter." I charge you all never in your trials to forget the griefs
"of the poor that cry, and of those that have none to help them."
I wrote most earnestly to my dear and afflicted wife not to come on
for the present, at any rate. I will now give her my reasons for doing
so. First, it would use up all the scanty means she has, or is at all likely
to have, to make herself and children comfortable hereafter. For let
me tell you that the sympathy that is now aroused in your behalf
may not always follow you. There is but little more of the romantic
about helping poor widows and their children than there is about
trying to relieve poor "niggers." Again, the little comfort it might
afford us to meet again would be dearly bought by the pains of a
final separation. We must part; and I feel assured for us to meet under
such dreadful circumstances would only add to our distress. If she
comes on here, she must be only a gazing-stock throughout the
whole journey, to be remarked upon in every look, word, and action,
and by all sorts of creatures, and by all sorts of papers, throughout
the whole country. Again, it is my most decided judgment that in

quietly and submissively staying at home vastly more of generous sympathy will reach her, without such dreadful sacrifice of feeling as she must put up with if she comes on. The visits of one or two female friends that have come on here have produced great excitement, which is very annoying; and they cannot possibly do me any good. Oh, Mary! do not come, but patiently wait for the meeting of those who love God and their fellow-men, where no separation must follow. "They shall go no more out forever." I greatly long to hear from some one of you, and to learn anything that in any way affects your welfare. I sent you ten dollars the other day; did you get it? I have also endeavored to stir up Christian friends to visit and write to you in your deep affliction. I have no doubt that some of them, at least, will heed the call. Write to me, care of Captain John Avis, Charlestown, Jefferson County, Virginia.

"Finally, my beloved, be of good comfort." May all your names be "written in the Lamb's book of life!"—may you all have the purifying and sustaining influence of the Christian religion!—is the earnest prayer of

Your affectionate husband and father,
John Brown

P.S. I cannot remember a night so dark as to have hindered the coming day, nor a storm so furious and dreadful as to prevent the return of warm sunshine and a cloudless sky. But, beloved ones, do remember that this is not your rest,—that in this world you have no abiding place or continuing city. To God and his infinite mercy I always commend you.

J.B.

Charlestown, Jefferson County, Va., Nov. 12, 1859.

Dear Brother Jeremiah,—Your kind letter of the 9th inst. is received, and also one from Mr. Tilden; for both of which I am greatly obliged. You inquire, "Can I do anything for you or your family?" I would answer that my sons, as well as my wife and daughters, are all very poor; and that anything that may hereafter be due me from my father's estate I wish paid to them, as I will endeavor hereafter to describe, without legal formalities to consume it all. One of my boys has been so entirely used up as very likely to be in want of comfortable clothing for the winter. I have, through the kindness of friends, fifteen dollars to send him, which I will remit shortly. If you know where to reach him, please send him that amount at once, as I shall remit the same to you by a safe conveyance. If I had a plain statement from Mr. Thompson of the state of my accounts with the estate of my father, I should then better know what to say about that matter. As it is, I have not the least memorandum left me to refer to. If Mr. Thompson will make me a statement, and charge my dividend fully for his trouble, I would be greatly obliged to him. In that case you can send me any remarks of your own. I am gaining in health slowly, and am quite cheerful in view of my approaching end,—being fully persuaded that I am worth inconceivably more to hang than for any other purpose. God Almighty bless and save you all!

Your affectionate brother,

John Brown.

November 13.

P. S. Say to my poor boys never to grieve for one moment on my account; and should many of you live to see the time when you will not blush to own your relation to Old John Brown, it will not be more strange than many things that have happened. I feel a thousand times more on account of my sorrowing friends than on my own account. So far as I am concerned, I "count it all joy." "I have fought the good fight," and have, as I trust, "finished my course." Please show this to any of my family that you may see. My love to all; and may God, in his infinite mercy, for Christ's sake, bless and save you all!

Your affectionate brother,

J. Brown.

Charlestown, Jefferson Co. Va, 15th. Nov. 1859.

Rev H L Vaill

My Dear stedfast Friend

Your *most kind & most welcome* letter of the 8th inst reached me in due time. *I am very grateful* for all the good feeling you express & also for the kind counsels you give together-with your prayers in my behalf. Allow me here to say that notwithstanding "my soul is amongst lions," still I believe that "God in very deed is with me." You will not therefore feel surprised when I tell you that I am "joyful in all my tribulations": that I do not feel condemned of Him whose judgment is just; nor of my own conscience. Nor do I feel degraded by my imprisonment, my chains or prospect of the Gallows. I have not only been (*though utterly unworthy*) permitted to suffer affliction with God's people," but have also had *a great many rare* opportunities for "preaching *righteousness* in the great congregation." I trust it will not all be lost. *The jailor* (in whose charge I am) *& his family; & assistants* have all been most kind: & notwithstanding he was one of the bravest of all who *fought me*: he is *now* being abused for his humanity. So far as my observation goes; *none but brave* men: are likely to be *humane*; to a fallen foe. "Cowards *prove* their *courage* by their *ferocity*." It may be done in that way with but little risk. I wish I could write you about a few only of the interesting times, I here experience with different classes of men; *clergymen* among others. Christ the great Captain of *liberty*; as well as of salvation; & who began his mission, as foretold of him; by proclaiming it, *saw fit* to take from me a sword of steel after I had carried it for a time but he has put another in my hand: ("The sword of the Spirit;") & I pray God to make me a faithful soldier wherever he may send me, not less on the scaffold, then when surrounded by my warmest sympathizers. My dear old friend I do assure you I have not forgotten our last meeting nor our retrospective look over the route by which God had then led us; & I bless his name that he has again enabled me to hear your words of cheering; & comfort, at a time when I at least am on the "brink of Jordan." See Bunyan's Pilgrim. God in Infinite mercy grant us *soon* another meeting on the opposite shore. I have often passed under the rod of him whom I *call my* Father; & certainly no son ever needed it oftener; & yet I have enjoyed much of life, as I was enabled to discover the secret of this; somewhat early. It has been in making the prosperity, & the happiness of others *my own*: so that really I have had a great deal of prosperity. I am very prosperous still; & looking forward to a time when "peace on Earth & good will to *men* shall every where prevail." I have no murmuring thoughts or *envyous* feelings to fret my mind. "I'll praise my *maker* with my *breath*." I am *an unworthy* nephew of Deacon John; & I loved him much; & in view of the many choice friends *I have had* here: I am led the more earnestly to pray; "gather *not* my soul with the *unrighteous*." Your assurance of the earnest sympathy of the friends in my native land is very greatful to my feelings; & allow me to say a word of comfort to them. As I believe most firmly that God reigns; I cannot believe that any thing I have *done suffered or may yet suffer will be lost*; to the *cause of God or of humanity*: & before I began my work at Harpers Ferry; I felt assured that in the *worst event*; it would certainly PAY. I often expressed that belief; & I can now see no possible cause to alter my mind. I am not as yet in the *maine* at all disappointed. I have been *a good deal* disappointed as it regards *myself* in not keeping up *to my own plans*; but I now feel entirely reconciled to that even: for Gods plan, was Infinitely better; *no doubt*; or I should have kept to my own. Had Samson kept to his *determination* of not telling Delilah wherein his great strength lay; he would probably have never over-turned the house. I did not tell Delilah; but I was induced to act very *contrary* to my *better judgment*; & I have lost my two noble boys; & *other friends, if not my two eyes*.

But "Gods will *not mine* be done." I feel a comfortable hope that like that *erring servant* of whom I have just been writing *even I* may (through Infinite mercy in Christ Jesus) yet *"die in faith."* As to both the time, & manner of my death: I have but very little trouble on that score; & *am able* to be (as you exhort) "of good cheer." I send through you my best wishes to Mrs. Woodruff & her son George; & to all dear friends. May the God of the *poor* and *oppressed*; be the God & Saveior of you all.

Farewell till we *"meet again."*

Your friend in truth
John Brown

Charlestown, Jefferson Co., Va., 16th Nov., 1859.

My Dear Wife:—I write you in answer to a most kind letter, of Nov. 13, from dear Mrs. Spring. I owe her ten thousand thanks; for her kindness to *you particularly and more especially* than for what she has done, and is doing, in a more direct way for me personally. Although I feel grateful for every expression of kindness or sympathy towards me, yet nothing can so effectually minister to my comfort as acts of kindness done to relieve the wants, or mitigate the sufferings of my poor distressed family. May *God Almighty* and *their own consciousness* be their eternal rewarders. I am exceedingly rejoiced to have you make the acquaintance and be surrounded by such choice friends, as I have *long known* some of those to be, with whom you are staying, by reputation. I am most glad to have you meet with one *of a family* (or I would rather say of two families) *most beloved and never to be forgotten by me.* I mean *dear gentle* Sarah Wattles. *Many and many* a time has *she, her father, mother, brothers, sisters, uncle and aunt,* (like angels of mercy) ministered to the wants of myself and of my poor sons, both in sickness and in health. Only last year I lay sick for quite a number of weeks with them, and was cared for *by all,* as though I had been a most affectionate brother or father. *Tell her* that I ask God to bless and reward them *all* forever. "I *was* a stranger, and they took me in." It may possibly be that Sarah would like to copy this letter, and send it to her home. If so, by all means, let her do so. *I would write them* if I had the power.

Now let me say a word about the effort to educate our daughters. I am no longer able to provide means to help towards that object, and it therefore becomes me not to dictate in the matter. I shall gratefully submit the direction of the whole thing to those whose generosity may lead them to undertake in their behalf, while I give *anew* a little expression of my own choice respecting it. You, my wife, *perfectly well* know that I have always expressed a decided preference for a very *plain but perfectly practical* education for both *sons and daughters.* I do not mean an education so very miserable as that *you* and *I* received in early life; nor as some of our children enjoyed. When I say plain but practical, I mean enough of the learning of the schools to enable them to transact the common business of life, comfortably and respectably, together with that thorough training to good business habits which prepares both men and women to be *useful though poor,* and to meet the *stern* Realities of life with a *good* grace. You well know that I always claimed that the *music* of the broom, washtub, needle, spindle, loom, axe, scythe, hoe, flail, etc., should first be learned, at all events, and that of the piano, etc., Afterwards. I put them in that order as most conducive to health of body and mind; and for the obvious reason, that after a life of some *experience and of much observation,* I have found *ten women* as well as *ten men* who have made their mark in life *Right,* whose early training was of that *plain, practical* kind, to *one* who had a more popular and fashionable *early* training. But enough of that.

Now, in regard to your coming here; If you feel sure that you can endure the trials and the shock, which will be *unavoidable* (if you come), I should be most glad to see you *once more*; but when I think of your being insulted on the road, and perhaps *while here,* and of only seeing your wretchedness made complete, I *shrink* from it. Your composure and fortitude of mind may be *quite equal to it all*; but I am in *dreadful* doubt of it. *If you do come,* defer your journey till about the 27th or 28th of this month. The scenes which you will have to pass through on coming here will be *anything but those* you now pass, with tender, kind-hearted friends, and kind faces to meet you everywhere. *Do consider the matter well* before you make the *plunge.* I think I had better say *no more* on this *most painful* subject. My health improves a little; my mind is very tranquil, I may say joyous, and I continue to receive every kind attention that I have any possible need of. I wish you to send copies of all my letters to all our poor children. What I write to one must answer for all, till I have more strength. I get numerous kind letters from friends in almost all directions, to encourage me to "be of good cheer," and I still have, *as I trust,* "the peace of God to rule in my heart." May God, for Christ's sake, ever make his face to shine on you all.

Your affectionate husband,
John Brown

Charlestown, Jefferson Co. Va. 17th Nov. 1859

J B Musgrave Esqr

My Dear Young Friend

I have just received your most kind; & welcome letter of the 15th inst but did not get any other from you. I am under many obligations *to you & to your Father* for all the kindness you have shown me, especially since my disaster. *May God* & your own conciousness ever be your rewarders. Tell your Father that I am quite cheerful that I do not feel myself in the least degraded by my imprisonment, my chain, or the *near prospect* of the Gallows. *Men* cannot *imprison,* or *chain*; or *hang* the *soul.* I go joyfuly in behalf of Millions that "have no rights" that this "great, & glorious"; "*this Christian* Republic," "is bound to respect." Strange *change in morals political*; as well as *Christian*; since 1776. I look forward *to other changes* to take place *in "Gods good time*;" fully believeing that "the fashion of this world passeth away." (I am unable *now* to tell you where my friend is; that you inquire after. Perhaps my Wife who I suppose is still with Mrs. Spring, may have some information of him. I think it quite uncertain however.) Farewell; May God abundantly bless You all.

Your Friend

John Brown

Charlestown, Jefferson Co. Va. 19th. Nov. 1859.
Rev. Luther Humphrey.

My dear friend,

Your kind letter of 12th inst. is now before me. So far as my knowledge goes as to our mutual kindred, I suppose *I am the* first since the landing of Peter Brown from the Mayflower that has *either been sentenced to imprisonment*; or to the Gallows. But my dear old friend, let not that fact *alone* grieve you. You cannot have forgotten *how; & where our Grandfather* (Capt. John Brown) fell in 1776; & *that he too* might have perished on the scaffold had circumstances been but *very little* different. *The fact* that a man dies under the hand of an executioner (or other wise) has but little to do with his true character, as I suppose. John Rogers perished at the stake *a great & good* man as I suppose: but *his being so* does *not prove* that any other man who has died in the same way was *good or otherwise*. Whether I have any reason to "be of good cheer" (or not) in view of my end; I can assure you that *I feel so; &* that I am totally *blinded* if I do not really *experience* that *strengthening; & consolation* you so faithfully implore in my behalf. God of *our Fathers*; reward your fidelity. I neither feel *mortified, degraded, nor in the least ashamed* of my imprisonment, my chain, or my near prospect *of death by hanging*. I feel assured "that not one hair shall fall from my head without my heavenly Father." I also feel that I have *long been endeavouring* to hold exactly "such a *fast* as God has chosen." See the passage in Isaiah which you have quoted. No part of my life has been more hapily spent; than that I have spent here; & I humbly *trust* that no past has been spent to better purpose. *I would not* say *boastingly*: but "thanks be unto God who giveth us the victory: *through infinite grace*." I should be sixty years old were I to live till May 9th 1860. I have enjoyed much of life as it is: & have been remarkably prosperous; having *early learned* to regard the welfare & prosperity of others as *my own*. I have never since I can remember required a great amount of sleep: so that I conclude that I have already enjoyed *full an average* number of waking hours with those who reach their "Three Score years, & ten." I have not as yet been driven to the use of glasses; but can still see to read, & write quite comfortably. But more than that I have *generally* enjoyed remarkably good health. I might go on to recount unnumbered *& unmerited* blessings among which would be some very severe afflictions: & those the most needed blessings of all. And now when I think how easily I might *be left to spoil* all I have done, or suffered in the cause of freedom; I hardly dare risk another voyage; if I even had the opportunity. It is a long time since we met; but we shall now soon come together in our "Fathers House," *I trust*. "Let us hold fast that we already have." "remembering that we shall reap in due time if we faint not." "Thanks be *ever* unto God; who giveth us the victory through Jesus Christ our Lord." And now my old warmhearted friend, "Good bye."

Your Affectionate Cousin

John Brown

Charlestown, Jefferson County, Va., Nov. 21, 1859.

My Dear Wife,—Your most welcome letter of the 13th instant I got yesterday. I am very glad to learn from yourself that you feel so much resigned to your circumstances, so much confidence in a wise and good Providence, and such composure of mind in the midst of all your deep afflictions. This is just as it should be; and let me still say, "Be of good cheer," for we shall soon "come out of all our great tribulations;" and very soon, if we trust in him, "God shall wipe away all tears from our eyes." Soon "we shall be satisfied when we are awake in His likeness." There is now here a source of disquietude to me,—namely, the fires which are almost of daily and nightly occurrence in this immediate neighborhood. While I well know that no one of them is the work of our friends, I know at the same time that by more or less of the inhabitants we shall be charged with them,—the same as with the ominous and threatening letters to Governor Wise. In the existing state of public feeling I can easily see a further objection to your coming here at present; but I did not intend saying another word to you on that subject.

Why will you not say to me whether you had any crops mature this season? If so, what ones? Although I may nevermore intermeddle with your worldly affairs, I have not yet lost all interest in them. A little history of your failures I should very much prize; and I would gratify you and other friends some way were it in my power. I am still quite cheerful, and by no means cast down. I "remember that the time is short." The little trunk and all its contents, so far as I can judge, reached me safe. May God reward all the contributors! I wrote you under cover to our excellent friend Mrs. Spring on the 16th instant. I presume you have it before now. When you return, it is most likely the lake will not be open; so you must get your ticket at Troy for Moreau Station or Glens Falls (for Glens Falls, if you can get one), or get one for Vergennes in Vermont, and take your chance of crossing over on the ice to Westport. If you go soon, the route by Glens Falls to Elizabethtown will probably be the best.

I have just learned that our poor Watson lingered until Wednesday about noon of the 19th of October. Oliver died near my side in a few moments after he was shot. Dauphin died the next morning after Oliver and William were killed,—namely, Monday. He died almost instantly; was by my side. William was shot by several persons. Anderson was killed with Dauphin.

Keep this letter to refer to. God Almighty bless and keep you all!

Your affectionate husband,
John Brown.

Dear Mrs. Spring,—I send this to your care, because I am at a loss where it will reach my wife.

Your friend in truth,
John Brown.

Charlestown, Jefferson County, Va., Nov. 22, 1859.

Dear Children, All,—I address this letter to you, supposing that your mother is not yet with you. She has not yet come here, as I have requested her not to do at present, if at all. She may think it best for her not to come at all. She has (or will), I presume, written you before this. Annie's letter to us both, of the 9th, has but just reached me. I am very glad to get it, and to learn that you are in any measure cheerful. This is the greatest comfort I can have, except it would be to know that you are all Christians. God in mercy grant you all may be so! That is what you all will certainly need. When and in what form death may come is but of small moment. I feel just as content to die for God's eternal truth and for suffering humanity on the scaffold as in any other way; and I do not say this from any disposition to "brave it out." No; I would readily own my wrong were I in the least convinced of it. I have now been confined over a month, with a good opportunity to look the whole thing as "fair in the face" as I am capable of doing; and I now feel it most grateful that I am counted in the least possible degree worthy to suffer for the truth. I want you all to "be of good cheer." This life is intended as a season of training, chastisement, temptation, affliction, and trial; and the "righteous shall come out of" it all. Oh, my dear children, let me again entreat you all to "forsake the foolish, and live." What can you possibly lose by such a course? "Godliness with contentment is great gain, having the promise of the life that now is, and of that which is to come." "Trust in the Lord and do good, so shalt thou dwell in the land; and verily thou shalt be fed." I have enjoyed life much; why should I complain on leaving it? I want some of you to write me a little more particularly about all that concerns your welfare. I intend to write you as often as I can. "To God and the word of his grace I commend you all."

Your affectionate father,
John Brown.

Charlestown, Jefferson County, Va., Nov. 22, 1859.
Dear Children,—Your most welcome letters of the 16th inst. I have just received, and I bless God that he has enabled you to bear the heavy tidings of our disaster with so much seeming resignation and composure of mind. That is exactly the thing I have wished you all to do for me,—to be cheerful and perfectly resigned to the holy will of a wise and good God. I bless his most holy name that I am, I trust, in some good measure able to do the same. I am even "joyful in all my tribulations" ever since my confinement, and I humbly trust that "I know in whom I have trusted." A calm peace, perhaps like that which your own dear mother felt in view of her last change, seems to fill my mind by day and by night. Of this neither the powers of "earth or hell" can deprive me. Do not, my dear children, any of you grieve for a single moment on my account. As I trust my life has not been thrown away, so I also humbly trust that my death will not be in vain. God can make it to be a thousand times more valuable to his own cause than all the miserable service (at best) that I have rendered it during my life. When I was first taken, I was too feeble to write much; so I wrote what I could to North Elba, requesting Ruth and Anne to send you copies of all my letters to them. I hope they have done so, and that you, Ellen, will do the same with what I may send to you, as it is still quite a labor for me to write all that I need to. I want your brothers to know what I write, if you know where to reach them. I wrote Jeremiah a few days since to supply a trifling assistance, fifteen dollars, to such of you as might be most destitute. I got his letter, but do not know as he got mine. I hope to get another letter from him soon. I also asked him to show you my letter. I know of nothing you can any of you now do for me, unless it is to comfort your own hearts, and cheer and encourage each other to trust in God and Jesus Christ whom he hath sent. If you will keep his sayings, you shall certainly "know of his doctrine, whether it be of God or no." Nothing can be more grateful to me than your earnest sympathy, except it be to know that you are fully persuaded to be Christians. And now, dear children, farewell for this time. I hope to be able to write you again. The God of my fathers take you for his children.

Your affectionate father,
John Brown.

Charlestown, Jefferson County, Va.,
November 22, 1859

Dear Sir: I have just had my attention called to a seeming confliction between the statement I at first made to Governor Wise and that which I made at the time I received my sentence, regarding my intentions respecting the slaves we took *about the Ferry.* There need be no such confliction, and a few words of explanation will, I think, be quite sufficient. I had given Governor Wise a *full and particular* account of that, and when called in court to say whether I had anything further to urge, I was taken wholly by surprise, as I did not expect my sentence before the others. In the hurry of the moment, I forgot much that I had before *intended to say,* and did *not* consider the full bearing of what *I then said.* I intended to convey this idea, that it was my object to place the slaves in a condition to defend their liberties, if they would, *without any bloodshed, but not* that I intended *to run them out of the slave States.* I was not *aware* of any such apparent confliction until my attention *was called* to it, and I do not suppose that a man in *my then circumstances* should be *superhuman* in respect to the *exact purport* of every word he might utter. What I said to Governor Wise was spoken with all the deliberation I was master of, *and was intended for truth*; and what I said in court was *equally intended for truth,* but required a more full explanation *than I then gave.* Please make such use of this as you think calculated to correct any *wrong* impressions I may have given.

Very respectfully, yours,

John Brown

Andrew Hunter, Esq., *Present.*

Charlestown, Jefferson Co. Va. 22d, Nov. 1859.
Rev T W Higginson
                    Dear Sir

I write you a few lines to express to you my deep feeling of gratitude for your journey to visit & comfort my family as well as myself in different ways & at different times; since my imprisonment here. Truly you have proved yourself to be "a friend in need;" & *I feel* my many obligations for all your kind *attentions, none the less*: for my wishing my Wife *not* to come on when she first set out. I would it were in my power to make *to all* my kind friends: some *other acknowledgements* than a mere tender of *our & my* thanks. I can assure *all*: Mrs. Stearns, my young friend Hoyt; & many others I have been unable to write as yet: that I *certainly do not forget*; their love, & kindness. *God Allmighty* bless; & save them *all*; & grant *them to see*; a fulfilment of all their reasonable desires. My Daughter writes me that you have sent $25. Twenty Five Dollars in a letter with a bundle of papers. I wish to thank you in particular for sending *them papers*; & hope you will continue this kindness. Friends in the cities who get more papers than they can read; cannot think how much it may add to the comfort of a bereaved family to receive a good paper from time to time from distant friends *even though* those friends may be entire strangers. I am getting much better of my wounds; but am *yet rather lame*. Am very cheerful & *trust* I may continue so "to the end." My Love to all dear friends.   Yours for *God & the right*.
                                                    John Brown

Jail, Charlestown, Wednesday, Nov. 23, 1859

Rev. McFarland.

Dear Friend: Although you write to me as a stranger, the spirit you show towards me and the cause for which I am in bonds, makes me feel towards you as a dear friend. I would be glad to have you, or any of my liberty-loving ministerial friends here, to talk and pray with me. I am not a stranger to the way of salvation by Christ. From my youth I have studied much on that subject, and at one time hoped to be a minister myself; but God had another work for me to do. To me it is given in behalf of Christ, not only to believe on him, but also to *suffer* for his sake. But while I trust that I have some experimental and saving knowledge of religion, it would be a great pleasure to me to have some one better qualified than myself to lead my mind in prayer and meditation, now that my time is so near a close. You may wonder, are there no ministers of the gospel here? I answer, No. There are no ministers of *Christ* here. These ministers who profess to be Christian, and hold slaves or advocate slavery, I cannot abide them. My knees will not bend in prayer with them while their hands are stained with the blood of souls. The subject you mention as having been preaching on, the day before you wrote to me, is one which I have often thought of since my imprisonment. I think I feel as happy as Paul did when he lay in prison. He knew if they killed him it would greatly advance the cause of Christ; that was the reason he rejoiced so. On that same ground "I do rejoice, yea, and will rejoice." Let them hang me; I forgive them, and may God forgive them, for they know not what they do. I have no regret for the transaction for which I am condemned. I went against the laws of men, it is true; but "whether it be right to obey *God* or *men,* judge ye." Christ told me to remember them that are in bonds, as *bound with them,* to do towards them as I would wish them to do towards me in similar circumstances. My conscience bade me do that. I tried to do it, but failed. Therefore I have no regret on that score. I have no sorrow either as to the result, only for my poor wife and children. They have suffered much, and it is hard to leave them uncared for. But God will be a husband to the widow, and a father to the fatherless.

I have frequently been in Wooster; and if any of my old friends from Akron are there, you can show them this letter. I have but a few more days, and I feel anxious to be away, "where the wicked cease from troubling, and the weary are at rest." Farewell.

Your friend, and the friend of all friends of liberty,

John Brown.

Charlestown, Jefferson County, Va., Nov. 24, 1859.

My Dear Mrs. Spring,—Your ever welcome letter of the 19th inst., together with the one now enclosed, were received by me last night too late for any reply. I am always grateful for anything you either do or write. I would most gladly express my gratitude to you and yours by something more than words; but it has come to that, I now have but little else to deal in, and sometimes they are not so kind as they should be. You have laid me and my family under many and great obligations. I hope they may not soon be forgotten. The same is also true of a vast many others, that I shall never be able even to thank. I feel disposed to leave the education of my dear children to their mother, and to those dear friends who bear the burden of it; only expressing my earnest hope that they may all become strong, intelligent, expert, industrious, Christian housekeepers. I would wish that, together with other studies, they may thoroughly study Dr. Franklin's "Poor Richard." I want them to become matter-of-fact women. Perhaps I have said too much about this already; I would not allude to this subject now but for the fact that you had most kindly expressed your generous feelings with regard to it.

I sent the letter to my wife to your care, because the address she sent me from Philadelphia was not sufficiently plain, and left me quite at a loss. I am still in the same predicament, and were I not ashamed to trouble you further, would ask you either to send this to her or a copy of it, in order that she may see something from me often.

I have very many interesting visits from proslavery persons almost daily, and I endeavor to improve them faithfully, plainly, and kindly. I do not think that I ever enjoyed life better than since my confinement here. For this I am indebted to Infinite Grace, and the kind letters of friends from different quarters. I wish I could only know that all my poor family were as much composed and happy as I. I think that nothing but the Christian religion can ever make any one so much composed.

> "My willing soul would stay
> In such a frame as this."

There are objections to my writing many things while here that I might be disposed to write were I under different circumstances. I do not know that my wife yet understands that prison rules require that all I write or receive should first be examined by the sheriff or State's attorney, and that all company I see should be attended by the jailer or some of his assistants. Yet such is the case; and did she know this, it might influence her mind somewhat about the opportunity she would have on coming here. We cannot expect the jailer to devote very much time to us, as he has now a very hard task on his hands. I have just learned how to send letters to my wife near Philadelphia.

I have a son at Akron, Ohio, that I greatly desire to have located in such a neighborhood as yours; and you will pardon me for giving you some account of him, making all needful allowance for the source the account comes from. His name is Jason; he is about thirty-six years old; has a wife and one little boy. He is a very laborious, ingenious, temperate, honest, and truthful man. He is very expert as a gardener, vine-dresser, and manager of fruit-trees, but does not pride himself on account of his skill in anything; always has underrated himself; is bashful and retiring in his habits; is not (like his father) too much inclined to assume and dictate; is too conscientious in his dealings and too tender of people's feelings to get from them his just deserts, and is very poor. He suffered almost everything on the way to and while in Kansas but death, and returned to Ohio not a spoiled but next to a ruined man. He never quarrels, and yet I know that he is both morally and physically brave. He will not deny his principles to save his life, and he "turned not back in the day of battle." At the battle of Osawatomie he fought by my side. He is a most tender, loving, and steadfast friend, and on the right side of things in general, a practical Samaritan (if not Christian); and could I know that he was located with a population who were disposed to encourage him, without expecting him to pay too dearly in the end for it, I should feel greatly relieved. His wife is a very neat, industrious, prudent woman, who has undergone a severe trial in "the school of affliction."

You make one request of me that I shall not be able to comply with. Am sorry that I cannot at least explain. Your own account of my plans is very well. The son I mentioned has now a small stock of choice vines and fruit-trees, and in them consists his worldly store mostly. I would give you some account of others, but I suppose my wife may have done so.

Your friend,
John Brown.

Charlestown, Jefferson County, Va., Nov. 25, 1859.
Rev. Heman Humphrey, D.D.

My Dear and Honored Kinsman,—Your very sorrowful, kind, and faithful letter of the 20th instant is now before me. I accept it with all kindness. I have honestly endeavored to profit by the faithful advice it contains. Indeed, such advice could never come amiss. You will allow me to say that I deeply sympathize with you and all my sorrowing friends in their grief and terrible mortification. I feel ten times more afflicted on their account than on account of my own circumstances. But I must say that I am neither conscious of being "infatuated" nor "mad." You will doubtless agree with me in this,—that neither imprisonment, irons, nor the gallows falling to one's lot are of themselves evidence of either guilt, "infatuation, or madness."

I discover that you labor under a mistaken impression as to some important facts, which my peculiar circumstances will in all probability prevent the possibility of my removing; and I do not propose to take up any argument to prove that any motion or act of my life is right. But I will here state that I know it to be wholly my own fault as a leader that caused our disaster. Of this you have no proper means of judging, not being on the ground, or a practical soldier. I will only add, that it was in yielding to my feelings of humanity (if I ever exercised such a feeling), in leaving my proper place and mingling with my prisoners to quiet their fears, that occasioned our being caught. I firmly believe that God reigns, and that he overrules all things in the best possible manner; and in that view of the subject I try to be in some degree reconciled to my own weaknesses and follies even.

If you were here on the spot, and could be with me by day and by night, and know the facts and how my time is spent here, I think you would find much to reconcile your own mind to the ignominious death I am about to suffer, and to mitigate your sorrow. I am, to say the least, quite cheerful. "He shall begin to deliver Israel out of the hand of the Philistines." This was said of a poor erring servant many years ago; and for many years I have felt a strong impression that God had given me powers and faculties, unworthy as I was, that he intended to use for a similar purpose. This most unmerited honor He has seen fit to bestow; and whether, like the same poor frail man to whom I allude, my death may not be of vastly more value than my life is, I think quite beyond all human foresight. I really have strong hopes that notwithstanding all my many sins, I too may yet die "in faith."

If you do not believe I had a murderous intention (while I *know* I had not), why grieve so terribly on my account? The scaffold has but few terrors for me. God has often covered my head in the day of battle, and granted me many times deliverances that were almost so miraculous that I can scarce realize their truth; and now, when it seems quite certain that he intends to use me in a different way, shall I not most cheerfully go? I may be deceived, but I humbly trust that he will not forsake me "till I have showed his favor to this generation and his strength to every one that is to come." Your letter is most faithfully and kindly written, and I mean to profit by it. I am certainly quite grateful for it. I feel that a great responsibility rests upon me as regards the lives of those who have fallen and may yet fall. I must in that view cast myself on the care of Him "whose mercy endureth forever." If the cause in which I engaged in any possible degree approximated to be "infinitely better" than the one which Saul of Tarsus undertook, I have no reason to be ashamed of it; and indeed I cannot now, after more than a month for reflection, find in my heart (before God in whose presence I expect to stand within another week) any cause for shame.

I got a long and most kind letter from your pure-hearted brother Luther, to which I replied at some length. The statement that seems to be going around in the newspapers that I told Governor Wise that I came on here to seek revenge for the wrongs of either myself or my family, is utterly false. I never intended to convey such an idea, and I bless God that I am able even now to say that I have never yet harbored such a feeling. See testimony of witnesses who were with me while I had one son lying dead by my side, and another mortally wounded and dying on my other side. I do not believe that Governor Wise so understood, and I think he ought to correct that impression. The impression that we intended a general insurrection is equally untrue.

Now, my much beloved and much respected kinsman, farewell. May the God of our fathers save and abundantly bless you and yours!

John Brown.

Charlestown, Jefferson Co. Va. 26th Nov. 1859
(Nov. 27th I mean to write again to some care

My dear Wife

I wrote our dear friend McKim a few lines yesterday saying I had got his kind letter informing me of where you then were; & how to direct to you while in his neighbourhood. I also said to him that I would be glad to have you rem[a]in about there; until I was disposed of: *or untill*; I could send you a few little articles by Express: & also write you further; if that (could be) without your becoming burdensome to friends. Our friend McKim wrote me you had gone; *or was going* to stay a while with *Lucretia Mott.* I remember the faithful old Lady well; but presume she has no recollection of me. I once set myself to oppose a *mob* at Boston; where she was. After I interfered the police immediately took up the matter; & soon put a stop to mob proceedings. The meeting was I think in *Marlboro Street* Church, or *Hotel perhaps.* I am glad to have you make the acquaintance of such old "Pioneers" in the cause. I have just received from Mr. John Jay of New York a draft for $50, Fifty Dollars for the benefit of my family; & will enclose *it*; made payable to your order. I have also $15, Fifteen Dollars to send to our *cripled, & destitute* unmarried son; when I can I intend to send you by Express Care of Mr. McKim Two or Three little articles to carry home. Should you happen to meet with Mr. Jay say to him that I fully appreciate his great kindness both to *me; & my family.* God bless *all* such friends. It is out of my power to reply to *all* the kind, & encourageing letters *I get*; *Wish* I could do so. I have been so much relieved from my lameness for the last Three or Four days as to be able to sit up to read; & write pretty much all day: as well as part of the Night; & I do assure you & *all other* friends that I am quite busy; & *none the less hapy* on that account. The time passes *quite pleasantly*; & the near aproach of my great change is not the occasion of any particular dread. I trust that *God* who has sustained me *so long*; will not *forsake* me when I most feel my need of *Fatherly aid; & support.* Should he hide his face; my spirit will droop, & die: *but not otherwise: be assured.* My only anxiety is to be properly assured of my *fitness* for the company of those who are "washed from *all filthiness:*" *& for the presence of Him who is Infinitely pure.* I certainly *think* I do have *some* "hunger, *& thirst* after righteousness." If it be only *genuine* I make *no doubt I "shall be filled."* Please let all our friends read my letters when you can; & ask them to accept of it *as in part for them.* I am inclined to think you will not be likely to succeed well about getting away the bodies of your family; but should that *be so: do not let that grieve you*. It can make but little difference *what is done with them*. I would advise that you take any little funds you may have to carry home in Gold (smallish sized) *in good part*; which some kind friend will obtain at a Bank for you. You can continue to carry (*the most of it*) about your person in some *safe way*: & it will not be best for me to advise you about making the little you now get; reach as far as you consistently can. You can well remember the changes you have passed through. Life is made up of a series of changes: & let us try to meet them in the best maner [sic] possible. You will not wish to make yourself & children any more burdensome to friends than you are really compelled to do. *I would not*.

I will close this by saying that if you *now feel* that you are *equal* to the undertaking do *exactly as you* FEEL *disposed to do* about coming to see me before I suffer. *I am entirely willing*.

Your Affectionate Husband

John Brown

          Charlestown, Jefferson Co. Va. 27th Nov. 1859. Sabbath
My dearly beloved Sisters *Mary A, & Martha*.

   I am obliged to occupy a part of what is probably (my last) Sabbath
on Earth in answering the *very kind & very comforting* letters of Sister
Hand & Son of the 23d inst or I must fail to do so at all. I do not
think it any violation of the day that "God made for man. [quote
missing.] Nothing could be more grateful to my feelings than to learn
that you do *not* feel *dreadfully mortified & even disgraced* on account of
your relation to one who is to *die on the Scaffold* I have really suffered
more by Ten fold since my confinement here; on account of what
I feared would be the *terible feelings of my kindred* on my account than
from *all other* causes. I am most glad to learn *from you* that my fears
on *your own* account were ill founded I was afraid that a little *seeming
present* prosperity might have carried you away from realities so that
the honor that comes from men might lead you in *some measure* to
undervalue that which "cometh from God." I bless God who has
most abundantly supported & comforted me; all along to find *you* are not
ensnared. Dr Heman Humphrey has just sent me a *most doleful
Lamentation* over my *"infatuation" & "madness"* (very kindly expressed:)
in which I cannot doubt he has given expression to the *extreme grief*
of others of our kindred. I have endeavoured to answer him kindly
also: & at the same time to deal faithfully with my old friend. I think
I will send you his letter; & if you deem it worth the trouble you
can probably get my reply or a copy of it. Suffise it for me to say
none of these things move me." I here experienced a consolation; &
peace which I fear he has not yet known. Luther Humphrey wrote
me a very comforting letter There are "things dear Sisters that God
hides *even* from the wise & prudent" I feel astonished that one *so
exceedingly vile & unworthy* as *I am* would even be suffered to have a
place *anyhow or any where* amongst the *very least of All* who when they
came to die (as all must:) *were permitted* to pay the debt of nature" in
defence of the *right*: & of Gods *eternal & immutable truth*. Oh my dear
friends can you believe *it possible* that the Scaffold *has no terrors* for
your *own* poor, old, unworthy brother? *I thank God* through Jesus Christ
my Lord: it is even so I am now sheding tears: but they *are no longer*
tears of *grief or sorrow*. I trust I have nearly DONE with those. I am
weeping for *joy*: & *gratitude* that I can *in no other way* express. I get
many *very kind & comforting* letters that I cannot possibly reply to.
Wish I had time & strength to answer all. I am obliged to ask those
to whom I do write to let friends read what I send as much as they
well can. *Do write* my deeply & oft afflicted Wife: It will greatly

comfort her to have you write her freely. She has born up *manfully* under accumulated trials. She will be most glad to know that she has not been entirely forgotten by relatives and say to all my friends that I am "waiting cheerfully" & "patiently the days of my appointed time": fully believing that for me now "to die will be to me an Infinite gain;" & of *untold* benefit to the cause *we love*. Wherefore "be of good cheer" & "let not your hearts be troubled." "To him that overcometh will I grant to sit with me;" in my throne even as I also overcame; & am set down with my Father in his throne." I wish my friends could know but a little of the same opportunities I now get for *Kind & faithful* labour in *Gods cause*. I hope they have not been entirely lost. Now dear friends I have done "May the God of peace bring us all again from the dead."

Your Affectionate Brother
John Brown

Charlestown, Jefferson Co., Va., Monday, Nov. 28, 1859.
Hon. D. R. Tilden.

My Dear Sir,—Your *most kind and comforting* letter of the 23d inst. is received.

I have no language to express the feelings of gratitude and obligation I am under for your kind interest in my behalf ever since my disaster.

The great bulk of mankind estimate each other's actions *and motives* by the measure of success or *otherwise* that attends them through life. By that rule I have been one of the *worst* and one of the *best* of men. I *do* not claim to have been one of the *latter*; and I leave it to an impartial tribunal to decide whether the world has been the *worse* or the better of my *living* and *dying* in it. My present great anxiety is to get as near in readiness for a different field of action as I well *can* since being in a good measure *relieved from the fear* that my poor, *broken-hearted wife and children* would come to immediate want. May God reward, *a thousand fold*, all the kind efforts made in their behalf. I have enjoyed *remarkable cheerfulness and composure of mind* ever since my confinement; and it is a great comfort to *feel assured* that I *am permitted* to die (for a *cause*) not *merely* to pay the debt of nature, (as all must.) I feel myself to be *most* unworthy of *so great* distinction. The particular manner of dying *assigned* to me, gives me but very little *uneasiness*. I wish I had the time and the ability to give you (my dear friend) some little idea of what is *daily, and, I might almost say, hourly,* passing within my *prison walls*; and could my friends but witness only a few of those scenes just as they occur, I think they would feel very well reconciled to my being here *just what I am, and just as I am*. My *whole* life *before* had not afforded me one half the opportunity to plead *for the right*. *In this*, also, *I find* much to reconcile me to both my present condition and my immediate prospect. I may be *very insane*, (and I *am so*, if insane at all.) But if that be so, *insanity* is like a very pleasant dream to me. I am not in the least degree conscious of my *ravings*, of my fears, or of any terrible visions whatever; but *fancy* myself entirely composed, and that my *sleep, in particular,* is as sweet as that of a healthy, joyous little infant. I pray God that he will grant me a continuance of the same calm, but delightful, *dream*, until I come to know of those realities which "eyes have not seen, and which ears have not heard." I have scarce realized that I am in prison, or in irons, at all. I certainly think I was never more cheerful in my life. I intend to take the liberty of sending, by express, to your care, some trifling articles for those of my family who may be in Ohio, which you can hand to my brother JEREMIAH, when you may see him, together with fifteen dollars I have asked him to advance to them. Please excuse me so often troubling you with my letters, or any of my matters. Please also remember me *most* kindly to Mr. GRISWOLD, and to all others who love their neighbors. I write JEREMIAH to your care.

Your friend, in truth,
John Brown.

Charlestown, Jefferson Co Va. 29th Nov. 1859.

Mrs George L Stearns
    Boston Mass
 My Dear Friend

  No letter I have received since my imprisonment here, has given me more satisfaction, or comfort; then yours of the 8th inst. I am quite cheerful: & was never more happy. Have only time [to] write you a word. May God forever reward you & *all yours. My love to All* who love their neighbors. I have asked to be *spared* from having any *mock*; *or hypocritical prayers made over me,* when I am publicly *murdered*: & that my only *religious attendants* be poor *little, dirty, ragged, bare headed, & barefooted Slave boys*; & *Girls*; led by some old *grey headed Slave Mother.*

  Farewell. Farewell.

Your Friend
John Brown.

Charlestown, Jefferson Co., Va., Nov. 29, 1859.

S. E. Sewall, Esq.

My dear Sir: Your most kind letter of the 24th inst. is received. It does, indeed, give me "pleasure," and the greatest encouragement to know of any efforts that have been made in behalf of my poor and deeply afflicted family. It takes from my mind the greatest cause of sadness I have experienced during my imprisonment here. I feel quite cheerful, and ready to die. I can only say, for want of time, may the *God of the oppressed* and the poor, *in great mercy, remember* all those to whom we are so deeply indebted!

  Farewell!   Your friend,   John Brown.

Charlestown, Prison, Jefferson Co. Va. 30th Nov 1859.
My Dearly beloved Wife, Sons: & Daughters, *every one*

As I now begin what is probably the last letter I shall ever write to any of you; I conclude to write you all at the same time. I will mention some little matters particularly applicable to little property concerns in another place. I yesterday received a letter from my wife from near Philadelphia: dated Nov 27th, by which it would seem that she has about given up the idea of seeing me again. I had written her to come on; if *she* felt equal to the undertaking: but I do not know as she will get my letter in time. It was on her *own account chiefly* that I asked her to stay *back* at first. I had a most strong desire to see her again; but there appeared to be very serious objections; & should we never meet in *this life*; I trust she will in the end be satisfied it was *for the best at least*; if not most for her comfort. I enclosed in my last letter to her a Draft of $50, Fifty Dollars from John Jay made payable to her order. I have now another to send her from my excellent old friend Edward Harris of Woonsocket Rhode Island for $100, One Hundred Dollars; which I shall *also make payable* to *her* order. I am waiting the hour of my public *murder* with great composure of mind, & cheerfulness: feeling the strongest assurance that in no other possible way could I be used to so much advance the cause of God; & of humanity: & that nothing that either I or all my family have sacrifised or suffered: *will be lost.* The reflection that a *wise, & merciful, as well as Just, & holy God*: rules not only the affairs of *this world*; but of all worlds; is a rock to set our feet upon; under all circumstances: *even* those more severely *trying ones*: into which our own follies; & [w]rongs have placed us. I have now no doubt but that our seeming *disaster*: will ultimately result in the most *glorious success.* So my dear *shattered; & broken* family; be of good cheer; & believe & trust in God; *"with all your heart: & with all your soul";* for he doeth *All things well."* Do not feel ashamed on my account; nor *for one moment* despair of the cause; or grow *weary* of *well doing.* I bless God; I never felt stronger confidence in the certain & near approach of a *bright Morning*; & a *glorious day*: than I have felt; & do now feel; since my confinement here. I am endeavouring to "return" like a "poor Prodigal" *as I am*; to my Father: against whom I have *always* sined: *in the hope*; that he may kindly, & forgivingly "meet me: though; *a verry great way off."* Oh my dear Wife & Children would "to God" you could know how I have been "traveling in birth for you" all; that no one of you "may fail of the grace of God, through Jesus Christ:" that no one of you may be blind to the truth: & glorious "light of *his* word;" in which Life; & Immortality; are brought to light." I beseech you *every one* to make the bible your *dayly & Nightly study*; with a *childlike honest, candid, teachable spirit*: out of love and respect for your Husband; & Father: & I beseech *the God of my Fathers*; to open all your eyes to a discovery of *the truth*. You *cannot immagine* how much *you* may *soon need* the consolations of the Christian religion.

Circumstances like my own; for more than a month past; convince me beyound *all doubt*; of our great need: of something more to rest our hopes on; than merely our own vague theories framed up, while our *prejudices* are excited; *or* our *Vanity* worked up to its highest pitch. Oh do not trust your eternal all uppon the boisterous Ocean, without *even* a *Helm*; or *Compass* to *aid* you in steering. I do *not ask any* of you; to throw *away your reason*: I only *ask* you, to make a candid, & sober *use of your reason*: My dear younger children will you listen to this last poor admonition of one who can *only* love you? Oh be determined at once to give your whole hearts to God; & let *nothing* shake; *or alter*, that resolution. You need have no fear of REGRETING *it*. Do not be vain; and thoughtless: but *sober minded*. And let me entreat you all to love *the whole remnant* of our once great family: "with a pure *heart fervently*." Try to *build again*: your broken walls: & to make *the utmost* of every *stone* that is left. Nothing can so tend to make life a blessing as the consciousness that you *love: & are beloved*: & "love ye the stranger" *still*. It is ground of the utmost comfort to *my mind*: to know that so many of you as have had *the opportunity*; have given full proof of your fidelity to the great family of man. *Be faithful* until *death*. From the exercise of habitual love to man: *it cannot* be very *hard*: to *learn to love* his *maker*. I must *yet* insert a reason for my firm belief in the Divine inspiration of the Bible: notwithstanding I am (perhaps naturally) skeptical. (certainly not, *credulous*.) I wish you all to consider *it most thoroughly*; when you read that blessed book; & see whether you *can not* discover such evidence yourselves. It is the purity of *heart, feeling, or motive*: as well as *word, & action* which is every where insisted on; that distinguish it from *all other teachings*; that *commends it* to *my conscience*: whether *my heart* be "willing, & obedient" *or not*. The inducements that it holds out; are another reason *of my conviction* of its *truth*: & *genuineness*; that I cannot here *omit*; in this my *last argument,* for the Bible *Eternal life*: is that my soul is "panting after" this moment. I mention this; as reason for endeavouring to leave a valuable copy of the Bible to be carefully *preserved* in remembrance of *me*: to so many of my posterity; *instead* of some *other* thing: of equal *cost*. I beseech you all to live in habitual contentment with verry *moderate* circumstances: & gains, of *worldly store*: & most earnestly to teach this: to your *children; & Childrens, Children*; after you: by *example: as well*; as precept. Be determined to know by experience *as soon as may be*: whether bible instruction is of *Divine origin* or not; *which says; "Owe no man anything but* to love one another." John Rogers wrote to his children, "Abhor that arrant whore of Rome." John Brown writes to his children to abhor with *undiing hatred,* also: that "sum of all vilanies;" Slavery. *Remember* that "he that is *slow* to *anger* is *better* than the mighty: and he that ruleth his *spirit*; than he that taketh a city." Remember also: *that* "they that be *wise* shall *shine*: and they that *turn* many to *righteousness*: as the stars forever; & ever." And now dearly beloved *Farewell* To God & the word of his grace I comme[n]d you all.

Your Affectionate Husband & Father
John Brown

Charlestown, Jefferson, Co Va, 2d, Dec. 1859.

Lora Case Esqr

My Dear Sir

Your most kind & cheering letter of the 28th Nov is received Such an outburst of warm hearted sympathy not only for myself; but also for those who *"have no helper"* compells me to steal a moment from those allowe[d] me; in which to prepare for my last great change to send you a few words. Such a feeling as you manifest makes you to *"shine* (in my estimation) in the midst of this wicked; & perverse generation as a light in the world"* May you ever prove yourself equal to the high estimate I have placed on you. Pure & undefiled religion befor God & the Father is as I understand it: an *active* (not a dormant) *principle*. I do not undertake to direct any more about my Children. I leave that now entirely to their excellent Mother from whom I have just parted. I send you my "salutation with my own hand." Remember me to all *yours, & my dear friends*.   Your Friend

John Brown

Charlestown, Va, 2d, December, 1859.

I John Brown am now quite *certain* that the crimes of this *guilty, land: will* never be purged *away*; but with Blood. I had *as I now think: vainly* flattered myself that without *verry much* bloodshed; it might be done.

Part 2

The Literary Heritage

Letter to the Editor

Victor Hugo

Hauteville House, Dec. 2, 1859.

SIR: When one thinks of the United States of America, a majestic figure rises to the mind—Washington. Now, in that country of Washington, see what is going on at this hour!

There are slaves in the Southern States, a fact which strikes with indignation, as the most monstrous of contradictions, the reasonable and freer conscience of the Northern States. These slaves, these negroes, a white man, a free man, one John Brown, wanted to deliver. Certainly, if insurrection be ever a sacred duty, it is against Slavery. Brown wished to begin the good work by the deliverance of the slaves in Virginia. Being a Puritan, a religious and austere man, and full of the Gospel, he cried aloud to these men—his brothers—the cry of emancipation "Christ has set us free!" The slaves, enervated by Slavery, made no response to his appeal—Slavery makes deafness in the soul. Brown, finding himself abandoned, fought with a handful of heroic men; he struggled; he fell, riddled with bullets; his two young sons, martyrs of a holy cause, dead at his side. This is what is called the Harper's Ferry affair.

John Brown, taken prisoner, has just been tried, with four of his fellows—Stephens, Coppoc, Green, and Copeland. What sort of trial it was, a word will tell.

Brown, stretched upon a truckle bed, with six half-closed wounds—a gun-shot wound in his arm, one in his loins, two in the chest, two in the head—almost bereft of hearing, bleeding through his mattress, the spirits of his two dead sons attending him; his four fellow-prisoners crawling around him; Stephens with four sabre wounds; "Justice" in a hurry to have done with the case; an attorney, Hunter, demanding that it be despatched with sharp speed; a Judge, Parker, assenting; the defence cut short; scarcely any delay allowed;

forged or garbled documents put in evidence; the witnesses for the prisoner shut out; the defence clogged; two guns, loaded with grape, brought into the court, with an order to the jailers to shoot the prisoners in case of an attempt at rescue; forty minutes' deliberation; three sentences to death. I affirm, on my honor, that all this took place, not in Turkey, but in America.

Such things are not done with impunity in the face of the civilized world. The universal conscience of mankind is an ever-watchful eye. Let the Judge of Charlestown, and Hunter, and Parker, and the slave-holding jurors, and the whole population of Virginia, ponder it well: they are seen! They are not alone in the world. At this moment the gaze of Europe is fixed on America.

John Brown, condemned to die, was to have been hanged on the 2d of December—this very day. But news has this instant reached us. A respite is granted him. It is not until the 16th that he is to die. The interval is short. Has a cry of mercy time to make itself heard? No matter. It is a duty to lift up the voice.

Perhaps a second respite may be granted. America is a noble land. The sentiment of humanity is soon quickened among a free people. We hope that Brown may be saved. If it were otherwise—if Brown should die on the scaffold on the 16th of December—what a terrible calamity!

The executioner of Brown—let us avow it openly (for the day of the kings is past, and the day of the people dawns, and to the people we are bound frankly to speak the truth)—the executioner of Brown would be neither the Attorney Hunter, nor the Judge Parker, nor the Governor Wise, nor the State of Virginia; it would be, we say it, and we think it with a shudder, the whole American Republic.

The more one loves, the more one admires, the more one reveres the Republic, the more heart-sick one feels at such a catastrophe. A single State ought not to have the power to dishonor all the rest, and in this case federal intervention is a clear right. Otherwise, by hesitating to interfere when it might prevent a crime, the Union becomes an accomplice. No matter how intense may be the indignation of the generous Northern States, the Southern States associate them with the disgrace of this murder. All of us, whosoever we may be—for whom the democratic cause is a common country—feel ourselves in a manner compromised and hurt. If the scaffold should be erected on the 16th of December, the incorruptible voices of history would thenceforward testify that the august confederation of the New World had added to all its ties of holy brotherhood a brotherhood of blood, and the *fasces* of that splendid Republic would be bound together with the running noose that hung from the gibbet of Brown.

This is a bond that kills.

When we reflect on what Brown, the liberator, the champion of Christ, has striven to effect, and when we remember that he is about to die, slaughtered by the American Republic, the crime assumes the proportions of the Nation which commits it; and when we say to ourselves that this Nation is a glory of the human race; that—like France, like England, like Germany—she is one of the organs of civilization; that she sometimes even out-marches Europe by the sublime audacity of her progress; that she is the queen of an entire world; and that she bears on her brow an immense light of freedom; we affirm that John Brown will not die; for we recoil, horror-struck, from the idea of so great a crime committed by so great a People.

In a political light, the murder of Brown would be an irreparable fault. It would penetrate the Union with a secret fissure, which would in the end tear it asunder. It is possible that the execution of Brown might consolidate Slavery in Virginia, but it is certain that it would convulse the entire American Democracy. You preserve your shame, but you sacrifice your glory.

In a moral light, it seems to me, that a portion of the light of humanity would be eclipsed; that even the idea of justice and injustice would be obscured on the day which should witness the assassination of Emancipation by Liberty.

As for myself, though I am but an atom, yet being, as I am, in common with all other men, inspired with the conscience of humanity, I kneel in tears before the great starry banner of the New World, and with clasped hands, and with profound and filial respect, I implore the illustrious American Republic, sister of the French Republic, to look to the safety of the universal moral law, to save Brown; to throw down the threatening scaffold of the 16th December, and not to suffer that, beneath its eyes, and, I add, with a shudder, almost by its fault, the first fratricide be outdone.

For—yes, let America know it, and ponder it well—there is something more terrible than Cain slaying Abel—it is Washington slaying Spartacus.

Victor Hugo.

To the Editor of the London News.

With a Rose

That Bloomed on the Day of
John Brown's Martyrdom.

Louisa May Alcott

In the long silence of the night,
   Nature's benignant power
Woke aspirations for the light
   Within the folded flower.
Its presence and the gracious day
   Made summer in the room,
But woman's eyes shed tender dew
   On the little rose in bloom.

Then blossomed forth a grander flower,
   In the wilderness of wrong,
Untouched by Slavery's bitter frost,
   A soul devout and strong.
God-watched, that century plant uprose,
   Far shining through the gloom,
Filling a nation with the breath
   Of a noble life in bloom.

A life so powerful in its truth,
   A nature so complete;
It conquered ruler, judge and priest,
   And held them at its feet.
Death seemed proud to take a soul
   So beautifully given,
And the gallows only proved to him
   A stepping-stone to heaven.

Each cheerful word, each valiant act,
   So simple, so sublime,
Spoke to us through the reverent hush
   Which sanctified that time.
That moment when the brave old man
   Went so serenely forth,
With footsteps whose unfaltering tread
   Reëchoed through the North.

The sword he wielded for the right
   Turns to a victor's palm;
His memory sounds forever more,
   A spirit-stirring psalm.
No breath of shame can touch his shield,
   Nor ages dim its shine;
Living, he made life beautiful,—
   Dying, made death divine.

No monument of quarried stone,
   No eloquence of speech,
Can grave the lessons on the land
   His martyrdom will teach.
No eulogy like his own words,
   With hero-spirit rife,
"I truly serve the cause I love,
   By yielding up my life."

The Portent

Herman Melville

Hanging from the beam,
  Slowly swaying (such the law),
Gaunt the shadow on your green,
  Shenandoah!
The cut is on the crown
(Lo, John Brown),
And the stabs shall heal no more.

Hidden in the cap
  Is the anguish none can draw;
So your future veils its face,
  Shenandoah!
But the streaming beard is shown
(Weird John Brown),
The meteor of the war.

O! never may yon blue-ridged hills
  The Northern rifle hear,
Nor see the light of blazing homes
  Flash on the negro's spear.
But let the free-winged angel Truth
  Their guarded passes scale,
To teach that Right is more than Might
  And Justice more than Mail!

So vainly shall Virginia set
 Her battle in array;
In vain her trampling squadrons knead
 The winter snow with clay.
She may strike the pouncing eagle,
 But she dare not harm the dove;
And every gate she bars to Hate
 Shall open wide to Love!

John Brown

Ralph Waldo Emerson

Mr. Chairman:

I have been struck with one fact, that the best orators who have added their praise to his fame,—and I need not go out of this house to find the purest eloquence in the country,—have one rival who comes off a little better, and that is *JOHN BROWN*. Every thing that is said of him leaves people a little dissatisfied; but as soon as they read his own speeches and letters they are heartily contented,—such is the singleness of purpose which justifies him to the head and the heart of all. Taught by this experience, I mean, in the few remarks I have to make, to cling to his history, or let him speak for himself.

John Brown, the founder of liberty in Kansas, was born in Torrington, Litchfield County, Conn., in 1800. When he was five years old his father emigrated to Ohio, and the boy was there set to keep sheep and to look after cattle and dress skins; he went bareheaded and barefooted, and clothed in buckskin. He said that he loved rough play, could never have rough play enough; could not see a seedy hat without wishing to pull it off. But for this it needed that the playmates should be equal; not one in fine clothes and the other in buckskin; not one his own master, hale and hearty, and the other watched and whipped. But it chanced that in Pennsylvania, where he was sent by his father to collect cattle, he fell in with a boy whom he heartily liked and whom he looked upon as his superior. This boy was a slave; he saw him beaten with an iron shovel, and otherwise maltreated; he saw that this boy had nothing better to look forward to in life, whilst he himself was petted and made much of; for he was much considered in the family where he then stayed, from the circumstance that this boy of twelve years had conducted alone a drove of cattle a hundred miles. But the colored boy had no friend, and no future. This worked such indignation in him that he swore an oath of resistance to Slavery as long as he lived. And thus his enterprise to go into Virginia and run off five hundred or a thousand slaves was not a piece of spite or revenge, a plot of two years or of twenty years, but the keeping of an oath made to Heaven and earth forty-seven years before. Forty-seven years at least, though I incline to accept his own account of the matter at Charlestown, which makes the date a little older, when he said, "This was all settled millions of years before the world was made."

He grew up a religious and manly person, in severe poverty; a fair specimen of the best stock of New England; having that force of thought and that sense of right which are the warp and woof of greatness. Our farmers were Orthodox Calvinists, mighty in the Scriptures; had learned that life was a preparation, a "probation," to use their word, for a higher world, and was to be spent in loving and serving mankind.

Thus was formed a romantic character absolutely without any vulgar traits; living to ideal ends, without any mixture of self-indulgence or compromise, such as lowers the value of benevolent and thoughtful men we know; abstemious, refusing luxuries, not sourly and reproachfully but simply as unfit for his habit; quiet and gentle as a child in the house. And, as happens usually to men of romantic character, his fortunes were romantic. Walter Scott would have delighted to draw his picture and trace his adventurous career. A shepherd and herdsman, he learned the manners of animals and knew the secret signals by which animals communicate. He made his hard bed on the mountains with them; he learned to drive his flock through thickets all but impassable; he had all the skill of a shepherd by choice of breed and by wise husbandry to obtain the best wool, and that for a course of years. And the anecdotes preserved show a far-seeing skill and conduct which, in spite of adverse accidents, should secure, one year with another, an honest reward, first to the farmer, and afterwards to the dealer. If he kept sheep, it was with a royal mind; and if he traded in wool, he was a merchant prince, not in the amount of wealth, but in the protection of the interests confided to him.

I am not a little surprised at the easy effrontery with which political gentlemen, in and out of Congress, take it upon them to say that there are not a thousand men in the North who sympathize with John Brown. It would be far safer and nearer the truth to say that all people, in proportion to their sensibility and self-respect, sympathize with him. For it is impossible to see courage, and disinterestedness, and the love that casts out fear, without sympathy. All women are drawn to him by their predominance of sentiment. All gentlemen, of course, are on his side. I do not mean by "gentlemen," people of scented hair and perfumed handkerchiefs, but men of gentle blood and generosity, "fulfilled with all nobleness," who, like the Cid, give the outcast leper a share of their bed; like the dying Sidney, pass the cup of cold water to the wounded soldier who needs it more. For what is the oath of gentle blood and knighthood? What but to protect the weak and lowly against the strong oppressor?

Nothing is more absurd than to complain of this sympathy, or to complain of a party of men united in opposition to Slavery. As well complain of gravity, or the ebb of the tide. Who makes the Abolitionist? The Slaveholder. The sentiment of mercy is the natural recoil which the laws of the universe provide to protect mankind from destruction by savage passions. And our blind statesmen go up and down, with committees of vigilance and safety, hunting for the origin of this new heresy. They will need a very vigilant committee indeed to find its birthplace, and a very strong force to root it out. For the arch-Abolitionist, older than Brown, and older than the Shenandoah Mountains, is Love, whose other name is Justice, which was before Alfred, before Lycurgus, before Slavery, and will be after it.

The Last Days of John Brown

Henry David Thoreau

John Brown's career for the last six weeks of his life was meteor-like, flashing through the darkness in which we live. I know of nothing so miraculous in our history.

If any person, in a lecture or conversation at that time, cited any ancient example of heroism, such as Cato or Tell or Winkelried, passing over the recent deeds and words of Brown, it was felt by any intelligent audience of Northern men to be tame and inexcusably far-fetched.

For my own part, I commonly attend more to nature than to man, but any affecting human event may blind our eyes to natural objects. I was so absorbed in him as to be surprised whenever I detected the routine of the natural world surviving still, or met persons going about their affairs indifferent. It appeared strange to me that the "little dipper" should be still diving quietly in the river, as of yore; and it suggested that this bird might continue to dive here when Concord should be no more.

I felt that he, a prisoner in the midst of his enemies and under sentence of death, if consulted as to his next step or resource, could answer more wisely than all his countrymen beside. He best understood his position; he contemplated it most calmly. Comparatively, all other men, North and South, were beside themselves. Our thoughts could not revert to any greater or wiser or better man with whom to contrast him, for he, then and there, was above them all. The man this country was about to hang appeared the greatest and best in it.

Years were not required for a revolution of public opinion; days, nay hours, produced marked changes in this case. Fifty who were ready to say, on going into our meeting in honor of him in Concord, that he ought to be hung, would not say it when they came out. They heard his words read; they saw the earnest faces of the congregation; and perhaps they joined at last in singing the hymn in his praise.

The order of instructors was reversed. I heard that one preacher, who at first was shocked and stood aloof, felt obliged at last, after he was hung, to make him the subject of a sermon, in which, to some extent, he eulogized the man, but said that his act was a failure. An influential class-teacher thought it necessary, after the services, to tell his grown-up pupils that at first he thought as the preacher did then, but now he thought that John Brown was right. But it was understood that his pupils were as much ahead of the teacher as he was ahead of the priest; and I know for a certainty that very little boys at home had already asked their parents, in a tone of surprise, why God did not interfere to save him. In each case, the constituted teachers were only half conscious that they were not *leading,* but being *dragged,* with some loss of time and power.

The more conscientious preachers, the Bible men, they who talk about principle, and doing to others as you would that they should do unto you,—how could they fail to recognize him, by far the greatest preacher of them all, with the Bible in his life and in his acts, the embodiment of principle, who actually carried out the golden rule? All whose moral sense had been aroused, who had a calling from on high to preach, sided with him. What confessions he extracted from the cold and conservative! It is remarkable, but on the whole it is well, that it did not prove the occasion for a new sect of *Brownites* being formed in our midst.

They, whether within the Church or out of it, who adhere to the spirit and let go the letter, and are accordingly called infidel, were as usual foremost to recognize him. Men have been hung in the South before for attempting to rescue slaves, and the North was not much stirred by it. Whence, then, this wonderful difference? We were not so sure of *their* devotion to principle. We made a subtle distinction, forgot human laws, and did homage to an idea. The North, I mean the *living* North, was suddenly all transcendental. It went behind the human law, it went behind the apparent failure, and recognized eternal justice and glory. Commonly, men live according to a formula, and are satisfied if the order of law is observed, but in this instance they, to some extent, returned to original perceptions, and there was a slight revival of old religion. They saw that what was called order was confusion, what was called justice, injustice, and that the best was deemed the worst. This attitude suggested a more intelligent and generous spirit than that which actuated our forefathers, and the possibility, in the course of ages, of a revolution in behalf of another and an oppressed people.

Most Northern men, and a few Southern ones, were wonderfully stirred by Brown's behavior and words. They saw and felt that they were heroic and noble, and that there had been nothing quite equal to them in their kind in this country, or in the recent history of the world. But the minority were unmoved by them. They were only surprised and provoked by the attitude of their neighbors. They saw that Brown was brave, and that he believed that he had done right, but they did not detect any further peculiarity in him. Not being accustomed to make fine distinctions, or to appreciate magnanimity, they read his letters and speeches as if they read them not. They were not aware when they *burned*. They did not feel that he spoke with authority, and hence they only remembered that the *law* must be executed. They remembered the old formula, but did not hear the new revelation. The man who does not recognize in Brown's words a wisdom and nobleness, and therefore an authority, superior to our laws, is a modern Democrat. This is the test by which to discover him. He is not willfully but constitutionally blind on this side, and he is consistent with himself. Such has been his past life; no doubt about it. In like manner he has read history and his Bible, and he accepts, or seems to accept, the last only as an established formula, and not because he has been convicted by it. You will not find kindred sentiments in his commonplace book, if he has one.

When a noble deed is done, who is likely to appreciate it? They who are noble themselves. I was not surprised that certain of my neighbors spoke of John Brown as an ordinary felon, for who are they? They have either much flesh, or much office, or much coarseness of some kind. They are not ethereal natures in any sense. The dark qualities predominate in them. Several of them are decidedly pachydermatous. I say it in sorrow, not in anger. How can a man behold the light who has no answering inward light? They are true to their *right,* but when they look this way they *see* nothing, they are blind. For the children of the light to contend with them is as if there should be a contest between eagles and owls. Show me a man who feels bitterly toward John Brown, and let me hear what noble verse he can repeat. He'll be as dumb as if his lips were stone.

It is not every man who can be a Christian, even in a very moderate sense, whatever education you give him. It is a matter of constitution and temperament, after all. He may have to be born again many times. I have known many a man who pretended to be a Christian, in whom it was ridiculous, for he had no genius for it. It is not every man who can be a freeman, even.

Editors persevered for a good while in saying that Brown was crazy; but at last they said only that it was "a crazy scheme," and the only evidence brought to prove it was that it cost him his life. I have no doubt that if he had gone with five thousand men, liberated a thousand slaves, killed a hundred or two slave-holders, and had as many more killed on his own side, but not lost his own life, these same editors would have called it by a more respectable name. Yet he has been far more successful than that. He has liberated many thousands of slaves, both North and South. They seem to have known nothing about living or dying for a principle. They all called him crazy then; who calls him crazy now?

All through the excitement occasioned by his remarkable attempt and subsequent behavior the Massachusetts Legislature, not taking any steps for the defense of her citizens who were likely to be carried to Virginia as witnesses and exposed to the violence of a slaveholding mob, was wholly absorbed in a liquor-agency question, and indulging in poor jokes on the word "extension." Bad spirits occupied their thoughts. I am sure that no statesman up to the occasion could have attended to that question at all at that time,—a very vulgar question to attend to at any time!

When I looked into a liturgy of the Church of England, printed near the end of the last century, in order to find a service applicable to the case of Brown, I found that the only martyr recognized and provided for by it was King Charles the First, an eminent scamp. Of all the inhabitants of England and of the world, he was the only one, according to this authority, whom that church had made a martyr and saint of; and for more than a century it had celebrated his martyrdom, so called, by an annual service. What a satire on the Church is that!

Look not to legislatures and churches for your guidance, nor to any soulless *incorporated* bodies, but to *inspirited* or inspired ones.

What avail all your scholarly accomplishments and learning, compared with wisdom and manhood? To omit his other behavior, see what a work this comparatively unread and unlettered man wrote within six weeks. Where is our professor of *belles-lettres,* or of logic and rhetoric, who can write so well? He wrote in prison, not a History of the World, like Raleigh, but an American book which I think will live longer than that. I do not know of such words, uttered under such circumstances, and so copiously withal, in Roman or English or any history. What a variety of themes he touched on in that short space! There are words in that letter to his wife, respecting the education of his daughters, which deserve to be framed and hung over every mantelpiece in the land. Compare this earnest wisdom with that of Poor Richard.

The death of Irving, which at any other time would have attracted universal attention, having occurred while these things were transpiring, went almost unobserved. I shall have to read of it in the biography of authors.

Literary gentlemen, editors, and critics think that they know how to write, because they have studied grammar and rhetoric; but they are egregiously mistaken. The *art* of composition is as simple as the discharge of a bullet from a rifle, and its masterpieces imply an infinitely greater force behind them. This unlettered man's speaking and writing are standard English. Some words and phrases deemed vulgarisms and Americanisms before, he has made standard American; such as *"It will pay."* It suggests that the one great rule of composition—and if I were a professor of rhetoric I should insist on this—is, to *speak the truth*. This first, this second, this third; pebbles in your mouth or not. This demands earnestness and manhood chiefly.

We seem to have forgotten that the expression, a *liberal* education, originally meant among the Romans one worthy of *free* men; while the learning of trades and professions by which to get your livelihood merely was considered worthy of *slaves* only. But taking a hint from the word, I would go a step further, and say that it is not the man of wealth and leisure simply, though devoted to art, or science, or literature, who, in a true sense, is *liberally* educated, but only the earnest and *free* man. In a slaveholding country like this, there can be no such thing as a *liberal* education tolerated by the State; and those scholars of Austria and France who, however learned they may be, are contented under their tyrannies have received only a *servile* education.

Nothing could his enemies do but it redounded to his infinite advantage,—that is, to the advantage of his cause. They did not hang him at once, but reserved him to preach to them. And then there was another great blunder. They did not hang his four followers with him; that scene was still postponed; and so his victory was prolonged and completed. No theatrical manager could have arranged things so wisely to give effect to his behavior and words. And who, think you, *was* the manager? *Who* placed the slave-woman and her child, whom he stooped to kiss for a symbol, between his prison and the gallows?

We soon saw, as he saw, that he was not to be pardoned or rescued by men. That would have been to disarm him, to restore to him a material weapon, a Sharps rifle, when he had taken up the sword of the spirit—the sword with which he has really won his greater and most memorable victories. Now he has not laid aside the sword of the spirit, for he is pure spirit himself, and his sword is pure spirit also.

> "He nothing common did or mean
>   Upon that memorable scene,
>   Nor called the gods with vulgar spite,
>   To vindicate his helpless right;
>   But bowed his comely head
>   Down as upon a bed."

What a transit was that of his horizontal body alone, but just cut down from the gallows-tree! We read that at such a time it passed through Philadelphia, and by Saturday night had reached New York. Thus like a meteor it shot through the Union from the Southern regions toward the North! No such freight had the cars borne since they carried him Southward alive.

On the day of his translation, I heard, to be sure, that he was *hung,* but I did not know what that meant; I felt no sorrow on that account; but not for a day or two did I even *hear* that he was *dead,* and not after any number of days shall I believe it. Of all the men who were said to be my contemporaries, it seemed to me that John Brown was the only one who *had not died.* I never hear of a man named Brown now,—and I hear of them pretty often,—I never hear of any particularly brave and earnest man, but my first thought is of John Brown, and what relation he may be to him. I meet him at every turn. He is more alive than ever he was. He has earned immortality. He is not confined to North Elba nor to Kansas. He is no longer working in secret. He works in public, and in the clearest light that shines on this land.

John Brown

Frederick Douglass

Not to fan the flame of sectional animosity now happily in the process of rapid and I hope permanent extinction; not to revive and keep alive a sense of shame and remorse for a great national crime, which has brought its own punishment, in loss of treasure, tears and blood; not to recount the long list of wrongs, inflicted on my race during more than two hundred years of merciless bondage; nor yet to draw, from the labyrinths of far-off centuries, incidents and achievements wherewith to rouse your passions, and enkindle your enthusiasm, but to pay a just debt long due, to vindicate in some degree a great historical character, of our own time and country, one with whom I was myself well acquainted, and whose friendship and confidence it was my good fortune to share, and to give you such recollections, impressions and facts, as I can, of a grand, brave and good old man, and especially to promote a better understanding of the raid upon Harper's Ferry of which he was the chief, is the object of this address.

In all the thirty years' conflict with slavery, if we except the late tremendous war, there is no subject which in its interest and importance will be remembered longer, or will form a more thrilling chapter in American history than this strange, wild, bloody and mournful drama. The story of it is still fresh in the minds of many who now hear me, but for the sake of those who may have forgotten its details, and in order to have our subject in its entire range more fully and clearly before us at the outset, I will briefly state the facts in that extraordinary transaction.

On the night of the 16th of October, 1859, there appeared near the confluence of the Potomac and Shenandoah rivers, a party of nineteen men—fourteen white and five colored. They were not only armed themselves, but had brought with them a large supply of arms for such persons as might join them. These men invaded Harper's Ferry, disarmed the watchman, took possession of the arsenal, rifle factory, armory and other government property at that place, arrested and made prisoners nearly all the prominent citizens of the neighborhood, collected about fifty slaves, put bayonets into the hands of such as were able and willing to fight for their liberty, killed three men, proclaimed a general emancipation, held the ground more than thirty hours, were subsequently overpowered and nearly all killed, wounded or captured, by a body of United States troops, under command of Colonel Robert E. Lee, since famous as the rebel Gen. Lee. Three out of the nineteen invaders were captured whilst fighting, and one of these was Captain John Brown, the man who originated, planned and commanded the expedition. At the time of his capture Capt. Brown was supposed to be mortally wounded, as he had several ugly gashes and bayonet wounds on his head and body; and apprehending that he might speedily die, or that he might be rescued by his friends, and thus the opportunity of making him a signal example of slave-holding vengeance would be lost, his captors hurried him to Charlestown two miles further within the border of Virginia, placed him in prison strongly guarded by troops, and before his wounds were healed he was brought into court, subjected to a nominal trial, convicted of high treason and inciting slaves to insurrection, and was executed. His corpse was given to his woe-stricken widow, and she, assisted by Anti-slavery friends, caused it to be borne to North Elba, Essex County, N. Y., and there his dust now reposes, amid the silent, solemn and snowy grandeur of the Adirondacks.

Such is the story; with no line softened or hardened to my inclining. It certainly is not a story to please, but to pain. It is not a story to increase our sense of social safety and security, but to fill the imagination with wild and troubled fancies of doubt and danger. It was a sudden and startling surprise to the people of Harper's Ferry, and it is not easy to conceive of a situation more abundant in all the elements of horror and consternation. They had retired as usual to rest, with no suspicion that an enemy lurked in the surrounding darkness. They had quietly and trustingly given themselves up to "tired Nature's sweet restorer, balmy sleep," and while thus all unconscious of danger, they were roused from their peaceful slumbers by the sharp crack of the invader's rifle, and felt the keen-edged sword of war at their throats, three of their number being already slain.

Every feeling of the human heart was naturally outraged at this occurrence, and hence at the moment the air was full of denunciation and execration. So intense was this feeling, that few ventured to whisper a word of apology. But happily reason has her voice as well as feeling, and though slower in deciding, her judgments are broader, deeper, clearer and more enduring. It is not easy to reconcile human feeling to the shedding of blood for any purpose, unless indeed in the excitement which the shedding of blood itself occasions. The knife is to feeling always an offence. Even when in the hands of a skillful surgeon, it refuses consent to the operation long after reason has demonstrated its necessity. It even pleads the cause of the known murderer on the day of his execution, and calls society half criminal when, in cold blood, it takes life as a protection of itself from crime. Let no word be said against this holy feeling; more than to law and government are we indebted to this tender sentiment of regard for human life for the safety with which we walk the streets by day and sleep secure in our beds at night. It is nature's grand police, vigilant and faithful, sentineled in the soul, guarding against violence to peace and life. But whilst so much is freely accorded to feeling in the economy of human welfare, something more than feeling is necessary to grapple with a fact so grim and significant as was this raid. Viewed apart and alone, as a transaction separate and distinct from its antecedents and bearings, it takes rank with the most cold-blooded and atrocious wrongs ever perpetrated; but just here is the trouble—this raid on Harper's Ferry, no more than Sherman's march to the sea can consent to be thus viewed alone.

There is, in the world's government, a force which has in all ages been recognized, sometimes as Nemesis, sometimes as the judgment of God and sometimes as retributive justice; but under whatever name, all history attests the wisdom and beneficence of its chastisements, and men become reconciled to the agents through whom it operates, and have extolled them as heroes, benefactors and demigods.

To the broad vision of a true philosophy, nothing in this world stands alone. Everything is a necessary part of everything else. The margin of chance is narrowed by every extension of reason and knowledge, and nothing comes unbidden to the feast of human experience. The universe, of which we are a part, is continually proving itself a stupendous whole, a system of law and order, eternal and perfect. Every seed bears fruit after its kind, and nothing is reaped which was not sowed. The distance between seed time and harvest, in the moral world, may not be quite so well defined or as clearly intelligible as in the physical, but there is a seed time, and there is a harvest time, and though ages may intervene, and neither he who ploughed nor he who sowed may reap in person, yet the harvest nevertheless will surely come; and as in the physical world there are century plants, so it may be in the moral world, and their fruitage is as certain in the one as in the other. The bloody harvest of Harper's Ferry was ripened by the heat and moisture of merciless bondage of more than two hundred years. That startling cry of alarm on the banks of the Potomac was but the answering back of the avenging angel to the midnight invasions of Christian slave-traders on the sleeping hamlets of Africa. The history of the African slave-trade furnishes many illustrations far more cruel and bloody.

Viewed thus broadly our subject is worthy of thoughtful and dispassionate consideration. It invites the study of the poet, scholar, philosopher and statesman. What the masters in natural science have done for man in the physical world, the masters of social science may yet do for him in the moral world. Science now tells us when storms are in the sky, and when and where their violence will be most felt. Why may we not yet know with equal certainty when storms are in the moral sky, and how to avoid their desolating force? But I can invite you to no such profound discussions. I am not the man, nor is this the occasion for such philosophical enquiry. Mine is the word of grateful memory to an old friend; to tell you what I knew of him—what I knew of his inner life—of what he did and what he attempted, and thus if possible to make the mainspring of his actions manifest and thereby give you a clearer view of his character and services.

It is said that next in value to the performance of great deeds ourselves, is the capacity to appreciate such when performed by others; to more than this I do not presume. Allow me one other personal word before I proceed. In the minds of some of the American people I was myself credited with an important agency in the John Brown raid. Governor Henry A. Wise was manifestly of that opinion. He was at the pains of having Mr. Buchanan send his Marshals to Rochester to invite me to acccompany them to Virginia. Fortunately I left town several hours previous to their arrival.

What ground there was for this distinguished consideration shall duly appear in the natural course of this lecture. I wish however to say just here that there was no foundation whatever for the charge that I in any wise urged or instigated John Brown to his dangerous work. I rejoice that it is my good fortune to have seen, not only the end of slavery, but to see the day when the whole truth can be told about this matter without prejudice to either the living or the dead. I shall however allow myself little prominence in these disclosures. Your interests, like mine, are in the all-commanding figure of the story, and to him I consecrate the hour. His zeal in the cause of my race was far greater than mine—it was the burning sun to my taper light—mine was bounded by time, his stretched away to the boundless shores of eternity. I could live for the slave, but he could die for him. The crown of martyrdom is high, far beyond the reach of ordinary mortals, and yet happily no special greatness or superior moral excellence is necessary to discern and in some measure appreciate a truly great soul. Cold, calculating and unspiritual as most of us are, we are not wholly insensible to real greatness; and when we are brought in contact with a man of commanding mold, towering high and alone above the millions, free from all conventional fetters, true to his own moral convictions, a "law unto himself," ready to suffer misconstruction, ignoring torture and death for what he believes to be right, we are compelled to do him homage.

In the stately shadow, in the sublime presence of such a soul I find myself standing to-night; and how to do it reverence, how to do it justice, how to honor the dead with due regard to the living, has been a matter of most anxious solicitude.

Much has been said of John Brown, much that is wise and beautiful, but in looking over what may be called the John Brown literature, I have been little assisted with material, and even less encouraged with any hope of success in treating the subject. Scholarship, genius and devotion have hastened with poetry and eloquence, story and song to this simple altar of human virtue, and have retired dissatisfied and distressed with the thinness and poverty of their offerings, as I shall with mine.

The difficulty in doing justice to the life and character of such a man is not altogether due to the quality of the zeal, or of the ability brought to the work, nor yet to any imperfections in the qualities of the man himself; the state of the moral atmosphere about us has much to do with it. The fault is not in our eyes, nor yet in the object, if under a murky sky we fail to discover the object. Wonderfully tenacious is the taint of a great wrong. The evil, as well as "the good that men do, lives after them." Slavery is indeed gone; but its long, black shadow yet falls broad and large over the face of the whole country. It is the old truth oft repeated, and never more fitly than now, "a prophet is without honor in his own country and among his own people." Though more than twenty years have rolled between us and the Harper's Ferry raid, though since then the armies of the nation have found it necessary to do on a large scale what John Brown attempted to do on a small one, and the great captain who fought his way through slavery has filled with honor the Presidential chair, we yet stand too near the days of slavery, and the life and times of John Brown, to see clearly the true martyr and hero that he was and rightly to estimate the value of the man and his works. Like the great and good of all ages—the men born in advance of their times, the men whose bleeding footprints attest the immense cost of reform, and show us the long and dreary spaces, between the luminous points in the progress of mankind,—this our noblest American hero must wait the polishing wheels of after-coming centuries to make his glory more manifest, and his worth more generally acknowledged. Such instances are abundant and familiar. If we go back four and twenty centuries, to the stately city of Athens, and search among her architectural splendor and her miracles of art for the Socrates of today, and as he stands in history, we shall find ourselves perplexed and disappointed. In Jerusalem Jesus himself was only the "carpenter's son"—a young man wonderfully destitute of worldly prudence—a pestilent fellow, "inexcusably and perpetually interfering in the world's business,"—"upsetting the tables of the money-changers"—preaching sedition, opposing the good old religion—"making himself greater than Abraham," and at the same time "keeping company" with very low people; but behold the change! He was a great miracle-worker, in his day, but time has worked for him a greater miracle than all his miracles, for now his name stands for all that is desirable in government, noble in life, orderly and beautiful in society. That which time has done for other great men of his class, that will time certainly do for John Brown. The brightest gems shine at first with subdued light, and the strongest characters are subject to the same limitations. Under the influence of adverse education and hereditary bias, few things are more difficult than to render impartial justice. Men hold up their hands to Heaven, and swear they will do justice, but what are oaths against prejudice and against inclination! In the face of high-sounding professions and affirmations we know well how hard it is for a Turk to do justice to a Christian, or for a Christian to do justice to a Jew. How hard for an Englishman to do justice to an Irishman, for an Irishman to do justice to an Englishman, harder still for an American tainted by slavery to do justice to the Negro or the Negro's friends. "John Brown," said the late Wm. H. Seward, "was justly hanged." "John Brown," said the late John A. Andrew, "was right." It is easy to perceive the sources of these two opposite judgments: the one was the verdict of slave-holding and panic-stricken Virginia, the other was the verdict of the best heart and brain of free old

Massachusetts. One was the heated judgment of the passing and passionate hour, and the other was the calm, clear, unimpeachable judgment of the broad, illimitable future.

There is, however, one aspect of the present subject quite worthy of notice, for it makes the hero of Harper's Ferry in some degree an exception to the general rules to which I have just now adverted. Despite the hold which slavery had at that time on the country, despite the popular prejudice against the Negro, despite the shock which the first alarm occasioned, almost from the first John Brown received a large measure of sympathy and appreciation. New England recognized in him the spirit which brought the pilgrims to Plymouth rock and hailed him as a martyr and saint. True he had broken the law, true he had struck for a despised people, true he had crept upon his foe stealthily, like a wolf upon the fold, and had dealt his blow in the dark whilst his enemy slept, but with all this and more to disturb the moral sense, men discerned in him the greatest and best qualities known to human nature, and pronounced him "good." Many consented to his death, and then went home and taught their children to sing his praise as one whose "soul is marching on" through the realms of endless bliss. One element in explanation of this somewhat anomalous circumstance will probably be found in the troubled times which immediately succeeded, for "when judgments are abroad in the world, men learn righteousness."

The country had before this learned the value of Brown's heroic character. He had shown boundless courage and skill in dealing with the enemies of liberty in Kansas. With men so few, and means so small, and odds against him so great, no captain ever surpassed him in achievements, some of which seem almost beyond belief. With only eight men in that bitter war, he met, fought and captured Henry Clay Pate, with twenty-five well armed and mounted men. In this memorable encounter, he selected his ground so wisely, handled his men so skillfully, and attacked the enemy so vigorously, that they could neither run nor fight, and were therefore compelled to surrender to a force less than one-third of their own. With just thirty men on another important occasion during the same border war, he met and vanquished four hundred Missourians under the command of General Read. These men had come into the territory under an oath never to return to their homes till they had stamped out the last vestige of free State spirit in Kansas; but a brush with old Brown took this high conceit out of them, and they were glad to get off upon any terms, without stopping to stipulate. With less than one hundred men to defend the town of Lawrence, he offered to lead them and give battle to fourteen hundred men on the banks of the Waukerusia [Wakarusa] river, and was much vexed when his offer was refused by Gen. Jim Lane and others to whom the defense of the town was confided. Before leaving Kansas, he went into the border of Missouri, and liberated a dozen slaves in a single night, and, in spite of slave laws and marshals, he brought these people through a half dozen States, and landed them safely in Canada. With eighteen men this man shook the whole social fabric of Virginia. With eighteen men he overpowered a town of nearly three thousand souls. With these eighteen men he held that large community firmly in his grasp for thirty long hours. With these eighteen men he rallied in a single night fifty slaves to his standard, and made prisoners of an equal number of the slave-holding class. With these eighteen men he defied the power and bravery of a dozen of the best militia companies that Virginia could send against him. Now, when slavery struck, as it certainly did strike, at the life of the country, it was not the fault of John Brown that our rulers did not at first know how to deal with it. He had already shown us the weak side of the rebellion, had shown us where to strike and how. It was not from lack of native courage that Virginia submitted for thirty long hours and at last was relieved only by Federal troops; but because the attack was made on the side of her conscience and thus armed her against herself. She beheld at her side the sullen brow of a black Ireland. When John Brown proclaimed emancipation to the slaves of Maryland and Virginia he added to his war power the force of a moral earthquake. Virginia felt all her strong-ribbed mountains to shake under the heavy tread of armed insurgents. Of his army of nineteen her conscience made an army of nineteen hundred.

Another feature of the times, worthy of notice, was the effect of this blow upon the country at large. At the first moment we were stunned and bewildered. Slavery had so benumbed the moral sense of the nation, that it never suspected the possibility of an explosion like this, and it was difficult for Captain Brown to get himself taken for what he really was. Few could seem to comprehend that freedom to the slaves was his only object. If you will go back with me to that time you will find that the most curious and contradictory versions of the affair were industriously circulated, and those which were the least rational and true seemed to command the readiest belief. In the view of some, it assumed tremendous proportions. To such it was nothing less than a wide-sweeping rebellion to overthrow the existing government, and construct another upon its ruins, with

Brown for its President and Commander-in-chief; the proof of this was found in the old man's carpet-bag in the shape of a constitution for a new Republic, an instrument which in reality had been executed to govern the conduct of his men in the mountains. Smaller and meaner natures saw in it nothing higher than a purpose to plunder. To them John Brown and his men were a gang of desperate robbers, who had learned by some means that government had sent a large sum of money to Harper's Ferry to pay off the workmen in its employ there, and they had gone thence to fill their pockets from this money. The fact is, that outside of a few friends, scattered in different parts of the country, and the slave-holders of Virginia, few persons understood the significance of the hour. That a man might do something very audacious and desperate for money, power or fame, was to the general apprehension quite possible; but, in face of plainly-written law, in face of constitutional guarantees protecting each State against domestic violence, in face of a nation of forty million of people, that nineteen men could invade a great State to liberate a despised and hated race, was to the average intellect and conscience, too monstrous for belief. In this respect the vision of Virginia was clearer than that of the nation. Conscious of her guilt and therefore full of suspicion, sleeping on pistols for pillows, startled at every unusual sound, constantly fearing and expecting a repetition of the Nat Turner insurrection, she at once understood the meaning, if not the magnitude of the affair. It was this understanding which caused her to raise the lusty and imploring cry to the Federal government for help, and it was not till he who struck the blow had fully explained his motives and object, that the incredulous nation in any wise comprehended the true spirit of the raid, or of its commander. Fortunate for his memory, fortunate for the brave men associated with him, fortunate for the truth of history, John Brown survived the saber gashes, bayonet wounds and bullet holes, and was able, though covered with blood, to tell his own story and make his own defense. Had he with all his men, as might have been the case, gone down in the shock of battle, the world would have had no true basis for its judgment, and one of the most heroic efforts ever witnessed in behalf of liberty would have been confounded with base and selfish purposes. When, like savages, the Wises, the Vallandinghams, the Washingtons, the Stuarts and others stood around the fallen and bleeding hero, and sought by torturing questions to wring from his supposed dying lips some word by which to soil the sublime undertaking, by implicating Gerrit Smith, Joshua R. Giddings, Dr. S. G. Howe, G. L. Stearns,

Edwin Morton, Frank Sanborn, and other prominent Anti-slavery men, the brave old man, not only avowed his object to be the emancipation of the slaves, but serenely and proudly announced himself as solely responsible for all that had happened. Though some thought of his own life might at such a moment have seemed natural and excusable, he showed none, and scornfully rejected the idea that he acted as the agent or instrument of any man or set of men. He admitted that he had friends and sympathizers, but to his own head he invited all the bolts of slave-holding wrath and fury, and welcomed them to do their worst. His manly courage and self-forgetful nobleness were not lost upon the crowd about him, nor upon the country. They drew applause from his bitterest enemies. Said Henry A. Wise, "He is the gamest man I ever met." "He was kind and humane to his prisoners," said Col. Lewis Washington.

To the outward eye of men, John Brown was a criminal, but to their inward eye he was a just man and true. His deeds might be disowned, but the spirit which made those deeds possible was worthy highest honor. It has been often asked, why did not Virginia spare the life of this man? why did she not avail herself of this grand opportunity to add to her other glory that of a lofty magnanimity? Had they spared the good old man's life—had they said to him, "You see we have you in our power, and could easily take your life, but we have no desire to hurt you in any way; you have committed a terrible crime against society; you have invaded us at midnight and attacked a sleeping community, but we recognize you as a fanatic, and in some sense instigated by others; and on this ground and others, we release you. Go about your business, and tell those who sent you that we can afford to be magnanimous to our enemies." I say, had Virginia held some such language as this to John Brown, she would have inflicted a heavy blow on the whole Northern abolition movement, one which only the omnipotence of truth and the force of truth could have overcome. I have no doubt Gov. Wise would have done so gladly, but, alas, he was the executive of a State which thought she could not afford such magnanimity. She had that within her bosom which could more safely tolerate the presence of a criminal than a saint, a highway robber than a moral hero. All her hills and valleys were studded with material for a disastrous conflagration, and one spark of the dauntless spirit of Brown might set the whole State in flames. A sense of this appalling liability put an end to every noble consideration. His death was a foregone conclusion, and his trial was simply one of form.

Honor to the brave young Col. Hoyt who hastened from Massachusetts to defend his friend's life at the peril of his own; but there would have been no hope of success had he been allowed to plead the case. He might have surpassed Choate or Webster in power—a thousand physicians might have sworn that Capt. Brown was insane, it would have been all to no purpose; neither eloquence nor testimony could have prevailed. Slavery was the idol of Virginia, and pardon and life to Brown meant condemnation and death to slavery. He had practically illustrated a truth stranger than fiction—a truth higher than Virginia had ever known,—a truth more noble and beautiful than Jefferson ever wrote. He had evinced a conception of the sacredness and value of liberty which transcended in sublimity that of her own Patrick Henry and made even his fire-flashing sentiment of "Liberty or Death" seem dark and tame and selfish. Henry loved liberty for himself, but this man loved liberty for all men, and for those most despised and scorned, as well as for those most esteemed and honored. Just here was the true glory of John Brown's mission. It was not for his own freedom that he was thus ready to lay down his life, for with Paul he could say, "I was born free." No chain had bound his ankle, no yoke had galled his neck. History has no better illustration of pure, disinterested benevolence. It was not Caucasian for Caucasian—white man for white man; not rich man for rich man, but Caucasian for Ethiopian—white man for black man—rich man for poor man—the man admitted and respected, for the man despised and rejected. "I want you to understand, gentlemen," he said to his persecutors, "that I respect the rights of the poorest and weakest of the colored people, oppressed by the slave system, as I do those of the most wealthy and powerful." In this we have the key to the whole life and career of the man. Than in this sentiment humanity has nothing more touching, reason nothing more noble, imagination nothing more sublime; and if we could reduce all the religions of the world to one essence we could find in it nothing more divine. It is much to be regretted that some great artist, in sympathy with the spirit of the occasion, had not been present when these and similar words were spoken. The situation was thrilling. An old man in the center of an excited and angry crowd, far away from home, in an enemy's country—with no friend near—overpowered, defeated, wounded, bleeding—covered with reproaches—his brave companions nearly all dead—his two faithful sons stark and cold by his side—reading his death-warrant in his fast-oozing blood and increasing weakness as in the faces of all around him—yet calm, collected, brave, with a heart for any fate—using his supposed dying moments to explain his course and vindicate his cause; such a subject would have been at once an inspiration and a power for one of the grandest historical pictures ever painted. . . .

With John Brown, as with every other man fit to die for a cause, the hour of his physical weakness was the hour of his moral strength—the hour of his defeat was the hour of his triumph—the moment of his capture was the crowning victory of his life. With the Alleghany mountains for his pulpit, the country for his church and the whole civilized world for his audience, he was a thousand times more effective as a preacher than as a warrior, and the consciousness of this fact was the secret of his amazing complacency. Mighty with the sword of steel, he was mightier with the sword of truth, and with this sword he literally swept the horizon. He was more than a match for all the Wises, Masons, Vallandinghams and Washingtons, who could rise against him. They could kill him, but they could not answer him.

In studying the character and works of a great man, it is always desirable to learn in what he is distinguished from others, and what have been the causes of this difference. Such men as he whom we are now considering, come on to the theater of life only at long intervals. It is not always easy to explain the exact and logical causes that produce them, or the subtle influences which sustain them, at the immense hights where we sometimes find them; but we know that the hour and the man are seldom far apart, and that here, as elsewhere, the demand may in some mysterious way, regulate the supply. A great iniquity, hoary with age, proud and defiant, tainting the whole moral atmosphere of the country, subjecting both church and state to its control, demanded the startling shock which John Brown seemed especially inspired to give it.

Apart from this mission there was nothing very remarkable about him. He was a wool-dealer, and a good judge of wool, as a wool-dealer ought to be. In all visible respects he was a man like unto other men. No outward sign of Kansas or Harper's Ferry was about him. As I knew him, he was an even-tempered man, neither morose, malicious nor misanthropic, but kind, amiable, courteous, and gentle in his intercourse with men. His words were few, well chosen and forcible. He was a good business man, and a good neighbor. A good friend, a good citizen, a good husband and father: a man apparently in every way calculated to make a smooth and pleasant path for himself through the world. He loved society, he loved little children, he liked music, and was fond of animals. To no one was the world more beautiful or life more sweet. How then as I have said shall we explain his apparent indifference to life? I can find but one answer, and that is, his intense hatred to oppression. I have talked with many men, but I remember none, who seemed so deeply excited upon the subject of slavery as he. He would walk the room in agitation at mention of the word. He saw the evil through no mist or haze, but in a light of infinite brightness, which left no line of its ten thousand horrors out of sight. Law, religion, learning, were interposed in its behalf in vain. His law in regard to it was that which Lord Brougham described, as "the law above all the enactments of human codes, the same in all time, the same throughout the world—the law unchangeable and eternal—the law written by the finger of God on the human heart—that law by which property in man is, and ever must remain a wild and guilty phantasy."

Against truth and right, legislative enactments were to his mind mere cobwebs—the pompous emptiness of human pride—the pitiful outbreathings of human nothingness. He used to say "whenever there is a right thing to be done, there is a 'thus saith the Lord' that it shall be done."

It must be admitted that Brown assumed tremendous responsibility in making war upon the peaceful people of Harper's Ferry, but it must be remembered also that in his eye a slave-holding community could not be peaceable, but was, in the nature of the case, in one incessant state of war. To him such a community was not more sacred than a band of robbers: it was the right of any one to assault it by day or night. He saw no hope that slavery would ever be abolished by moral or political means: "he knew," he said, "the proud and hard hearts of the slave-holders, and that they never would consent to give up their slaves, till they felt a big stick about their heads."

It was five years before this event at Harper's Ferry, while the conflict between freedom and slavery was waxing hotter and hotter with every hour, that the blundering statesmanship of the National Government repealed the Missouri Compromise, and thus launched the territory of Kansas as a prize to be battled for between the North and the South. The remarkable part taken in this contest by Brown has been already referred to, and it doubtless helped to prepare him for the final tragedy, and though it did not by any means originate the plan, it confirmed him in it and hastened its execution.

During his four years' service in Kansas it was my good fortune to see him often. On his trips to and from the territory he sometimes stopped several days at my house, and at one time several weeks. It was on this last occasion that liberty had been victorious in Kansas, and he felt that he must hereafter devote himself to what he considered his larger work. It was the theme of all his conversation, filling his nights with dreams and his days with visions. An incident of his boyhood may explain, in some measure, the intense abhorrence he felt to slavery. He had for some reason been sent into the State of Kentucky, where he made the acquaintance of a slave boy, about his own age, of whom he became very fond. For some petty offense this boy was one day subjected to a brutal beating. The blows were dealt with an iron shovel and fell fast and furiously upon his slender body. Born in a free State and unaccustomed to such scenes of cruelty, young Brown's pure and sensitive soul revolted at the shocking spectacle and at that early age he swore eternal hatred to slavery. After years never obliterated the impression, and he found in this early experience an argument against contempt for small things. It is true that the boy is the father of the man. From the acorn comes the oak. The impression of a horse's foot in the sand suggested the art of printing. The fall of an apple intimated the law of gravitation. A word dropped in the woods of Vincennes, by royal hunters, gave Europe and the world a "William the Silent," and a thirty years' War. The beating of a Hebrew bondsman, by an Egyptian, created a Moses, and the infliction of a similar outrage on a helpless slave boy in our own land may have caused, forty years afterwards, a John Brown and a Harper's Ferry Raid.

Most of us can remember some event or incident which has at some time come to us, and made itself a permanent part of our lives. Such an incident came to me in the year 1847. I had then the honor of spending a day and a night under the roof of a man, whose character and conversation made a very deep impression on my mind and heart; and as the circumstance does not lie entirely out of the range of our present observations, you will pardon for a moment a seeming digression. The name of the person alluded to had been several times mentioned to me, in a tone that made me curious to see him and to make his acquaintance. It was a merchant, and our first meeting was at his store—a substantial brick building, giving evidence of a flourishing business. After a few minutes' detention here, long enough for me to observe the neatness and order of the place, I was conducted by him to his residence where I was kindly received by his family as an expected guest. I was a little disappointed at the appearance of this man's house, for after seeing his fine store, I was prepared to see a fine residence; but this logic was entirely contra-dicted by the facts. The house was a small, wooden one, on a back street in a neighborhood of laboring men and mechanics, respectable enough, but not just the spot where one would expect to find the home of a successful merchant. Plain as was the outside, the inside was plainer. Its furniture might have pleased a Spartan. It would take longer to tell what was not in it, than what was; no sofas, no cushions, no curtains, no carpets, no easy rocking chairs inviting to enervation or rest or repose. My first meal passed under the misnomer of tea. It was none of your tea and toast sort, but potatoes and cabbage, and beef soup; such a meal as a man might relish after following the plough all day, or after performing a forced march of a dozen miles over rough ground in frosty weather. Innocent of paint, veneering, varnish or tablecloth, the table announced itself unmistakably and hon-estly pine and of the plainest workmanship. No hired help passed from kitchen to dining room, staring in amazement at the colored man at the white man's table. The mother, daughters and sons did the serving, and did it well. I heard no apology for doing their own work; they went through it as if used to it, untouched by any thought of degradation or impropriety. Supper over, the boys helped to clear the table and wash the dishes. This style of housekeeping struck me as a little odd. I mention it because household management is wor-thy of thought. A house is more than brick and mortar, wood or paint; this to me at least was. In its plainness it was a truthful reflec-tion of its inmates: no disguises, no illusions, no make-believes here, but stern truth and solid purpose breathed in all its arrangements. I was not long in company with the master of this house before I dis-covered that he was indeed the master of it, and likely to become mine too, if I staid long with him. He fulfilled St. Paul's idea of the head of the family—his wife believed in him, and his children observed him with reverence. Whenever he spoke, his words commanded earnest attention. His arguments which I ventured at some points to oppose, seemed to convince all, his appeals touched all, and his will impressed all. Certainly I never felt myself in the presence of a stron-ger religious influence than while in this house. "God and duty, God and duty," run like a thread of gold through all his utterances, and his family supplied a ready "Amen." In person he was lean and sinewy, of the best new England mould, built for times of trouble, fitted to grapple with the flintiest hardships. Clad in plain American woolen, shod in boots of cowhide leather, and wearing a cravat of the same substantial material, under six feet high, less than one hundred and fifty lbs. in weight, aged about fifty, he presented a figure straight and symmetrical as a mountain pine. His bearing was singularly impressive. His head was not large, but compact and high. His hair was coarse, strong, slightly gray and closely trimmed and grew close to his forehead. His face was smoothly shaved and revealed a strong square mouth, supported by a broad and prominent chin. His eyes were clear and grey, and in conversation they alternated with tears and fire. When on the street, he moved with a long springing, race-horse step, absorbed by his own reflections, neither seeking nor shunning observation. Such was the man whose name I heard uttered in whispers—such was the house in which he lived—such were his family and household management—and such was Captain John Brown.

He said to me at this meeting, that he had invited me to his house for the especial purpose of laying before me his plan for the speedy emancipation of my race. He seemed to apprehend opposition on my part as he opened the subject and touched my vanity by saying, that he had observed my course at home and abroad, and wanted my co-operation. He said he had been for the last thirty years looking for colored men to whom he could safely reveal his secret, and had almost despaired, at times, of finding such, but that now he was encouraged for he saw heads rising up in all directions, to whom he thought he could with safety impart his plan. As this plan then lay in his mind it was very simple, and had much to commend it. It did not, as was supposed by many, contemplate a general rising among the slaves, and a general slaughter of the slave masters (an insurrection he thought would only defeat the object), but it did contemplate the creating of an armed force which should act in the very heart of the South. He was not averse to the shedding of blood, and thought the practice of carrying arms would be a good one for the colored people to adopt, as it would give them a sense of manhood. No people he said could have self-respect or be respected who would not fight for their freedom. He called my attention to a large map of the U. States, and pointed out to me the far-reaching Alleghanies, stretching away from the borders of New York into the Southern States. "These mountains," he said, "are the basis of my plan. God has given the strength of these hills to freedom; they were placed here to aid the emancipation of your race; they are full of natural forts, where one man for defense would be equal to a hundred for attack; they are also full of good hiding places where a large number of men could be concealed and baffle and elude pursuit for a long time. I know these mountains well and could take a body of men into them and keep them there in spite of all the efforts of Virginia to dislodge me, and drive me out. I would take at first about twenty-five picked men and begin on a small scale, supply them arms and ammunition, post them in squads of fives on a line of twenty-five miles, these squads to busy themselves for a time in gathering recruits from the surrounding farms, seeking and selecting the most restless and daring." He saw that in this part of the work the utmost care must be used to guard against treachery and disclosure; only the most conscientious and skillful should be sent on this perilous duty. With care and enterprise he thought he could soon gather a force of one hundred hardy men, men who would be content to lead the free and adventurous life to which he proposed to train them. When once properly drilled and each had found the place for which he was best suited, they would begin work in earnest; they would run off the slaves in large numbers, retain the strong and brave ones in the mountains, and send the weak and timid ones to the North by the underground Rail-road; his operations would be enlarged with increasing numbers and would not be confined to one locality. Slave-holders should in some cases be approached at midnight and told to give up their slaves and to let them have their best horses to ride away upon. Slavery was a state of war, he said, to which the slaves were unwilling parties and consequently they had a right to anything necessary to their peace and freedom. He would shed no blood and would avoid a fight except in self-defense, when he would of course do his best. He believed this movement would weaken slavery in two ways—first by making slave property insecure, it would become undesirable; and secondly it would keep the anti-slavery agitation alive and public attention fixed upon it, and thus lead to the adoption of measures to abolish the evil altogether. He held that there was need of something startling to prevent the agitation of the question from dying out; that slavery had come near being abolished in Virginia by the Nat Turner insurrection, and he thought his method would speedily put an end to it, both in Maryland and Virginia. The trouble was to get the right men to start with and money to equip them. He had adopted the simple and economical mode of living to which I have referred with a view to save money for this purpose. This was said in no boastful tone, for he felt that he had delayed already too long and had no room to boast either his zeal or his self-denial.

From 8 o'clock in the evening till 3 in the morning, Capt. Brown and I sat face to face, he arguing in favor of his plan, and I finding all the objections I could against it. Now mark! this meeting of ours was full twelve years before the strike at Harper's Ferry. He had been watching and waiting all that time for suitable heads to rise or "pop up" as he said among the sable millions in whom he could confide; hence forty years had passed between his thought and his act. Forty years, though not a long time in the life of a nation, is a long time in the life of a man; and here forty long years, this man was struggling with this one idea; like Moses he was forty years in the wilderness. Youth, manhood, middle age had come and gone; two marriages had been consummated, twenty children had called him father; and through all the storms and vicissitudes of busy life, this one thought, like the angel in the burning bush, had confronted him with its blazing light, bidding him on to his work. Like Moses he had made excuses, and as with Moses his excuses were overruled. Nothing should postpone further what was to him a divine command, the performance of which seemed to him his only apology for existence. He often said to me, though life was sweet to him, he would willingly lay it down for the freedom of my people; and on one occasion he added, that he had already lived about as long as most men, since he had slept less, and if he should now lay down his life the loss would not be great, for in fact he knew no better use for it. During his last visit to us in Rochester there appeared in the newspapers a touching story connected with the horrors of the Sepoy War in British India. A Scotch missionary and his family were in the hands of the enemy, and were to be massacred the next morning. During the night, when they had given up every hope of rescue, suddenly the wife insisted that relief would come. Placing her ear close to the ground she declared she heard the Slogan—the Scotch war song. For long hours in the night no member of the family could hear the advancing music but herself. "Dinna ye hear it? Dinna ye hear it?" she would say, but they could not hear it. As the morning slowly dawned a Scotch regiment was found encamped indeed about them, and they were saved from the threatened slaughter. This circumstance, coming at such a time, gave Capt. Brown a new word of cheer. He would come to the table in the morning his countenance fairly illuminated, saying that he had heard the Slogan, and he would add, "Dinna ye hear it?" "*Dinna* ye hear it?" Alas! like the Scotch missionary I was obliged to say "No." Two weeks prior to the meditated attack, Capt. Brown summoned me to meet him in an old stone quarry on the Conecochequi river, near the town of Chambersburg, Penn. His arms and ammunition were stored in that town and were to be moved on to Harper's Ferry. In company with Shields Green I obeyed the summons, and prompt to the hour we met the dear old man, with Kagi, his secretary, at the appointed place. Our meeting was in some sense a council of war. We spent the Saturday and succeeding Sunday in conference on the question, whether the desperate step should then be taken, or the old plan as already described should be carried out. He was for boldly striking Harper's Ferry at once and running the risk of getting into the mountains afterwards. I was for avoiding Harper's Ferry altogether. Shields Green and Mr. Kagi remained silent listeners throughout. It is needless to repeat here what was said, after what has happened. Suffice it, that after all I could say, I saw that my old friend had resolved on his course and that it was idle to parley. I told him finally that it was impossible for me to join him. I could see Harper's Ferry only as a trap of steel, and ourselves in the wrong side of it. He regretted my decision and we parted.

Thus far, I have spoken exclusively of Capt. Brown. Let me say a word or two of his brave and devoted men, and first of Shields Green. He was a fugitive slave from Charleston, South Carolina, and had attested his love of liberty by escaping from slavery and making his way through many dangers to Rochester, where he had lived in my family, and where he met the man with whom he went to the scaffold. I said to him, as I was about to leave, "Now Shields, you have heard our discussion. If in view of it, you do not wish to stay, you have but to say so, and you can go back with me." He answered, "I b'l'eve I'll go wid de old man;" and go with him he did, into the fight, and to the gallows, and bore himself as grandly as any of the number. At the moment when Capt. Brown was surrounded, and all chance of escape was cut off, Green was in the mountains and could have made his escape as Osborne Anderson did, but when asked to do so, he made the same answer he did at Chamberburg, "I b'l'eve I'll go down wid de ole man." When in prison at Charlestown, and he was not allowed to see his old friend, his fidelity to him was in no wise weakened, and no complaint against Brown could be extorted from him by those who talked with him.

If a monument should be erected to the memory of John Brown, as there ought to be, the form and name of Shields Green should have a conspicuous place upon it. It is a remarkable fact, that in this small company of men, but one showed any sign of weakness or regret for what he did or attempted to do. Poor Cook broke down and sought to save his life by representing that he had been deceived, and allured by false promises. But Stephens, Hazlett and

Green went to their doom like the heroes they were, without a murmur, without a regret, believing alike in their captain and their cause.

For the disastrous termination of this invasion, several causes have been assigned. It has been said that Capt. Brown found it necessary to strike before he was ready; that men had promised to join him from the North who failed to arrive; that the cowardly negroes did not rally to his support as he expected, but the true cause as stated by himself, contradicts all these theories, and from his statement there is no appeal. Among the questions put to him by Mr. Vallandingham after his capture were the following: "Did you expect a general uprising of the slaves in case of your success?" To this he answered, "No, sir, nor did I wish it. I expected to gather strength from time to time and then to set them free." "Did you expect to hold possession here until then?" Answer, "Well, probably I had quite a different idea. I do not know as I ought to reveal my plans. I am here wounded and a prisoner because I foolishly permitted myself to be so. You overstate your strength when you suppose I could have been taken if I had not allowed it. I was too tardy after commencing the open attack in delaying my movements through Monday night and up to the time of the arrival of government troops. It was all because of my desire to spare the feelings of my prisoners and their families."

But the question is, Did John Brown fail? He certainly did fail to get out of Harper's Ferry before being beaten down by United States soldiers; he did fail to save his own life, and to lead a liberating army into the mountains of Virginia. But he did not go to Harper's Ferry to save his life. The true question is, Did John Brown draw his sword against slavery and thereby lose his life in vain? and to this I answer ten thousand times, No! No man fails, or can fail who so grandly gives himself and all he has to a righteous cause. No man, who in his hour of extremest need, when on his way to meet an ignominious death, could so forget himself as to stop and kiss a little child, one of the hated race for whom he was about to die, could by any possibility fail. Did John Brown fail? Ask Henry A. Wise in whose house less than two years after, a school for the emancipated slaves was taught. Did John Brown fail? Ask James M. Mason, the author of the inhuman fugitive slave bill, who was cooped up in Fort Warren, as a traitor less than two years from the time that he stood over the prostrate body of John Brown. Did John Brown fail? Ask Clement C. Vallandingham, one other of the inquisitorial party; for he too went down in the tremendous whirlpool created by the powerful hand of this bold invader. If John Brown did not end the war that ended slavery, he did at least begin the war that ended slavery. If we look over the dates, places and men, for which this honor is claimed, we shall find that not Carolina, but Virginia—not Fort Sumpter [Sumter], but Harper's Ferry and the arsenal—not Col. Anderson, but John Brown, began the war that ended American slavery and made this a free Republic. Until this blow was struck, the prospect for freedom was dim, shadowy and uncertain. The irrepressible conflict was one of words, votes and compromises. When John Brown stretched forth his arm the sky was cleared. The time for compromises was gone—the armed hosts of freedom stood face to face over the chasm of a broken Union—and the clash of arms was at hand. The South staked all upon getting possession of the Federal Government, and failing to do that, drew the sword of rebellion and thus made her own, and not Brown's, the lost cause of the century.

Osawatomie

Carl Sandburg

I don't know how he came,
shambling, dark, and strong.

He stood in the city and told men:
My people are fools, my people are young and strong, my people
    must learn, my people are terrible workers and fighters.
Always he kept on asking: Where did that blood come from?

        They said: You for the fool killer,
                  you for the booby hatch
                  and a necktie party.

    They hauled him into jail.
    They sneered at him and spit on him,
    And he wrecked their jails,
    Singing, "God damn your jails,"
    And when he was most in jail
    Crummy among the crazy in the dark
    Then he was most of all out of jail
    Shambling, dark, and strong,
Always asking: Where did that blood come from?
    They laid hands on him
    And the fool killers had a laugh
    And the necktie party was a go, by God.
They laid hands on him and he was a goner.
    They hammered him to pieces and he stood up.
They buried him and he walked out of the grave, by God,
    Asking again: Where did that blood come from?

John Brown's Prayer

Stephen Vincent Benet

Omnipotent and steadfast God,
Who, in Thy mercy, hath
Upheaved in me Jehovah's rod
And his chastising wrath,

For fifty-nine unsparing years
Thy Grace hath worked apart
To mould a man of iron tears
With a bullet for a heart.

Yet, since this body may be weak
With all it has to bear,
Once more, before Thy thunders speak,
Almighty, hear my prayer.

I saw Thee when Thou did display
The black man and his lord
To bid me free the one, and slay
The other with the sword.

I heard Thee when Thou bade me spurn
Destruction from my hand
And, though all Kansas bleed and burn.
It was at Thy command.

I hear the rolling of the wheels,
The chariots of war!
I hear the breaking of the seals
And the opening of the door!

The glorious beasts with many eyes
Exult before the Crowned.
The buried saints arise, arise
Like incense from the ground!

Before them march the martyr-kings,
In bloody sunsets drest,
O, Kansas, bleeding Kansas,
You will not let me rest!

I hear your sighing corn again,
I smell your prairie-sky,
And I remember five dead men
By Pottawattomie.

Lord God it was a work of Thine,
And how might I refrain?
But Kansas, bleeding Kansas,
I hear her in her pain.

Her corn is rustling in the ground,
An arrow in my flesh.
And all night long I staunch a wound
That ever bleeds afresh.

Get up, get up, my hardy sons,
From this time forth we are
No longer men, but pikes and guns
In God's advancing war.

And if we live, we free the slave,
And if we die, we die.
But God has digged His saints a grave
Beyond the western sky.

Oh, fairer than the bugle-call
Its walls of jasper shine!
And Joshua's sword is on the wall
With space beside for mine.

And should the Philistine defend
His strength against our blows,
The God who doth not spare His friend,
Will not forget His foes.

Part 3

W.E.B. Du Bois on John Brown

The Blow

"Woe unto them that call evil, good; and good, evil."

"At eight o'clock on Sunday evening, Captain Brown said: 'Men, get on your arms; we will proceed to the Ferry.' His horse and wagon were brought out before the door, and some pikes, a sledge-hammer and a crowbar were placed in it. The captain then put on his old Kansas cap, and said: 'Come, boys!' when we marched out of the camp behind him, into the lane leading down the hill to the main road."

The orders given commanded Owen Brown, Merriam and Barclay Coppoc to watch the house and arms until ordered to bring them toward the Ferry. Tidd and Cook were to cut the telegraph lines and Kagi and Stephens to detain the bridge guard. Watson Brown and Taylor were to hold the bridge over the Potomac, and Oliver Brown and William Thompson the bridge over the Shenandoah. Jerry Anderson and Dauphin Thompson were to occupy the engine-house in the arsenal yard, while Hazlett and Edwin Coppoc were to hold the armory.

During the night Kagi and Copeland were to seize and guard the rifle factory, and others were to go out in the country and bring in certain masters and their slaves.

It was a cold dark night when the band started. Ahead was John Brown in his one-horse farm-wagon, with pikes, a sledge-hammer and a crowbar. Behind him marched the men silently and at intervals, Cook and Tidd leading. They had five miles to go, over rolling hills and through woods and then down to a narrow road between the cliffs and the Cincinnati and Ohio canal. As they approached the railroad, Cook and Tidd cut the telegraph wires which led to Baltimore and Washington. At the bridge they halted and made ready their arms. At ten o'clock William Williams, one of the watchmen there, was surprised to find himself a prisoner in the hands of Kagi and Stevens, who took him through the covered structure to the town, leaving Watson Brown and Steward Taylor to guard the bridge. The rest of the company entered Harper's Ferry.

The land between the rivers is itself high, though dwarfed by the mountains and running down to a low point where the rivers join. At this place the bridge leads to Maryland. After crossing the bridge to Virginia, about sixty yards up the street, running parallel to the Potomac, was the gate of the armory where the arms were made. On the Shenandoah side about sixty yards from the armory gate is the arsenal, where the arms were stored. The company proceeded to the armory gate. The watchman tells how the place was captured:

"'Open the gate,' said they; I said, 'I could not if I was stuck,' and one of them jumped up on the pier of the gate over my head, and another fellow ran and put his hand on me and caught me by the coat and held me; I was inside and they were outside, and the fellow standing over my head upon the pier, and then when I would not open the gate for them, five or six ran in from the wagon, clapped their guns against my breast, and told me I should deliver up the key; I told them I could not; and another fellow made an answer and said they had not time now to be waiting for the key, but to go to the wagon and bring out the crowbar and large hammer, and they would soon get in; they went to the little wagon and brought a large crowbar out of it; there is a large chain around the two sides of the wagon-gate going in; they twisted the crowbar in the chain and they opened it, and in they ran and got in the wagon; one fellow took me; they all gathered about me and looked in my face; I was nearly scared to death with so many guns about me."

The two captured watchmen, Anderson says, "were left in the custody of Jerry Anderson and Dauphin Thompson, and A. D. Stevens arranged the men to take possession of the armory and rifle factory. About this time, there was apparently much excitement. People were passing back and forth in the town, and before we could do much, we had to take several prisoners. After the prisoners were secured, we passed to the opposite side of the street and took the armory, and Albert Hazlett and Edwin Coppoc were ordered to hold it for the time being."

The other fourteen men quickly dispersed through the village. Oliver Brown and William Thompson seized and guarded the bridge across the Shenandoah. This bridge was sixty rods from the railway bridge up the river and was the direct route to Loudoun Heights, the slave-filled lower valley, and the Great Black Way. It was, however, not the only way across the Shenandoah: a little more than half a mile farther up were the rifle works, where the stream could be easily forded. Kagi and Copeland went there, captured the watchman and took possession.

"These places were all taken, and the prisoners secured, without the snap of a gun, or any violence whatever," says Anderson, and he continues: "The town being taken, Brown, Stevens, and the men who had no post in charge, returned to the engine-house, where council was held, after which Captain Stevens, Tidd, Cook, Shields Green, Leary and myself went to the country. On the road we met some colored men, to whom we made known our purpose, when they immediately agreed to join us. They said they had been long waiting for an opportunity of the kind. Stevens then asked them to go around among the colored people and circulate the news, when each started off in a different direction. The result was that many colored men gathered to the scene of action. The first prisoner taken by us was Colonel Lewis Washington (a relative of George Washington). When we neared his house, Captain Stevens placed Leary and Shields Green to guard the approaches to the house, the one at the side, and the other in front. We then knocked, but no one answering, although females were looking from upper windows, we entered the building and commenced a search for the proprietor. Colonel Washington opened his room door, and begged us not to kill him. Captain Stevens replied, 'You are our prisoner,' when he stood as if speechless or petrified. Stevens further told him to get ready to go to the Ferry; that he had come to abolish slavery, not to take life but in self-defense, but that he must go along. The colonel replied: 'You can have my slaves, if you will let me remain.' 'No,' said the captain, 'you must go along too; so get ready.'"

He and his male slaves were thus taken, together with a large four horse wagon and some arms, including the Lafayette sword. Away the party went and after capturing another planter and his slaves, arrived at the Ferry before daybreak.

Meantime the citizens of the Ferry, returning late from protracted Methodist meeting, were being taken prisoners and about one o'clock in the morning the east-bound Baltimore and Ohio train arrived. This was detained and the local colored porter shot dead by Brown's guards on the bridge. The passengers were greatly excited, but at first thought it was a strike of some kind. After sunrise the train was allowed to proceed, John Brown himself walking ahead across the bridge to reassure the conductor. So Monday, October 17th, began and Anderson says it "was a time of stirring and exciting events. In consequence of the movements of the night before we were prepared for commotion and tumult, but certainly not for more than we beheld around us. Gray dawn and yet brighter daylight revealed great confusion, and as the sun arose, the panic spread like wild-fire. Men, women and children could be seen leaving their homes in every direction; some seeking refuge among residents, and in quarters further away; others climbing up the hillsides, and hurrying off in various directions, evidently impelled by a sudden fear, which was plainly visible in their countenances or in their movements.

"Captain Brown was all activity, though I could not help thinking that at times he appeared somewhat puzzled. He ordered Lewis Sherrard Leary and four slaves, and a free man belonging in the neighborhood, to join John Henry Kagi and John Copeland at the rifle factory, which they immediately did. . . . After the departure of the train, quietness prevailed for a short time; a number of prisoners were already in the engine-house, and of the many colored men living in the neighborhood, who had assembled in the town, a number were armed."

Up to this point everything in John Brown's plan had worked like clockwork, and there had been but one death. The armory was captured, from twenty-five to fifty slaves had been armed, several masters were in custody and the next move was to get the arms and ammunition from the farm. Cook says that when the party returned from the country at dawn, "I stayed a short while in the engine-house to get warm, as I was chilled through. After I got warm, Captain Brown ordered me to go with C. P. Tidd, who was to take William H. Leeman, and I think, four slaves [Anderson says fourteen slaves] with him, in Colonel Washington's large wagon, across the river, and to take Terrence Burns and his brother and their slaves prisoners. My orders were to hold Burns and brother as prisoners at their own house, while Tidd and the slaves who accompanied him were to go to Captain Brown's house and to load in arms and bring them down to the schoolhouse, stopping for the Burnses and their guard. William H. Leeman remained with me to guard the prisoners. On return of the wagon, in compliance with orders, we all started for the schoolhouse. When we got there, I was to remain, by Captain Brown's orders, with one of the slaves to guard the arms, while C. P. Tidd, with the other Negroes, was to go back for the rest of the arms, and Burns was to be sent with William H. Leeman to Captain Brown at the armory. It was at this time that William Thompson came up from the Ferry and reported that everything was all right, and then hurried on to overtake William H. Leeman. A short time after the departure of Tidd, I heard a good deal of firing and became anxious to know the cause, but my orders were strict to remain in the schoolhouse and guard the arms, and I obeyed the orders to the letter. About four o'clock in the evening C. P. Tidd came with the second load."

Here, in all probability, was the fatal hitch. The farm was not over three miles from the schoolhouse, and there was a heavy farm-wagon with four large strong horses and a dozen men or more to help. The fact that it took these men eleven hours to move two wagon-loads of material less than three miles is the secret of the extraordinary failure of Brown's foray at a time when victory was in his grasp. That Cook was needlessly dilatory in the moving is certain. He sat down in Byrnes's house and made a speech on human equality. Then Tidd went on to the farm with the wagon and brought a load of arms, which he deposited at the point where the Kennedy farm road meets the Potomac almost at right angles, about three miles or less from the Ferry. The schoolhouse stood here and the children were frightened half to death. Cook stopped at this place and unloaded the wagon, and then Leeman went with Byrnes to the guard-house, lingering and actually sitting beside the road. Even then they arrived before ten o'clock. With haste it is certain that, despite the muddy road, the first load of arms could have been at the schoolhouse before eight o'clock in the morning, and the whole of the stores by ten o'clock. That Brown expected this is shown by his sending William Thompson to reassure the men at the farm of his safety and probably to urge haste; yet when the second load of arms appeared, it was four o'clock in the afternoon, at least three hours after Brown had been completely surrounded. Judging from Cook's narrative, it is likely that Thompson did not see Tidd at all. It was this inexcusable delay on the part of Tidd and Cook and, possibly, William Thompson that undoubtedly made the raid a failure. To be sure, John Brown never said so—never hinted that any one was to blame but himself. But that was John Brown's way.

Events in the town had moved quickly. After Cook had departed, Brown ordered O. P. Anderson "to take the pikes out of the wagon in which he rode to the Ferry, and to place them in the hands of the colored men who had come with us from the plantations, and others who had come forward without having had communication with any of our party."

The citizens were "wild with fright and excitement. . . . The prisoners were also terror-stricken. Some wanted to go home to see their families, as if for the last time. The privilege was granted them, under escort, and they were brought back again. Edwin Coppoc, one of the sentinels at the armory gate, was fired at by one of the citizens, but the ball did not reach him, when one of the insurgents close by put up his rifle, and made the enemy bite the dust. Among the arms taken from Colonel Washington was one double barreled gun. This weapon was loaded by Leeman with buck-shot, and placed in the hands of an elderly slave man, early in the morning. After the cowardly charge upon Coppoc, this old man was ordered by Captain Stevens to arrest a citizen. The old man ordered him to halt, which he refused to do, when instantly the terrible load was discharged into him, and he fell, and expired without a struggle."

The next step which John Brown had in mind is unknown, but there were two safe movements at 9 a.m. Monday morning:

(*a*) The arms could have been brought across the Potomac bridge and then across the Shenandoah, and so up Loudoun Heights. The men from the Maryland side could have joined, and Brown and his men covered their retreat by compelling the hostages to march with them. Kagi and his men, by wading the Shenandoah, could have supported them.

(*b*) The arms could have been taken down to the Potomac from the schoolhouse, ferried across and moved over to Kagi. Brown and his men could have joined the party there and all retreated up Loudoun Heights. From the fact that Brown had the arms stopped at the schoolhouse, this seems probably to have been the thought in his mind.

On the other hand, the plan usually attributed to Brown is unthinkable; viz., that he intended retreating across the Potomac into the Maryland mountains. First, he had just come out of the Maryland mountains and had moved down his arms and ammunition; and second, this manœuvre would have cut his band off from the Great Black Way to the South unless he captured the Ferry a second time. Manifestly this, then, was not Brown's idea. It has, however, been suggested that the arms had been moved down to the schoolhouse to be placed in the hands of slaves there. But why were they left on the Maryland side? In the whole Maryland country west of the mountains were less than a thousand able-bodied Negroes, of whom not a tenth could have been cognizant of the uprising, while Brown had arms for 1,200 men or more. No, Brown intended to move the arms in bulk. He had perhaps a ton, or a ton and a half of baggage. He wished it moved first to the schoolhouse, and then if all was well to the Ferry, or straight across to the mountains. Cook started before

five o'clock in the morning, and Brown no doubt expected to hear
that the arms were at the schoolhouse by ten. At eleven o'clock he
dispatched William Thompson to Kennedy farm. Anderson thinks
that Thompson's message made the farm party even more leisurely
because it told of success so far. This is surely impossible. The veri-
est tyro must have known that minutes were golden despite the
tremendous fortune of the expedition. Did Thompson misapprehend
his message? Was the delay Tidd's and what was Owen Brown
thinking and doing? It is a curious puzzle, but it is the puzzle of the
foray. If the party with the arms had arrived at the bridge any time
before noon, the raid would have been successful. Even as it was,
Brown still had three courses open to him, all of which promised a
measure of success:

(a) He could have gotten his band and crossed back to Maryland,—
although this meant the abandonment of the main features of his
whole plan. As time waned Stevens and Kagi urged this but Brown
refused.

(b) He could have gone to Loudoun Heights, but this would have
involved abandoning his arms and stores and above all, one of his
sons, Cook, Tidd, Merriam, Coppoc and the slaves. This was
unthinkable.

(c) He could have used his hostages to force terms. For not doing
this he afterward repeatedly blamed himself, but characteristically
blamed no one else for anything.

Meantime every minute of delay aroused the country and brought
the citizens to their senses. "The train that left Harper's Ferry carried
a panic to Virginia, Maryland and Washington with it. The passengers, taking all the paper they could find, wrote accounts of the
insurrection, which they threw from the windows as the train rushed
onward."

A local physician says: "I went back to the hillside then, and tried to
get the citizens together, to see what we could do to get rid of these
fellows. They seemed to be very troublesome. When I got on the
hill I learned that they had shot Boerly. That was probably about
seven o'clock. . . . I had ordered the Lutheran church bell to be rung
to get the citizens together to see what sort of arms they had. I found
one or two squirrel rifles and a few shotguns. I had sent a messenger
to Charlestown in the meantime for Captain Rowan, commander
of a volunteer company there. I also sent messengers to the Baltimore
and Ohio Railroad to stop the trains coming east, and not let them
approach the Ferry, and also a messenger to Shepherdstown."

Another eye-witness adds: "There was unavoidable delay in the preparations for a fight, because of the scarcity of weapons; for only a few squirrel guns and fowling-pieces could be found. There were then at Harper's Ferry thousands and tens of thousands of muskets and rifles of the most approved patterns, but they were all boxed up in the arsenal, and the arsenal was in the hands of the enemy. And such, too, was the scarcity of the ammunition that, after using up the limited supply of lead found in the village stores, pewter plates and spoons had to be melted and molded into bullets for the occasion.

"By nine o'clock a number of indifferently armed citizens assembled on Camp Hill and decided that the party, consisting of half a dozen men, should cross the Potomac a short distance above the Ferry, and, going down the tow-path of the Chesapeake and Ohio Canal as far as the railway bridge, should attack the two sentinels stationed there, who, by the way, had been reinforced by four more of Brown's party. Another small party under Captain Medler was to cross the Shenandoah and take position opposite the rifle works, while Captain Avis, with a sufficient force, should take possession of the Shenandoah bridge, and Captain Roderick, with some of the armorers, should post themselves on the Baltimore and Ohio Railway west of the Ferry just above the armories."

At last the militia commenced to arrive and the movements to cut off Brown's men began. The Jefferson Guards crossed the Potomac, came down to the Maryland side and seized the Potomac bridge. The local company was sent to take the Shenandoah bridge, leave a guard and march to the rear of the arsenal, while another local company was to seize the houses in front of the arsenal.

"As strangers poured in," says Anderson, "the enemy took positions round about, so as to prevent any escape, within shooting distance of the engine-house and arsenal. Captain Brown, seeing their manœuvres, said, 'We will hold on to our three positions, if they are unwilling to come to terms, and die like men.'"

The attack came at noon from the Jefferson Guards, who started across the Potomac bridge from Maryland. This is Anderson's story:

"It was about twelve o'clock in the day when we were first attacked by the troops. Prior to that, Captain Brown, in anticipation of further trouble, had girded to his side the famous sword taken from Colonel Lewis Washington the night before, and with that memorable weapon, he commanded his men against General Washington's own state. When the captain received the news that the troops had entered the bridge from the Maryland side, he, with some of his men, went into the street, and sent a message to the arsenal for us to come forth also. We hastened to the street as ordered, when he said—'The troops are on the bridge, coming into town; we will give them a warm reception.' He then walked around amongst us, giving us words of encouragement, in this wise:—'Men! be cool! Don't waste your powder and shot! Take aim, and make every shot count!' 'The troops will look for us to retreat on their first appearance; be careful to shoot first.' Our men were well supplied with firearms, but Captain Brown had no rifle at that time; his only weapon was the sword before mentioned.

"The troops soon came out of the bridge, and up the street facing us, we occupying an irregular position. When they got within sixty or seventy yards, Captain Brown said, 'Let go upon them!' which we did, when several of them fell. Again and again the dose was repeated. There was now consternation among the troops. From marching in solid martial columns, they became scattered. Some hastened to seize upon and bear up the wounded and dying,—several lay dead upon the ground. They seemed not to realize, at first, that we would fire upon them, but evidently expected that we would be driven out by them without firing. Captain Brown seemed fully to understand the matter, and hence, very properly and in our defense, undertook to forestall their movements. The consequence of their unexpected reception was, after leaving several of their dead on the field, they beat a confused retreat into the bridge, and there stayed under cover until reinforcements came to the Ferry. On the retreat of the troops, we were ordered back to our former posts."

At this time the Negro, Newby, was killed and his assailant shot in turn by Green. Two slaves also died fighting. Now "there was comparative quiet for a time, except that the citizens seemed to be wild with terror. Men, women and children forsook the place in great haste, climbing up hillsides, and scaling the mountains. The latter seemed to be alive with white fugitives, fleeing from their doomed city. During this time, William Thompson, who was returning from his errand to the Kennedy farm, was surrounded on the bridge by railroad men, who next came up, and taken a prisoner to the Wager house."

It was now one o'clock in the day and while things were going against Brown, his cause was not desperate. His Maryland men might yet attack the disorganized Jefferson Guards in the rear and the arsenal was full of hostages. But militia and citizens kept pouring into the town and by three o'clock "could be seen coming from every direction." Kagi sent word to Brown, urging retreat; but Brown faced a difficult dilemma: Should he go to Loudoun Heights and lose half his men and all his munitions? or should he retreat to Maryland? This latter path lay open, he was sure, by means of his hostages. Meantime the Maryland party might appear at any moment. Indeed, the Jefferson Guards had once been mistaken for them. On this account the message was sent back to Kagi "to hold out for a few minutes, when we would all evacuate the place." Still the Maryland party lingered with the stubborn Tidd somewhere up the road, and Cook idly kicking his heels at the schoolhouse.

The messenger, Jerry Anderson, was fired on and mortally wounded before he reached Kagi, and the latter's party was attacked by a large force and driven into the river.

"The river at that point runs rippling over a rocky bed," writes a Virginian, "and at ordinary stages of the water is easily forded. The raiders, finding their retreat to the opposite shore intercepted by Medler's men, made for a large flat rock near the middle of the stream. Before reaching it, however, Kagi fell and died in the water, apparently without a struggle. Four others reached the rock, where, for a while, they made an ineffectual stand, returning the fire of the citizens. But it was not long before two of them were killed outright and another prostrated by a mortal wound, leaving Copeland, a mulatto, standing alone unharmed upon their rock of refuge.

"Thereupon, a Harper's Ferry man, James H. Holt, dashed into the river, gun in hand, to capture Copeland, who, as he approached him, made a show of fight by pointing his gun at Holt, who halted and leveled his; but, to the surprise of the lookers-on, neither of their weapons were discharged, both having been rendered temporarily useless, as I afterward learned, from being wet. Holt, however, as he again advanced, continued to snap his gun, while Copeland did the same."

Copeland was taken alive and Leeman, with a second message from Kagi to Brown, was killed. Matters were now getting desperate, but the armory was full of prisoners and therein lay John Brown's final hope. Easily as a last resort he could use these citizens as a screen and so escape to the mountains. In attempting this, however, some of the prisoners were bound to be killed and Brown hesitated at sacrificing innocent blood to save himself. He thought that the same end might be accomplished by negotiation. His first move, therefore, was to withdraw all his force and the important prisoners to a small brick building near the armory gate called the "engine-house."

Captain Daingerfield, one of the prisoners, says: "He entered the engine-house, carrying his prisoners along, or rather part of them, for he made selections. After getting into the engine-house he made this speech: 'Gentlemen, perhaps you wonder why I have selected you from the others. It is because I believe you to be the most influential; and I have only to say now, that you will have to share precisely the same fate that your friends extend to my men.' He began at once to bar the doors and windows, and to cut port-holes through the brick wall."

This evident weakening of the raiders let pandemonium loose. The citizens realized how small a force Brown had and were filled with fury at his presumption. His men began to fight desperately for their lives.

"About the time when Brown immured himself," a narrator reports, "a company of Berkeley County militia arrived from Martinsburg who, with some citizens of Harper's Ferry and the surrounding country, made a rush on the armory and released the great mass of the prisoners outside of the engine-house, not, however, without suffering some loss from a galling fire kept up by the enemy from 'the fort.'"

This released the arms and one of the Virginia watchmen says: "The people, who came pouring into town, broke into liquor saloons, filled up, and then got into the arsenal, arming themselves with United States guns and ammunition. They kept shooting at random and howling."

The prisoners within the engine-house heard "a terrible firing from without, at every point from which the windows could be seen, and in a few minutes every window was shattered, and hundreds of balls came through the doors. These shots were answered from within whenever the attacking party could be seen. This was kept up most of the day, and, strange to say, not a prisoner was hurt, though thousands of balls were imbedded in the walls, and holes shot in the doors almost large enough for a man to creep through."

The doomed raiders saw "volley upon volley" discharged, while "the echoes from the hills, the shrieks of the townspeople, and the groans of their wounded and dying, all of which filled the air, were truly frightful." Yet "no powder and ball were wasted. We shot from under cover, and took deadly aim. For an hour before the flag of truce was sent out, the firing was uninterrupted, and one and another of the enemy were constantly dropping to the earth."

Oliver Brown was shot and died without a word and Taylor was mortally wounded. The mayor of the city ventured out, unarmed, to reconnoitre and was killed. Immediately the son of Andrew Hunter, who afterward was state's attorney against Brown, rushed into the hotel after the prisoner William Thompson:

"We burst into the room where he was, and found several around him, but they offered only a feeble resistance; we brought our guns down to his head repeatedly,—myself and another person,—for the purpose of shooting him in the room.

"There was a young lady there, the sister of Mr. Fouke, the hotel-keeper, who sat in this man's lap, covered his face with her arms, and shielded him with her person whenever we brought our guns to bear. She said to us, 'For God's sake, wait and let the law take its course.' My associate shouted to kill him. 'Let us shed his blood,' were his words. All round were shouting, 'Mr. Beckham's life was worth ten thousand of these vile Abolitionists.' I was cool about it, and deliberate. My gun was pushed by some one who seized the barrel, and I then moved to the back part of the room, still with purpose unchanged, but with a view to divert attention from me, in order to get an opportunity, at some moment when the crowd would be less dense, to shoot him. After a moment's thought it occurred to me that that was not the proper place to kill him. We then proposed to take him out and hang him. Some portion of our band then opened a way to him, and first pushing Miss Fouke aside, we slung him out-of-doors. I gave him a push, and many others did the same. We then shoved him along the platform and down to the trestle work of the bridge; he begged for his life all the time, very piteously at first."

Thus he was shot to death as he crawled in the trestle work. The prisoners in the engine-house now urged Brown to make terms with the citizens, representing that this was possible and that he and his men could escape. Brown sent out his son Watson with a white flag, but the maddened citizens paid no attention to it and shot him down. A lull in the fighting came a little later, and Stevens took a second flag of truce, but was captured and held prisoner. Daingerfield says:

"At night the firing ceased, for we were in total darkness, and nothing could be seen in the engine-house. During the day and night I talked much with Brown. I found him as brave as a man could be, and sensible upon all subjects except slavery. He believed it was his duty to free the slaves, even if in doing so he lost his own life. During a sharp fight one of Brown's sons was killed. He fell; then trying to raise himself, he said, 'It is all over with me,' and died instantly. Brown did not leave his post at the port-hole; but when the fighting was over he walked to his son's body, straightened out his limbs, took off his trappings, and then, turning to me, said, 'This is the third son I have lost in this cause.' Another son had been shot in the morning, and was then dying, having been brought in from the street. Often during the affair at the engine-house, when his men would want to fire upon some one who might be seen passing, Brown would stop them, saying, 'Don't shoot; that man is unarmed.' The firing was kept up by our men all day and until late at night, and during this time several of his men were killed, but none of the prisoners were hurt, though in great danger. During the day and night many propositions, pro and con, were made, looking to Brown's surrender and the release of the prisoners, but without result."

Another eye-witness says:

"A little before night Brown asked if any of his captives would volunteer to go out among the citizens and induce them to cease firing on the fort, as they were endangering the lives of their friends— the prisoners. He promised on his part that, if there was no more firing on his men, there should be none by them on the besiegers. Mr. Israel Russel undertook the dangerous duty; the risk arose from the excited state of the people who would be likely to fire on anything seen stirring around the prison-house, and the citizens were persuaded to stop firing in consideration of the danger incurred of injuring the prisoners. . . .

"It was now dark and the wildest excitement existed in the town, especially among the friends of the killed, wounded and prisoners of the citizens' party. It had rained some little all day and the atmosphere was raw and cold. Now, a cloudy and moonless sky hung like a pall over the scene of war, and, on the whole, a more dismal night cannot be imagined. Guards were stationed round the engine-house to prevent Brown's escape and, as forces were constantly arriving from Winchester, Frederick City, Baltimore and other places to help the Harper's Ferry people, the town soon assumed quite a military appearance. The United States authorities in Washington had been notified in the meantime, and, in the course of the night, Colonel Robert E. Lee, afterward the famous General Lee of the Southern Confederacy, arrived with a force of United States marines, to protect the interests of the government, and kill or capture the invaders."

Meantime Cook had awakened to the fact that something was wrong. He left Tidd at the schoolhouse and started toward the Ferry; finding it surrounded, he fired one volley from a tree and fled. He found no one at the schoolhouse, but met Tidd, and the whole farm guard, and one Negro on the road beyond. They all turned and fled north, Tidd and Cook quarreling. They wandered fourteen days in rain and snow, and finally all escaped except Cook who went into a town for food and was arrested.

Robert E. Lee, with 100 marines, arrived just before midnight on Monday and one of the prisoners tells the story of the last stand:

"When Colonel Lee came with the government troops in the night, he at once sent a flag of truce by his aid, J. E. B. Stuart, to notify Brown of his arrival, and in the name of the United States to demand his surrender, advising him to throw himself on the clemency of the government. Brown declined to accept Colonel Lee's terms, and determined to await the attack. When Stuart was admitted and a light brought, he exclaimed, 'Why, aren't you old Osawatomie Brown of Kansas, whom I once had there as my prisoner?' 'Yes,' was the answer, 'but you did not keep me.' This was the first intimation we had of Brown's real name. When Colonel Lee advised Brown to trust to the clemency of the government, Brown responded that he knew what that meant,—a rope for his men and himself; adding, 'I prefer to die just here.' Stuart told him he would return at early morning for his final reply, and left him. When he had gone, Brown at once proceeded to barricade the doors, windows, etc., endeavoring to make the place as strong as possible. All this time no one of Brown's men showed the slightest fear, but calmly awaited the attack, selecting the best situations to fire from, and arranging their guns and pistols so that a fresh one could be taken up as soon as one was discharged. . . .

"When Lieutenant Stuart came in the morning for the final reply to the demand to surrender, I got up and went to Brown's side to hear his answer. Stuart asked, 'Are you ready to surrender, and trust to the mercy of the government?' Brown answered, 'No, I prefer to die here.' His manner did not betray the least alarm. Stuart stepped aside and made a signal for the attack, which was instantly begun with sledge-hammers to break down the door. Finding it would not yield, the soldiers seized a long ladder for a battering-ram, and commenced beating the door with that, the party within firing incessantly. I had assisted in the barricading, fixing the fastenings so that I could remove them on the first effort to get in. But I was not at the door when the battering began, and could not get to the fastenings till the ladder was used. I then quickly removed the fastenings; and, after two or three strokes of the ladder, the engine rolled partially back, making a small aperture, through which Lieutenant Green of the marines forced his way, jumped on top of the engine, and stood a second, amidst a shower of balls, looking for John Brown. When he saw Brown, he sprang about twelve feet at him, giving an under-thrust of his sword, striking Brown about midway the body, and raising him completely from the ground. Brown fell forward, with his head between his knees, while Green struck him several times over the head, and, as I then supposed, split his skull at every stroke. I was not two feet from Brown at that time. Of course, I got out of the building as soon as possible, and did not know till some time later that Brown was not killed. It seems that Green's sword, in making the thrust, struck Brown's belt and did not penetrate the body. The sword was bent double. The reason that Brown was not killed when struck on the head was, that Green was holding his sword in the middle, striking with the hilt, and making only scalp wounds."

After the attack on the troops at the bridge, Brown had ordered O. P. Anderson, Hazlett and Green back to the arsenal. But Green saw the desperate strait of Brown and chose voluntarily to go into the engine-house and fight until the last. Anderson and Hazlett, when they saw the door battered in, went to the back of the arsenal, climbed the wall and fled along the railway that goes up the Shenandoah. Here in the cliffs they had a skirmish with the troops but finally escaped in the night, crossed the town and the Potomac and so got into Maryland and went to the farm. It was deserted and pillaged. Then they came back to the schoolhouse and found that empty. In the morning they heard firing and Anderson's narrative continues:

"Hazlett thought it must be Owen Brown and his men trying to force their way into the town, as they had been informed that a number of us had been taken prisoners, and we started down along the ridge to join them. When we got in sight of the Ferry, we saw the troops firing across the river to the Maryland side with consider-able spirit. Looking closely, we saw, to our surprise, that they were firing upon a few of the colored men, who had been armed the day before by our men, at the Kennedy farm, and stationed down at the schoolhouse by C. P. Tidd. They were in the bushes on the edge of the mountains, dodging about, occasionally exposing themselves to the enemy. The troops crossed the bridge in pursuit of them, but they retreated in different directions. Being further in the mountains, and more secure, we could see without personal harm befalling us. One of the colored men came toward where we were, when we hailed him, and inquired the particulars. He said that one of his comrades had been shot, and was lying on the side of the mountains; that they thought the men who had armed them the day before must be in the Ferry. That opinion, we told him, was not correct. We asked him to join with us in hunting up the rest of the party, but he declined, and went his way.

"While we were in this part of the mountains, some of the troops went to the schoolhouse, and took possession of it. On our return along up the ridge, from our position, screened by the bushes, we could see them as they invested it. Our last hope of shelter or of meeting our companions, now being destroyed, we concluded to make our escape north."

Anderson managed to get away, but Hazlett was captured in Pennsylvania and was returned to Virginia. Thus John Brown's raid ended. Seven of the men—John Brown himself, Shields Green, Edwin Coppoc, Stevens and Copeland and eventually Cook and Hazlett—were captured and hanged. Watson and Oliver Brown, the two Thompsons, Kagi, Jerry Anderson, Taylor, Newby, Leary, and John Anderson, ten in all, were killed in the fight, and six others—Owen Brown, Tidd, Leeman, Barclay Coppoc, Merriam and O. Anderson escaped.

At high noon on Tuesday, October 18th, the raid was over. John Brown lay wounded and blood-stained on the floor and the governor of Virginia bent over him.

"Who are you?" he asked.

"My name is John Brown; I have been well known as old John Brown of Kansas. Two of my sons were killed here today, and I'm dying too. I came here to liberate slaves, and was to receive no reward. I have acted from a sense of duty, and am content to await my fate; but I think the crowd have treated me badly. I am an old man. Yesterday I could have killed whom I chose; but I had no desire to kill any person, and would not have killed a man had they not tried to kill me and my men. I could have sacked and burned the town, but did not; I have treated the persons whom I took as hostages kindly, and I appeal to them for the truth of what I say. If I had succeeded in running off slaves this time, I could have raised twenty times as many men as I have now, for a similar expedition. But I have failed."

The Riddle of the Sphinx

"Surely He hath borne our griefs, and carried our sorrows; yet we did esteem Him stricken, smitten of God, and afflicted.

"But He was wounded for our transgressions, He was bruised for our iniquities: the chastisement of our peace was upon Him; and with His stripes we are healed."

The deed was done. The next day the world knew and the world sat in puzzled amazement. It was ever so and ever will be. When a prophet like John Brown appears, how must we of the world receive him? Must we follow out the drear, dread logic of surrounding facts, as did the South, even if they crucify a clean and pure soul, simply because consistent allegiance to our cherished, chosen ideal demands it? If we do, the shame will brand our latest history. Shall we hesitate and waver before his clear white logic, now helping, now fearing to help, now believing, now doubting? Yes, this we must do so long as the doubt and hesitation are genuine; but we must not lie. If we are human, we must thus hesitate until we know the right. How shall we know it? That is the Riddle of the Sphinx. We are but darkened groping souls, that know not light often because of its very blinding radiance. Only in time is truth revealed. To-day at last we know: John Brown was right.

Yet there are some great principles to guide us. That there are in this world matters of vast human import which are eternally right or eternally wrong, all men believe. Whether that great right comes, as the simpler, clearer minded think, from the spoken word of God, or whether it is simply another way of saying: this deed makes for the good of mankind, or that, for the ill—however it may be, all men know that there are in this world here and there and again and again great partings of the ways—the one way wrong, the other right, in some vast and eternal sense. This certainly is true at times—in the mighty crises of lives and nations. On the other hand, it is also true, as human experience again and again shows, that the usual matters

211

of human debate and difference of opinion are not so vitally important, or so easily classified; that in most cases there is much of right
and wrong on both sides and, so usual is it to find this true, that men
tend to argue it always so. Their life morality becomes always a
wavering path of expediency, not necessarily the best or the worst
path, as they freely even smilingly admit, but a good path, a safe path,
a path of little resistance and one that leads to the good if not to the
theoretical (but usually impracticable) best. Such philosophy of the
world's ways is common, and probably it is well that thus it is. And
yet we all feel its temporary, tentative character; we instinctively
distrust its comfortable tone, and listen almost fearfully for the greater
voice; its better is often so far below that which we feel is a possible
best, that its present temporizing seems evil to us, and ever and again
after the world has complacently dodged and compromised with,
and skilfully evaded a great evil, there shines, suddenly, a great white
light—an unwavering, unflickering brightness, blinding by its all-
seeing brilliance, making the whole world simply a light and a
darkness—a right and a wrong. Then men tremble and writhe and
waver. They whisper, "But—but—of course"; "the thing is plain,
but it is too plain to be true—it is true but truth is not the only thing
in the world." Thus they hide from the light, they burrow and grovel,
and yet ever in, and through, and on them blazes that mighty light
with its horror of darkness and behind it peals the voice—the Riddle
of the Sphinx, that must be answered.

Such a light was the soul of John Brown. He was simple, exasper-
atingly simple; unlettered, plain, and homely. No casuistry of culture
or of learning, of well-being or tradition moved him in the slightest
degree: "Slavery is wrong," he said,—"kill it." Destroy it—uproot
it, stem, blossom, and branch; give it no quarter, exterminate it and
do it now. Was he wrong? No. The forcible staying of human uplift
by barriers of law, and might, and tradition is the most wicked thing
on earth. It is wrong, eternally wrong. It is wrong by whatever name
it is called, or in whatever guise it lurks, and whenever it appears.
But it is especially heinous, black, and cruel when it masquerades in
the robes of law and justice and patriotism. So was American slavery
clothed in 1859, and it had to die by revolution, not by milder means.
And this men knew. They had known it a hundred years. Yet they
shrank and trembled. From round about the white and blinding path
of this soul flew equivocations, lies, thievings and red murders. And
yet all men instinctively felt that these things were not of the light
but of the surrounding darkness. It is at once surprising, baffling and

pitiable to see the way in which men—honest American citizens—faced this light. Many types met and answered the argument, John Brown (for he did not use argument, he was himself an argument). First there was the Western American—the typical American, like Charles Robinson—one to whose imagination the empire of the vale of the Mississippi appealed with tremendous force. Then there was the Abolitionist—shading away from him who held slavery an incubus to him who saw its sin, of whom Gerrit Smith was a fair type. Then there was the lover of men, like Dr. Howe, and the merchant-errant like Stearns. Finally, there were the two great fateful types—the master and the slave.

To Robinson, Brown was simply a means to an end—beyond that he was whatever prevailing public opinion indicated. When the gratitude of Osawatomie swelled high, Brown was fit to be named with Jesus Christ; when the wave of Southern reaction subjugated the nation, he was something less than a fanatic. But whatever he was, he was the sword on which struggling Kansas and its leaders could depend, the untarnished doer of its darker deeds, when they that knew them necessary cowered and held their hands. Brown's was not the only hand that freed Kansas, but his hand was indispensable, and not the first time, nor the last, has a cool and skilful politician, like Robinson, climbed to power on the heads of those helpers of his, whose half-realized ideals he bartered for present possibilities—human freedom for statehood. For the Abolitionist of the Garrison type Brown had a contempt, as undeserved as it was natural to his genius. To recognize an evil and not strike it was to John Brown sinful. "Talk, talk, talk," he said derisively. Nor did he rightly gauge the value of spiritual as contrasted with physical blows, until the day when he himself struck the greatest on the Charlestown scaffold.

But if John Brown failed rightly to gauge the movement of the Abolitionists, few of them failed to appreciate him when they met him. Instinctively they knew him as one who grasped the very pith and kernel of the evil which they fought. They asked no proofs or credentials; they asked John Brown. So it was with Gerrit Smith. He saw Brown and believed in him. He entertained him at his house. He heard his detailed plans for striking slavery a heart blow. He gave him in all over a thousand dollars, and bade him Godspeed! Yet when the blow was struck, he was filled with immeasurable consternation. He equivocated and even denied knowledge of Brown's plans. To be sure, he, his family, his fortune were in the shadow of danger—but where was John Brown? So with Dr. Howe, whose memory was painfully poor on the witness stand and who fluttered from enthusiastic support of Brown to a weak wavering when once he had tasted the famous Southern hospitality. He found slavery, to his own intense surprise, human: not ideally and horribly devilish, but only humanly bad. Was a bad human institution to be attacked *vi et armis?* Or was it not rather to be with persuasive argument in the soft shade of a Carolina veranda? Dr. Howe inclined to the latter thought, after his Cuban visit, and he was exceedingly annoyed and scared after the raid. He fled precipitately to Canada. Of the Boston committee only Stearns stood up and out in the public glare and said unequivocally, then and there: "I believe John Brown to be the representative man of this century, as Washington was of the last—the Harper's Ferry affair, and the capacity shown by the Italiens for self-government, the great events of this age. One will free Europe and the other America."

The attitude of the black man toward John Brown is typified by Frederick Douglass and Shields Green. Said Douglass: "On the evening when the news came that John Brown had taken and was then holding the town of Harper's Ferry, it so happened that I was speaking to a large audience in National Hall, Philadelphia. The announcement came upon us with the startling effect of an earthquake. It was something to make the boldest hold his breath."

Wise and Buchanan started immediately on Douglass's track and he fled to Canada and eventually to England. Why did not Douglass join John Brown? Because, first, he was of an entirely different cast of temperament and mind; and because, secondly, he knew, as only a Negro slave can know, the tremendous might and organization of the slave power. Brown's plan never in the slightest degree appealed to Douglass's reason. That the Underground Railroad methods could be enlarged and systematized, Douglass believed, but any further plan he did not think possible. Only national force could dislodge national slavery. As it was with Douglass, so it was practically with the Negro race. They believed in John Brown but not in his plan. He touched their warm loving hearts but not their hard heads. The Canadian Negroes, for instance, were men who knew what slavery meant. They had suffered its degradation, its repression and its still more fatal license. They knew the slave system. They had been slaves. They had risked life to help loved ones to escape its far-reaching tentacles. They had reached a land of freedom and had begun to taste the joy of being human. Their little homes were clustering about—they had their churches, lodges, social gatherings, and newspaper. Then came the call. They loved the old man and cherished him, helped and forwarded his work in a thousand little ways. But the call? Were they asked to sacrifice themselves to free their fellow-slaves? Were they not quite ready? No—to do that they stood ever ready. But here they were asked to sacrifice themselves for the sake of possibly free-ing a few slaves and certainly arousing the nation. They saw what John Brown did not fully realize until the last: the tremendous mean-ing of sacrifice even though his enterprise failed and they were sure it would fail. Yet in truth it need not have failed. History and mili-tary science prove its essential soundness. But the Negro knew little of history and military science. He did know slavery and the slave power, and they loomed large and invincible in his fertile imagination. He could not conceive their overthrow by anything short of the direct voice of God. That a supreme sacrifice of human beings on the altar of Moloch might hasten the day of emancipation was pos-sible, but were they called to give their lives to this forlorn hope? Most of them said no, as most of their fellows, black and white, ever answer to the "voice, without reply." They said it reluctantly, slowly, even hesitatingly, but they said it even as their leader Douglass said it. And why not, they argued? Was not their whole life already a sacrifice? Were they called by any right of God or man to give more than they already had given? What more did they owe the world? Did not the world owe them an unpayable amount?

Then, too, the sacrifice demanded of black men in this raid was far more than that demanded of whites. In 1859 it was a crime for a free black man even to set foot on Virginia soil, and it was slavery or death for a fugitive to return. If worse came to worst, the Negro stood the least chance of escape and the least consideration on capture. Yet despite all this and despite the terrible training of slavery in cowardice, submission and fatality; the systematic elimination, by death and cruelty, of strength and self-respect and bravery, there were in Canada and in the United States scores of Negroes ready for the sacrifice. But the necessary secrecy, vagueness and intangibility of the summons, the repeated changes of date, the difficulty of com-munication and the poverty of black men, all made effective coöper-ation exceedingly difficult.

Even as it was, fifteen or twenty Negroes had enlisted and would probably have been present had they had the time. Five, probably six, actually came in time, and thirty or forty slaves actively helped. Considering the mass of Negroes in the land and the character of the leader, this was an insignificant number. But what it lacked in number it made up in characters like Shields Green. He was a poor, unlettered fugitive, ignorant by the law of the land, stricken in life and homely in body. He sat and listened as Douglass and Brown argued amid the boulders of that old Chambersburg quarry. Some things he understood, some he did not. But one thing he did understand and that was the soul of John Brown, so he said, "I guess I'll go with the old man." Again in the sickening fury of that fatal Monday, a white man and a black man found themselves standing with freedom before them. The white man was John Brown's truest companion and the black man was Shields Green. "I told him to come," said the white man afterward, "that we could do nothing more," but he simply said, "I must go down to the old man." And he went down to John Brown and to death.

If this was the attitude of the slave, what was that of the master? It was when John Brown faced the indignant, self-satisfied and arrogant slave power of the South, flanked by its Northern Vallandighams, that the mighty paradox and burning farce of the situation revealed itself. Picture the situation: An old and blood-bespattered man, half-dead from the wounds inflicted but a few hours before; a man lying in the cold and dirt, without sleep for fifty-five nerve-wrecking hours, without food for nearly as long, with the dead bodies of two sons almost before his eyes, the piled corpses of his seven slain comrades near and afar, a wife and a bereaved family listening in vain, and a Lost Cause, the dream of a lifetime, lying dead in his heart. Around him was a group of bitter, inquisitive Southern aristocrats and their satellites, headed by one of the foremost leaders of subsequent secession.

"Who sent you—who sent you?" these inquisitors insisted.

"No man sent me—I acknowledge no master in human form!"

"What was your object in coming?"

"We came to free the slaves."

"How do you justify your acts?"

"You are guilty of a great wrong against God and humanity and it would be perfectly right for any one to interfere with you so far as to free those you wilfully and wickedly hold in bondage. I think I did right; and that others will do right who interfere with you at any time and at all times. I hold that the Golden Rule, 'Do unto others as ye would that others should do unto you,' applies to all who would help others to gain their liberty."

"But don't you believe in the Bible?"

"Certainly, I do."

"Do you consider this a religious movement?"

"It is in my opinion the greatest service man can render to God."

"Do you consider yourself an instrument in the hands of Providence?"

"I do."

"Upon what principles do you justify your acts?"

"Upon the Golden Rule. I pity the poor in bondage that have none to help them. That is why I am here; not to gratify any personal animosity, revenge, or vindictive spirit. It is my sympathy with the oppressed and the wronged, that are as good as you and as precious in the sight of God."

"Certainly. But why take the slaves against their will?"

"I never did." . . .

"Who are your advisers in this movement?"

"I have numerous sympathizers throughout the entire North. . . . I want you to understand that I respect the rights of the poorest and the weakest of colored people, oppressed by the slave system, just as much as I do those of the most wealthy and powerful. That is the idea that has moved me, and that alone. We expected no reward except satisfaction of endeavoring to do for those in distress and greatly oppressed as we would be done by. The cry of distress of the oppressed is my reason, and the only thing that prompted me to come here."

"Why did you do it secretly?"

"Because I thought that necessary to success; no other reason. . . . I agree with Mr. Smith that moral suasion is hopeless. I don't think the people of the slave states will ever consider the subject of slavery in its true light till some other argument is resorted to than moral suasion."

"Did you expect a general rising of the slaves in case of your success?"

"No, sir; nor did I wish it. I expected to gather them up from time to time, and set them free."

"Did you expect to hold possession here till then?"

"You overrate your strength in supposing I could have been taken if I had not allowed it. I was too tardy after commencing the open attack—in delaying my movements through Monday night, and up to the time I was attacked by the government troops."

"Where did you get arms?"

"I bought them."

"In what state?"

"That I will not state. I have nothing to say, only that I claim to be here in carrying out a measure I believe perfectly justifiable, and not to act the part of an incendiary or ruffian, but to aid those suffering great wrong. I wish to say, furthermore, that you had better—all you people at the South—prepare yourselves for a settlement of this question, that must come up for settlement sooner than you are prepared for it. The sooner you are prepared the better. You may dispose of me very easily,—I am nearly disposed of now, but this question is still to be settled,—this Negro question, I mean; the end of that is not yet."

"Brown, suppose you had every nigger in the United States, what would you do with them?"

"Set them free."

"Your intention was to carry them off and free them?"

"Not at all."

"To set them free would sacrifice the life of every man in this community."

"I do not think so."

"I know it; I think you are fanatical."

"And I think you are fanatical. Whom the gods would destroy they first make mad, and you are mad."

"Was it your only object to free the Negroes?"

"Absolutely our only object." . . .

"You are a robber," cried some voice in the crowd.

"You slaveholders are robbers," retorted Brown.

But Governor Wise interrupted: "Mr. Brown, the silver of your hair is reddened by the blood of crime, and you should eschew these hard words and think upon eternity. You are suffering from wounds, perhaps fatal; and should you escape death from these causes, you must submit to a trial which may involve death. Your confessions justify the presumption that you will be found guilty; and even now you are committing a felony under the laws of Virginia, by uttering sentiments like these. It is better you should turn your attention to your eternal future than be dealing in denunciations which can only injure you."

John Brown replied: "Governor, I have from all appearances not more than fifteen or twenty years the start of you in the journey to that eternity of which you kindly warn me; and whether my time here shall be fifteen months, or fifteen days, or fifteen hours, I am equally prepared to go. There is an eternity behind and an eternity before; and this little speck in the centre, however long, is but comparatively a minute. The difference between your tenure and mine is trifling, and I therefore tell you to be prepared. I am prepared. You have a heavy responsibility, and it behooves you to prepare more than it does me."

Thus from the day John Brown was captured to the day he died, and after, it was the South and slavery that was on trial—not John Brown. Indeed, the dilemma into which John Brown's raid threw the state of Virginia was perfect. If his foray was the work of a handful of fanatics, led by a lunatic and repudiated by the slaves to a man, then the proper procedure would have been to ignore the incident, quietly punish the worst offenders and either pardon the misguided leader, or send him to an asylum. If, on the other hand, Virginia faced a conspiracy that threatened her social existence, aroused dangerous unrest in her slave population, and was full of portent for the future, then extraordinary precaution, swift and extreme punishment, and bitter complaint were only natural. But both these situations could not be true—both horns of the dilemma could not be logically seized. Yet this was precisely what the South and Virginia sought. While insisting that the raid was too hopelessly and ridiculously small to accomplish anything, and saying, with Andrew Hunter, that "not a single one of the slaves" joined John Brown "except by coercion," the state nevertheless spent $250,000 to punish the invaders, stationed from one to three thousand soldiers in the vicinity and threw the nation into turmoil. When the inconsistency of this action struck various minds, the attempt was made to exaggerate the danger of the invading white men. The presiding judge at the trial wrote, as late as 1889, that the number in Brown's party was proven by witnesses to have been seventy-five to one hundred and he "expected large reinforcements"; while Andrew Hunter, the state's attorney, saw nation-wide conspiracies.

What, then, was the truth about the matter? It was as Frederick Douglass said twenty-two years later on the very spot: "If John Brown did not end the war that ended slavery, he did, at least, begin the war that ended slavery. If we look over the dates, places, and men for which this honor is claimed, we shall find that not Carolina, but Virginia, not Fort Sumter, but Harper's Ferry and the arsenal, not Major Anderson, but John Brown began the war that ended American slavery, and made this a free republic. Until this blow was struck, the prospect for freedom was dim, shadowy, and uncertain. The irrepressible conflict was one of words, votes, and compromises. When John Brown stretched forth his arm the sky was cleared,—the armed hosts of freedom stood face to face over the chasm of a broken Union, and the clash of arms was at hand."

The paths by which John Brown's raid precipitated civil war were these: In the first place, he aroused the Negroes of Virginia. How far the knowledge of his plan had penetrated is of course only to be conjectured. Evidently few knew that the foray would take place on October 17th. But when the movement had once made a successful start, there is no doubt that Osborne Anderson knew whereof he spoke, when he said that slaves were ready to coöperate. His words were proven by the 200,000 black soldiers in the Civil War. That something was wrong was shown, too, by five incendiary fires in a single week after the raid. Hunter sought to attribute these to "Northern emissaries," but this charge was unproven and extremely improbable. The only other possible perpetrators were slaves and free Negroes. That Virginians believed this is shown by Hinton's declaration that the loss in 1859 by the sale of Virginia slaves alone was $ 10,000,000. A lady who visited John Brown said, "It was hard for me to forget the presence of the jailer (I had that morning seen his advertisement of 'fifty Negroes for sale')." It is impossible to prove the extent of this clearing-out of suspected slaves but the census reports indicate something of it. The Negro population of Maryland and Virginia increased a little over four per cent, between 1850 and 1860. But in the three counties bordering on Harper's Ferry—Loudoun and Jefferson in Virginia and Washington in Maryland, the 17,647 slaves of 1850 had shrunk to 15,996 in 1860, a decrease of nearly ten per cent. This means a disappearance of 2,400 slaves and is very significant.

Secondly, long before John Brown appeared at Harper's Ferry, Southern leaders like Mason, the author of the Fugitive Slave Bill, and chairman of the Harper's Ferry investigating committee; Jefferson Davis, who was a member of this committee; Wise, Hunter and other Virginians, had set their faces toward secession as the only method of protecting slavery. Into the mouths of these men John Brown put a tremendous argument and a fearful warning. The argument they used, the warning they suppressed and hushed. The argument was: This is Abolitionism; this is the North. This is the kind of treatment which the South and its cherished institution can expect unless it resorts to extreme measures. Proceeding along these lines, they emphasized and enlarged the raid so far as its white participants and Northern sympathizers were concerned. Governor Wise, on November 25th, issued a burning manifesto for the ears of the South and the eyes of President Buchanan, and the majority report of the Senate Committee closed with ominous words. On the other hand, the warning of John Brown's raid—the danger of Negro insurrection, was but whispered.

Third, and this was the path that led to Civil War and far beyond: The raid aroused and directed the conscience of the nation. Strange it was to watch its work. Some, impulsive, eager to justify themselves, rushed into print. To Garrison, the non-resistant, the sword of Gideon was abhorrent; Beecher thundered against John Brown and Seward bitterly traduced him. Then came an ominous silence in the land while his voice, in his own defense, was heard over the whole country. A great surging throb of sympathy arose and swept the world. That John Brown was legally a lawbreaker and a murderer all men knew. But wider and wider circles were beginning dimly and more clearly to recognize that his lawlessness was in obedience to the highest call of self-sacrifice for the welfare of his fellow men. They began to ask themselves, What is this cause that can inspire such devotion? The reiteration of the simple statement of "the brother in bonds" could not help but attract attention. The beauty of the conception despite its possible unearthliness and impracticability attracted poet and philosopher and common man.

To be sure, the nation had long been thinking over the problem of the black man, but never before had its attention been held by such deep dramatic and personal interest as in the forty days from mid-October to December, 1859. This arresting of national attention was due to Virginia and to John Brown:—to Virginia by reason of its exaggerated plaint; to John Brown whose strength, simplicity and acumen made his trial, incarceration and execution the most powerful Abolition argument yet offered. The very processes by which Virginia used John Brown to "fire the Southern heart" were used by John Brown to fire the Northern conscience. Andrew Hunter, the prosecuting state's attorney, of right demanded that the trial should be short and the punishment swift and in this John Brown fully agreed. He had no desire to escape the consequences of his act or to clog the wheels of Virginia justice. After a certain moral bewilderment there in the old engine-house at his failure on the brink of success, the true significance of his mission of sacrifice slowly rose before him. In the face of proposals to rescue him he said at first thoughtfully: "I do not know that I ought to encourage any attempt to save my life. I am not sure that it would not be better for me to die at this time. I am not incapable of error, and I may be wrong;

but I think that perhaps my object would be nearer fulfilment if I should die. I must give it some thought." And more and more this conviction seized and thrilled him, and he began to say decisively: "I think I cannot now better serve the cause I love so much than to die for it; and in my death I may do more than in my life."

And again: "I can trust God with both the time and the manner of my death, believing, as I now do, that for me at this time to seal my testimony for God and humanity with my blood will do vastly more toward advancing the cause I have earnestly endeavored to promote, than all I have done in my life before." And then finally came that last great hymn of utter sacrifice: "I feel astonished that one so vile and unworthy as I am would even be suffered to have a place anyhow or anywhere amongst the very least of all who when they came to die (as all must) were permitted to pay the debt of nature in defense of the right and of God's eternal and immutable truth."

The trial was a difficult experience. Virginia attempted to hold scales of even justice between mob violence and the world-wide sympathy of all good men. To defend its domestic institutions, it must try a man for murder when that very man, sitting as self-appointed judge of those very institutions, had convicted them before a jury of mankind. To defend the good name of the state, Virginia had to restrain the violent blood vengeance of men whose kin had been killed in the raid, and who had sworn that no prisoner should escape the extreme penalty. The trial was legally fair but pressed to a conclusion in unseemly haste, and in obedience to a threatening public opinion and a great hovering dread. Only against this unfair haste did John Brown protest, for he wanted the world to understand why he had done the deed. On the other hand, Hunter not only feared the local mob but the slowly arising sentiment for this white-haired crusader. He therefore pushed the proceedings legally, but with almost brutal pertinacity. The prisoner was arraigned while wounded and in bed; the lawyers, hurriedly chosen, were given scant time for consultation or preparation. John Brown was formally committed to jail at Charlestown, the county seat, on October 20th, had a preliminary examination October 25th, and was indicted by the grand jury October 26th, for "conspiracy with slaves for the purpose of insurrection; with treason against the commonwealth of Virginia; and with murder in the first degree."

Thursday, October 27th, his trial was begun. A jury was impaneled without challenge and Brown's lawyers, ignoring his outline of defense, brought in the plea of insanity. The old man arose from his couch and said: "I look upon it as a miserable artifice and pretext of those who ought to take a different course in regard to me, if they took any at all, and I view it with contempt more than otherwise. . . . I am perfectly unconscious of insanity, and I reject, so far as I am capable, any attempts to interfere in my behalf on that score."

On Friday a Massachusetts lawyer arrived to help in the trial and also privately to suggest methods of escape. John Brown quietly refused to contemplate any such attempt, but was glad to accept the aid of this lawyer and two others, who were sent by John A. Andrew and his friends. The judge curtly refused these men any time to prepare their case, but in spite of this it ran over until Monday when the jury retired. Late Monday afternoon they returned. Redpath says:

"At this moment the crowd filled all the space from the couch inside the bar, around the prisoner, beyond the railing in the body of the court, out through the wide hall, and beyond the doors. There stood the anxious but perfectly silent and attentive populace, stretching head and neck to witness the closing scene of old Brown's trial."

The clerk of the court read the indictment and asked: "Gentlemen of the jury, what say you? Is the prisoner at the bar, John Brown, guilty or not guilty?"

"Guilty," answered the foreman.

"Guilty of treason, and conspiring and advising with slaves and others to rebel, and murder in the first degree?"

"Yes."

Redpath continues: "Not the slightest sound was heard in this vast crowd as this verdict was thus returned and read. Not the slightest expression of elation or triumph was uttered from the hundreds present, who, a moment before, outside the court, joined in heaping threats and imprecations on his head; nor was this strange silence interrupted during the whole of the time occupied by the forms of the court. Old Brown himself said not even a word, but, as on any previous day, turned to adjust his pallet, and then composedly stretched himself upon it."

The following Wednesday John Brown was sentenced. Moving with painful steps and pale face, he took his seat under the gaslight in the great square room and remained motionless. The judge read his decision on the points of exception and the clerk asked: "Have you anything to say why sentence of death should not be passed upon you?" Then rising and leaning forward, John Brown made that last great speech, in a voice at once gentle and firm:

"I have, may it please the court, a few words to say.

"In the first place, I deny everything but what I have all along admitted,—the design on my part to free the slaves. I intended certainly to have made a clean thing of that matter, as I did last winter, when I went into Missouri and there took slaves without the snapping of a gun on either side, moved them through the country and finally left them in Canada. I designed to have done the same thing again, on a larger scale. That was all I intended. I never did intend murder, or treason, or the destruction of property, or to excite or incite slaves to rebellion, or to make insurrection.

"I have another objection; and that is, it is unjust that I should suffer such a penalty. Had I interfered in the manner which I admit, and which I admit has been fairly proved (for I admire the truthfulness and candor of the greater portion of the witnesses who have testified in this case),—had I so interfered in behalf of the rich, the powerful, the intelligent, the so-called great, or in behalf of any of their friends,—either father, mother, brother, sister, wife, or children, or any of that class,—and suffered and sacrificed what I have in this interference, it would have been all right; and every man in this court would have deemed it an act worthy of reward rather than punishment.

"This court acknowledges, as I suppose, the validity of the law of God. I see a book kissed here which I suppose to be the Bible, or at least the New Testament. That teaches me that all things whatsoever I would that men should do to me, I should do even so to them. It teaches me, further, to 'remember them that are in bonds, as bound with them.' I endeavored to act up to that instruction. I say, I am yet too young to understand that God is any respecter of persons. I believe that to have interfered as I have done—as I have always freely admitted I have done—in behalf of His despised poor, was not wrong, but right. Now, if it is deemed necessary that I should forfeit my life for the furtherance of the ends of justice, and mingle my blood further with the blood of my children and with the blood of millions in this slave country whose rights are disregarded by wicked, cruel, and unjust enactments,—I submit; so let it be done! Let me say one word further.

"I feel entirely satisfied with the treatment I have received on my trial. Considering all the circumstances, it has been more generous than I expected. But I feel no consciousness of guilt. I have stated from the first what was my intention, and what was not. I never had any design against the life of any person, nor any disposition to commit treason, or excite slaves to rebel, or make any general insurrection. I never encouraged any man to do so, but always discouraged any idea of that kind.

"Let me say, also, a word in regard to the statements made by some of those connected with me. I hear it has been stated by some of them that I have induced them to join me. But the contrary is true. I do not say this to injure them, but as regretting their weakness. There is not one of them but that joined me of his own accord, and the greater part at their own expense. A number of them I never saw, and never had a word of conversation with, till the day they came to me; and that was for the purpose I have stated.

"Now I have done."

The day of his dying, December 2d, dawned glorious; twenty-four hours before he had kissed his wife good-bye, and on this morning he visited his doomed companions—Shields Green and Copeland first; then the wavering Cook and Coppoc and the unmovable Stevens. At last he turned toward the place of his hanging. Since early morning three thousand soldiers had been marching and counter-marching around the scaffold, which had been erected a half mile from Charlestown, encircling it for fifteen miles; a hush sat on the hearts of men. John Brown rode out into the morning. "This is a beautiful land," he said. It was beautiful. Wide, glistening, rolling fields flickered in the sunlight. Beyond, the Shenandoah went rolling northward, and still afar rose the mighty masses of the Blue Ridge, where Nat Turner had fought and died, where Gabriel had looked for refuge and where John Brown had builded his awful dream. Some say he kissed a Negro child as he passed, but Andrew Hunter vehemently denies it. "No Negro could get access to him," he says, and he is probably right; and yet all about him as he hung there knelt the funeral guard he prayed for when he said:

"My love to all who love their neighbors. I have asked to be spared from having any weak or hypocritical prayers made over me when I am publicly murdered, and that my only religious attendants be poor little dirty, ragged, bare-headed, and barefooted slave boys and girls, led by some gray-headed slave mother. Farewell! Farewell!"

The Legacy of John Brown

"Ho, every one that thirsteth, come ye to the waters, and he that hath no money; come ye, buy, and eat; yea, come, buy wine and milk without money and without price."

"I, John Brown, am quite certain that the crimes of this guilty land will never be purged away but with blood. I had, as I now think vainly, flattered myself that without very much bloodshed it might be done."

These were the last written words of John Brown, set down the day he died—the culminating of that wonderful message of his forty days in prison, which all in all made the mightiest Abolition document that America has known. Uttered in chains and solemnity, spoken in the very shadow of death, its dramatic intensity after that wild and puzzling raid, its deep earnestness as embodied in the character of the man, did more to shake the foundations of slavery than any single thing that ever happened in America. Of himself he speaks simply and with satisfaction: "I should be sixty years old were I to live to May 9, 1860. I have enjoyed much of life as it is, and have been remarkably prosperous, having early learned to regard the welfare and prosperity of others as my own. I have never, since I can remember, required a great amount of sleep; so that I conclude that I have already enjoyed full an average number of working hours with those who reach their threescore years and ten. I have not yet been driven to the use of glasses, but can see to read and write quite comfortably. But more than that, I have generally enjoyed remarkably good health. I might go on to recount unnumbered and unmerited blessings, among which would be some very severe afflictions and those the most needed blessings of all. And now, when I think how easily I might be left to spoil all I have done or suffered in the cause of freedom, I hardly dare wish another voyage even if I had the opportunity."

After a surging, trouble-tossed voyage he is at last at peace in body and mind. He asserts that he is and has been in his right mind: "I may be very insane; and I am so, if insane at all. But if that be so, insanity is like a very pleasant dream to me. I am not in the least degree conscious of my ravings, of my fears, or of any terrible visions whatever; but fancy myself entirely composed, and that my sleep, in particular, is as sweet as that of a healthy, joyous little infant. I pray God that He will grant me a continuance of the same calm but delightful dream, until I come to know of those realities which eyes have not seen and which ears have not heard. I have scarce realized that I am in prison or in irons at all. I certainly think I was never more cheerful in my life."

To his family he hands down the legacy of his faith and works: "I beseech you all to live in habitual contentment with moderate circumstances and gains of worldly store, and earnestly to teach this to your children and children's children after you, by example as well as precept." And again: "Be sure to remember and follow my advice, and my example too, so far as it has been consistent with the holy religion of Jesus Christ, in which I remain a most firm and humble believer. Never forget the poor, nor think anything you bestow on them to be lost to you, even though they may be black as Ebedmelech, the Ethiopian eunuch, who cared for Jeremiah in the pit of the dungeon; or as black as the one to whom Philip preached Christ. Be sure to entertain strangers, for thereby some have . . . Remember them that are in bonds as bound with them."

Of his own merit and desert he is modest but firm: "The great bulk of mankind estimate each other's actions and motives by the measure of success or otherwise that attends them through life. By that rule, I have been one of the worst and one of the best of men. I do not claim to have been one of the latter, and I leave it to an impartial tribunal to decide whether the world has been the worse or the better for my living and dying in it."

He has no sense of shame for his action: "I feel no consciousness of guilt in that matter, nor even mortification on account of my imprisonment and irons; I feel perfectly sure that very soon no member of my family will feel any possible disposition to blush on my account."

"I do not feel conscious of guilt in taking up arms; and had it been in behalf of the rich and powerful, the intelligent, the great (as men count greatness), or those who form enactments to suit themselves and corrupt others, or some of their friends, that I interfered, suffered, sacrificed, and fell, it would have been doing very well. But enough of this. These light afflictions, which endure for a moment, shall but work for me a far more exceeding and eternal weight of glory."

With desperate faith he clings to his belief in the providence of an all-wise God: "Under all these terrible calamities, I feel quite cheerful in the assurance that God reigns and will overrule all for His glory and the best possible good."

True is it that the night is dark and his faith at first wavers, yet it rises ever again triumphant: "As I believe most firmly that God reigns, I cannot believe that anything I have done, suffered, or may yet suffer, will be lost to the cause of God or of humanity. And before I began my work at Harper's Ferry, I felt assured that in the worst event it would certainly pay. I often expressed that belief; and I can now see no possible cause to alter my mind. I am not as yet, in the main, at all disappointed. I have been a good deal disappointed as it regards myself in not keeping up to my own plans; but I now feel entirely reconciled to that, even,—for God's plan was infinitely better, no doubt, or I should have kept to my own."

He is, after all, the servant and instrument of the Almighty: "If you do not believe I had a murderous intention (while I know I had not), why grieve so terribly on my account? The scaffold has but few terrors for me. God has often covered my head in the day of battle, and granted me many times deliverances that were almost so miraculous that I can scarce realize their truth; and now, when it seems quite certain that He intends to use me in a different way, shall I not most cheerfully go?"

"I have often passed under the rod of Him whom I call my Father,—and certainly no son ever needed it oftener; and yet I have enjoyed much of life, as I was enabled to discover the secret of this somewhat early. It has been in making the prosperity and happiness of others my own; so that really I have had a great deal of prosperity. I am very prosperous still; and looking forward to a time when 'peace on earth and good-will to men' shall everywhere prevail, I have no murmuring thoughts or envious feelings to fret my mind. I'll praise my Maker with my breath."

"Success is in general the standard of all merit. I have passed my time quite cheerfully; still trusting that neither my life nor my death will prove a total loss. As regards both, however, I am liable to mistake. It affords me some satisfaction to feel conscious of having at least tried to better the condition of those who are always on the under-hill side, and am in hopes of being able to meet the consequences without a murmur. I am endeavoring to get ready for another field of action, where no defeat befalls the truly brave. That 'God reigns,' and most wisely, and controls all events, might, it would seem, reconcile those who believe it to much that appears to be very disastrous. I am one who has tried to believe that, and still keep trying."

"I cannot remember a night so dark as to have hindered the coming day, nor a storm so furious or dreadful as to prevent the return of warm sunshine and a cloudless sky."

More and more his eyes pierce the gloom and see the vast plan for which God has used him and the glory of his sacrifice:

"'He shall begin to deliver Israel out of the hands of the Philistines.' This was said of a poor erring servant many years ago; and for many years I have felt a strong impression that God had given me powers and faculties, unworthy as I was, that He intended to use for a similar purpose. This most unmerited honor He has seen fit to bestow; and whether, like the same poor frail man to whom I allude, my death may not be of vastly more value than my life is, I think quite beyond all human foresight."

"I think I feel as happy as Paul did when he lay in prison. He knew if they killed him, it would greatly advance the cause of Christ; that was the reason he rejoiced so. On that same ground 'I do rejoice, yea, and will rejoice.' Let them hang me; I forgive them, and may God forgive them, for they know not what they do. I have no regret for the transaction for which I am condemned. I went against the laws of men, it is true, but 'whether it be right to obey God or men, judge ye.'"

"When and in what form death may come is but of small moment. I feel just as content to die for God's eternal truth and for suffering humanity on the scaffold as in any other way; and I do not say this from disposition to 'brave it out.' No; I would readily own my wrong were I in the least convinced of it. I have now been confined over a month, with a good opportunity to look the whole thing as 'fair in the face' as I am capable of doing; and I feel it most grateful that I am counted in the least possible degree worthy to suffer for the truth."

"I can trust God with both the time and the manner of my death, believing, as I now do, that for me at this time to seal my testimony for God and humanity with my blood will do vastly more toward advancing the cause I have earnestly endeavored to promote, than all I have done in my life before."

"My whole life before had not afforded me one-half the opportunity to plead for the right. In this, also, I find much to reconcile me to both my present condition and my immediate prospect."

Against slavery his face is set like flint: "There are no ministers of Christ here. These ministers who profess to be Christian, and hold slaves or advocate slavery, I cannot abide them. My knees will not bend in prayer with them, while their hands are stained with the blood of souls." He said to one Southern clergyman: "I will thank you to leave me alone; your prayers would be an abomination to God." To another he said, "I would not insult God by bowing down in prayer with any one who had the blood of the slave on his skirts."

And to a third who argued in favor of slavery as "a Christian institution," John Brown replied impatiently: "My dear sir, you know nothing about Christianity; you will have to learn its A, B, C; I find you quite ignorant of what the word Christianity means. . . I respect you as a gentleman, of course; but it is as a heathen gentleman."

To his children he wrote: "Be determined to know by experience, as soon as may be, whether Bible instruction is of divine origin or not. Be sure to owe no man anything, but to love one another. John Rogers wrote his children, 'Abhor that arrant whore of Rome.' John Brown writes to his children to abhor, with undying hatred also, that sum of all villanies,—slavery."

And finally he rejoiced: "Men cannot imprison, or chain, or hang the soul. I go joyfully in behalf of millions that 'have no rights' that this great and glorious, this Christian republic 'is bound to respect.' Strange change in morals, political as well as Christian, since 1776."

"No formal will can be of use," he wrote on his dooms-day, "when my expressed wishes are made known to my dutiful and beloved family."

This was the man. His family is the world. What legacy did he leave? It was soon seen that his voice was a call to the great final battle with slavery.

In the spring of 1861 the Boston Light Infantry was sent to Fort Warren in Boston harbor to drill. A quartette was formed among the soldiers to sing patriotic songs and for them was contrived the verses,

> "John Brown's body lies a-mouldering in the grave,
>   His soul is marching on," etc.

This was set to the music of an old camp-meeting tune—possibly of Negro origin—called, "Say, Brother, Will You Meet Us?" The regiment learned it and first sang it publicly when it came up from Fort Warren and marched past the scene where Crispus Attucks fell.

Gilmore's Band learned and played it and thus "the song of John Brown was started on its eternal way!"

Was John Brown simply an episode, or was he an eternal truth? And if a truth, how speaks that truth to-day? John Brown loved his neighbor as himself. He could not endure therefore to see his neighbor, poor, unfortunate or oppressed. This natural sympathy was strengthened by a saturation in Hebrew religion which stressed the personal responsibility of every human soul to a just God. To this religion of equality and sympathy with misfortune, was added the strong influence of the social doctrines of the French Revolution with its emphasis on freedom and power in political life. And on all this was built John Brown's own inchoate but growing belief in a more just and a more equal distribution of property. From this he concluded,— and acted on that conclusion—that all men are created free and equal and that the cost of liberty is less than the price of repression.

Up to the time of John Brown's death this doctrine was a growing, conquering, social thing. Since then there has come a change and many would rightly find reason for that change in the coincidence that the year in which John Brown suffered martyrdom was the year that first published the *Origin of Species*. Since that day tremendous scientific and economic advance has been accompanied by distinct signs of moral retrogression in social philosophy. Strong arguments have been made for the fostering of war, the utility of human degradation and disease, and the inevitable and known inferiority of certain classes and races of men. While such arguments have not stopped the efforts of the advocates of peace, the workers for social uplift and the believers in human brotherhood, they have, it must be confessed, made their voices falter and tinged their arguments with apology.

Why is this? It is because the splendid scientific work of Darwin, Weissman, Galton and others has been widely interpreted as meaning that there is essential and inevitable inequality among men and races of men, which no philanthropy can or ought to eliminate; that civilization is a struggle for existence whereby the weaker nations and individuals will gradually succumb, and the strong will inherit the earth. With this interpretation has gone the silent assumption that the white European stock represents the strong surviving peoples, and that the swarthy, yellow and black peoples are the ones rightly doomed to eventual extinction.

One can easily see what influence such a doctrine would have on the race problem in America. It meant moral revolution in the attitude of the nation. Those that stepped into the pathway marked by men like John Brown faltered and large numbers turned back. They said: He was a good man—even great, but he has no message for us to-day—he was a "belated Covenanter," an anachronism in the age of Darwin, one who gave his life to lift not the unlifted but the unliftable. We have consequently the present reaction—a reaction which says in effect, Keep these black people in their places, and do not attempt to treat a Negro simply as a white man with a black face; to do this would mean the moral deterioration of the race and the nation—a fate against which a divine racial prejudice is successfully fighting. This is the attitude of the larger portion of our thinking people.

It is not, however, an attitude that has brought mental rest or social peace. On the contrary, it is to-day involving a degree of moral strain and political and social anomaly that gives the wisest pause. The chief difficulty has been that the natural place in which by scientific law the black race in America should stay, cannot easily be determined. To be sure, the freedmen did not, as the philanthropists of the sixties apparently expected, step in forty years from slavery to nineteenth century civilization. Neither, on the other hand, did they, as the ex-masters confidently predicted, retrograde and die. Contrary to both these views, they chose a third and apparently quite unawaited way. From the great, sluggish, almost imperceptibly moving mass, they sent off larger and larger numbers of faithful workmen and artisans, some merchants and professional men, and even men of educational ability and discernment. They developed no world geniuses, no millionaires, no great captains of industry, no artists of the first rank; but they did in forty years get rid of the greater part of their total illiteracy, accumulate a half-billion dollars of property in small homesteads, and gain now and then respectful attention in the world's ears and eyes. It has been argued that this progress of the black man in America is due to the exceptional men among them and does not measure the ability of the mass. Such an admission is, however, fatal to the whole argument. If the doomed races of men are going to develop exceptions to the rule of inferiority, then no rule, scientific or moral, should or can proscribe the race as such.

To meet this difficulty in racial philosophy, a step has been taken in America fraught with the gravest social consequences to the world, and threatening not simply the political but the moral integrity of the nation; that step is denying in the case of black men the validity of those evidences of culture, ability, and decency which are accepted unquestionably in the case of other people; and by vague assertions, unprovable assumptions, unjust emphasis, and now and then by deliberate untruth, aiming to secure not only the continued proscription of all these people, but, by caste distinction, to shut in the faces of their rising classes many of the paths to further advance.

When a social policy, based on a supposed scientific sanction, leads to such a moral anomaly, it is time to examine rather carefully the logical foundations of the argument. And as soon as we do this many things are clear: First, assuming the truth of the unproved dictum that there are stocks of human beings whose elimination the best welfare of the world demands, it is certainly questionable if these stocks include the majority of mankind; and it is indefensible and monstrous to pretend that we know to-day with any reasonable assurance which these stocks are. We can point to degenerate individuals and families here and there among all races, but there is not the slightest warrant for assuming that there does not lie among the Chinese and Hindus, the African Bantus and American Indians as lofty possibilities of human culture as any European race has ever exhibited. It is, to be sure, puzzling to know why the Soudan should linger a thousand years in culture behind the valley of the Seine, but it is no more puzzling than the fact that the valley of the Thames was miserably backward as compared with the banks of the Tiber. Climate, human contact, facilities of communication and what we call accident, have played a great part in the rise of culture among nations: to ignore these and assert dogmatically that the present distribution of culture is a fair index of the distribution of human ability and desert, is to make an assertion for which there is not the slightest scientific warrant.

What the age of Darwin has done is to add to the eighteenth century idea of individual worth the complementary idea of physical immortality. And this, far from annulling or contracting the idea of human freedom, rather emphasizes its necessity and eternal possibility— the boundlessness and endlessness of human achievement. Freedom has come to mean not individual caprice or aberration, but social self-realization in an endless chain of selves; and freedom for such development is not the denial but the central assertion of the evolutionary theory. So, too, the doctrine of human equality passes through the fire of scientific inquiry, not obliterated but transfigured: not equality of present attainment but equality of opportunity, for unbounded future attainment is the rightful demand of mankind.

What now does the present hegemony of the white races threaten? It threatens by means of brute force a survival of some of the worst stocks of mankind. It attempts to people the best parts of the earth and put in absolute authority over the rest, not usually (and indeed not mainly) the culture of Europe but its greed and degradation—not only some representatives of the best stocks of the West End of London, upper New York and the Champs Elysées, but also, in as large if not larger numbers, the worst stocks of Whitechapel, the East Side and Montmartre; and it essays to make the slums of white society in all cases and under all circumstances the superior of any colored group, no matter what its ability or culture. To be sure, this outrageous program of wholesale human degeneration is not outspoken yet, save in the backward civilizations of the Southern United States, South Africa and Australia. But its enunciation is listened to with respect and tolerance in England, Germany, and the Northern states by those very persons who accuse philanthropy with seeking to degrade holy white blood by an infiltration of colored strains. And the average citizen is voting ships and guns to carry out this program.

This movement gathered force and strength during the latter half of the nineteenth century and reached its culmination when France, Germany, England and Russia began the partition of China and the East. With the sudden self-assertion of Japan, its wildest dreams collapsed, but it is still to-day a living, virile, potent force and motive, the most subtle and dangerous enemy of world peace and the dream of human brotherhood. It has a whole vocabulary of its own: the strong races, superior peoples, race preservation, the struggle for survival and a variety of terms meaning the right of white men of any kind to beat blacks into submission, make them surrender their wealth and the use of their women and submit to dictation without murmur, for the sake of being swept off the fairest portions of the earth or held there in perpetual serfdom or guardianship. Ignoring the fact that the era of physical struggle for survival has passed away among human beings, and that there is plenty of room accessible on earth for all, this theory makes the possession of Krupp guns the main criterion of mental stamina and moral fitness.

Even armed with this morality of the club, and every advantage of modern culture, the white races have been unable to possess the earth. Many signs of degeneracy have appeared among them: their birth-rate is falling, their average ability is not increasing, their physical stamina is impaired, and their social condition is not reassuring. Lacking the physical ability to take possession of the world, they are to-day fencing in America, Australia, and South Africa and declaring that no dark race shall occupy or develop the land which they themselves are unable to use. And all this on the plea that their stock is threatened with deterioration from without, when in reality its most dangerous threat is deterioration from within.

We are, in fact, to-day repeating in our intercourse between races all the former evils of class distinction within the nation: personal hatred and abuse, mutual injustice, unequal taxation and rigid caste. Individual nations outgrew these fatal things by breaking down the horizontal barriers between classes. We are bringing them back by seeking to erect vertical barriers between races. Men were told that abolition of compulsory class distinction meant leveling down, degradation, disappearance of culture and genius and the triumph of the mob. As a matter of fact, it has been the salvation of European civilization. Some deterioration and leveling there was but it was more than balanced by the discovery of new reservoirs of ability and strength. So to-day we are told that free racial contact—or "social equality" as Southern *patois* has it—means contamination of blood and lowering of ability and culture. It need mean nothing of the sort. Abolition of class distinction did not mean universal intermarriage of stocks, but rather the survival of the fittest by peaceful, personal and social selection—a selection all the more effective because free democracy and equality of opportunity allow the best to rise to their rightful place. The same is true in racial contact. Vertical race distinctions are even more emphatic hindrances to human evolution than horizontal class distinctions, and their tearing away involves fewer chances of degradation and greater opportunities of human betterment than in case of class lines. On the other hand, persistence in racial distinction spells disaster sooner or later. The earth is growing smaller and more accessible. Race contact will become in the future increasingly inevitable not only in America, Asia, and Africa but even in Europe. The color line will mean not simply a return to the absurdities of class as exhibited in the sixteenth and seventeenth centuries, but even to the caste of ancient days. This, however, the Japanese, the Chinese, the East Indians and the Negroes are going to resent in just such proportion as they gain the power; and they are gaining the power, and they cannot be kept from gaining more power. The price of repression will then be hypocrisy and slavery and blood.

This is the situation to-day. Has John Brown no message—no legacy, then, to the twentieth century? He has and it is this great word: the cost of liberty is less than the price of repression. The price of repressing the world's darker races is shown in a moral retrogression and an economic waste unparalelled since the age of the African slave-trade. What would be the cost of liberty? what would be the cost of giving the great stocks of mankind every reasonable help and incentive to self-development—opening the avenues of opportunity freely, spreading knowledge, suppressing war and cheating, and treating men and women as equals the world over whenever and wherever they attain equality? It would cost something. It would cost something in pride and prejudice, for eventually many a white man would be blacking black men's boots; but this cost we may ignore— its greatest cost would be the new problems of racial intercourse and intermarriage which would come to the front. Freedom and equal opportunity in this respect would inevitably bring some intermarriage of whites and yellows and browns and blacks. This might be a good thing and it might not be. We do not know. Our belief on the matter may be strong and even frantic, but it has no adequate scientific foundation. If such marriages are proven inadvisable, how could they be stopped? Easily. We associate with cats and cows, but we do not fear intermarriage with them, even though they be given all freedom of development. So, too, intelligent human beings can be trained to breed intelligently without the degradation of such of their fellows as they may not wish to breed with. In the Southern United States, on the contrary, it is assumed that unwise marriages can be stopped only by the degradation of the blacks—the classing of all darker women with prostitutes, the loading of a whole race with every badge of public isolation, degradation and contempt, and by burning offenders at the stake. Is this civilization? No. The civilized method of preventing ill-advised marriage lies in the training of mankind in the ethics of sex and child-bearing. We cannot ensure the survival of the best blood by the public murder and degradation of unworthy suitors, but we can substitute a civilized human selection of husbands and wives which shall ensure the survival of the fittest. Not the methods of the jungle, not even the careless choices of the drawing-room, but the thoughtful selection of the schools and laboratory is the ideal of future marriage. This will cost something in ingenuity, self-control and toleration, but it will cost less than forcible repression.

Not only is the cost of repression to-day large—it is a continually increasing cost: the procuring of coolie labor, the ruling of India, the exploitation of Africa, the problem of the unemployed, and the curbing of the corporations, are a tremendous drain on modern society with no near end in sight. The cost is not merely in wealth but in social progress and spiritual strength, and it tends ever to explosion, murder, and war. All these things but increase the difficulty of beginning a regime of freedom in human growth and development—they raise the cost of liberty. Not only that but the very explosions, like the Russo-Japanese War, which bring partial freedom, tend in the complacent current philosophy to prove the wisdom of repression. "Blood will tell," men say. "The fit will survive; stop up the tea-kettle and eventually the steam will burst the iron," and therefore only the steam that bursts is worth the generating; only organized murder proves the fitness of a people for liberty. This is a fearful and dangerous doctrine. It encourages wrong leadership and perverted ideals at the very time when loftiest and most unselfish striving is called for—as witness Japan after her emancipation, or America after the Civil War. Conversely, it leads the shallow and unthinking to brand as demagogue and radical every group leader who in the day of slavery and struggle cries out for freedom.

For such reasons it is that the memory of John Brown stands to-day as a mighty warning to his country. He saw, he felt in his soul the wrong and danger of that most daring and insolent system of human repression known as American slavery. He knew that in 1700 it would have cost something to overthrow slavery and establish liberty; and that by reason of cowardice and blindness the cost in 1800 was vastly larger but still not unpayable. He felt that by 1900 no human hand could pluck the vampire from the body of the land without doing the nation to death. He said, in 1859, "Now is the accepted time." Now is the day to strike for a free nation. It will cost something—even blood and suffering, but it will not cost as much as waiting. And he was right. Repression bred repression—serfdom bred slavery until in 1861 the South was farther from freedom than in 1800.

The edict of 1863 was the first step in emancipation and its cost in blood and treasure was staggering. But that was not all—it was only a first step. There were other bills to pay of material reconstruction, social regeneration, mental training and moral uplift. These the nation started to meet in the Fifteenth Amendment, the Freedman's Bureau, the crusade of school-teachers and the Civil Rights Bill. But the effort was great and the determination of the South to pay no single cent or deed for past error save by force, led in the revolution of 1876 to the triumph of reaction. Reaction meant and means a policy of state, society and individual, whereby no American of Negro blood shall ever come into the full freedom of modern culture. In the carrying out of this program by certain groups and sections, no pains have been spared—no expenditure of money, ingenuity, physical or moral strength. The building of barriers around these black men has been pushed with an energy so desperate and unflagging that it has seriously checked the great outpouring of benevolence and sympathy that greeted the freedman in 1863. It has come so swathed and gowned in graciousness as to disarm philanthropy and chill enthusiasm. It has used double-tongued argument with deadly effect. Has the Negro advanced? Beware his further strides. Has the Negro retrograded? It is his fate, why seek to help him? Thus has the spirit of repression gained attention, complacent acquiescence, and even coöperation. To be sure, there still stand staunch souls who cannot yet believe the doctrine of human repression, and who pour out their wealth for Negro training and freedom in the face of the common cry. But the majority of Americans seem to have forgotten the foundation principles of their government and the recklessly destructive effect of the blows meant to bind and tether their fellows. We have come to see a day here in America when one citizen can deprive another of his vote at his discretion; can restrict the education of his neighbors' children as he sees fit; can with impunity load his neighbor with public insult on the king's highway; can deprive him of his property without due process of law; can deny him the right of trial by his peers, or of any trial whatsoever if he can get a large enough group of men to join him; can refuse to protect or safeguard the integrity of the family of some men whom he dislikes; finally, can not only close the door of opportunity in commercial and social lines in a fully competent neighbor's face, but can actually count on the national and state governments to help and make effective this discrimination.

Such a state of affairs is not simply disgraceful; it is deeply and increasingly dangerous. Not only does the whole nation feel already the loosening of joints which these vicious blows on human liberty have caused—lynching, lawlessness, lying and stealing, bribery and divorce—but it can look for darker deeds to come.

And this not merely because of the positive harm of this upbuilding of barriers, but above all because within these bursting barriers are men—human forces which no human hand can hold. It is human force and aspiration and endeavor which are moving there amid the creaking of timbers and writhing of souls. It is human force that has already done in a generation the work of many centuries. It has saved over a half-billion dollars in property, bought and paid for landed estate half the size of all England, and put homes thereon as good and as pure as the homes of any corresponding economic class the world around; it has crowded eager children through a wretched and half-furnished school system until from an illiteracy of seventy per cent., two-thirds of the living adults can read and write. These proscribed millions have 50,000 professional men, 200,000 men in trade and transportation, 275,000 artisans and mechanics, 1,250,000 servants and 2,000,000 farmers working with the nation to earn its daily bread. These farmers raise yearly on their own and hired farms over 4,000,000 bales of cotton, 25,000,000 pounds of rice, 10,000,000 bushels of potatoes, 90,000,000 pounds of tobacco and 100,000,000 bushels of corn, besides that for which they labor on the farms of others. They have given America music, inspired art and literature, made its bread, dug its ditches, fought its battles, and suffered in its misfortunes. The great mass of these men is becoming daily more thoroughly organized, more deeply self-critical, more conscious of its power. Threatened though it has been naturally, as a proletariat, with degeneration and disease, it is to-day reducing its death-rate and beginning organized rescue of its delinquents and defectives. The mass can still to-day be called ignorant, poor and but moderately efficient, but it is daily growing better trained, richer and more intelligent. And as it grows it is sensing more and more the vantage-ground which it holds as a defender of the right of the freedom of human development for black men in the midst of a centre of modern culture. It sees its brothers in yellow, black and brown held physically at arms' length from civilization lest they become civilized and less liable to conquest and exploitation. It sees the world-wide effort to build an aristocracy of races and nations on a foundation of darker half-enslaved and tributary peoples. It knows that the last great battle of the West is to vindicate the right of any man of any nation, race, or color to share in the world's goods and thoughts and efforts to the extent of his effort and ability.

Thus to-day the Negro American faces his destiny and doggedly strives to realize it. He has his tempters and temptations. There are ever those about him whispering: "You are nobody; why strive to be somebody? The odds are overwhelming against you—wealth, tradition, learning and guns. Be reasonable. Accept the dole of charity and the cant of missionaries and sink contentedly to your place as humble servants and helpers of the white world." If this has not been effective, threats have been used: "If you continue to complain, we will withdraw all aid, boycott your labor, cease to help support your schools and let you die and disappear from the land in ignorance, crime and disease." Still the black man has pushed on, has continued to protest, has refused to die out and disappear, and to-day stands as physically the most virile element in America, intellectually among the most promising, and morally the most tremendous and insistent of the social problems of the New World. Not even the silence of his friends, or of those who ought to be the friends of struggling humanity, has silenced him. Not even the wealth of modern Golconda has induced him to believe that life without liberty is worth living.

On the other side heart-searching is in order. It is not well with this land of ours: poverty is certainly not growing less, wealth is being wantonly wasted, business honesty is far too rare, family integrity is threatened, bribery is poisoning our public life, theft is honeycombing our private business, and voting is largely unintelligent. Not that these evils are unopposed. There are brave men and women striving for social betterment, for the curbing of the vicious power of wealth, for the uplift of women and the downfall of thieves. But their battle is hard, and how much harder because of the race problem—because of the calloused conscience of caste, the peonage of black labor hands, the insulting of black women, and the stealing of black votes? How far are business dishonesty and civic degradation in America the direct result of racial prejudice?

Well do I know that many persons defend their treatment of undeveloped peoples on the highest grounds. They say, as Jefferson Davis intimated, that liberty is for the full-grown; not for children. It was during Senator Mason's inquisition after the hanging of John Brown, whereby the Southern leader hoped to entrap the Abolitionists. Joshua R. Giddings, keen, impetuous and fiery, was on the rack. Senator Davis, pale, sallow and imperturbable, with all the aristocratic poise and dignity built on the unpaid toil of two centuries of slaves, said:

"Did you, in inculcating, by popular lectures, the doctrine of a law higher than that of the social compact, make your application exclusively to Negro slaves, or did you also include minors, convicts, and lunatics, who might be restrained of their liberty by the laws of the land?"

Mr. Giddings smiled. "Permit me," he said, ". . . with all due deference, to suggest, so that I may understand you, do you intend to inquire whether those lectures would indicate whether your slaves of the slave states had a right at all times to their liberty?"

"I will put the question in that form if you like it," answered Davis, and then Giddings flashed:

"My lectures, in all instances, would indicate the right of every human soul in the enjoyment of reason, while he is charged with no crime or offense, to maintain his life, his liberty, the pursuit of his own happiness; that this has reference to the enslaved of all the states as much as it had reference to our own people while enslaved by the Algerines in Africa."

But Mr. Davis suavely pressed his point: "Then the next question is, whether the same right was asserted for minors and apprentices, being men in good reason, yet restrained of their liberty by the laws of the land."

Giddings replied: "I will answer at once that the proposition or comparison is conflicting with the dictates of truth. The minor is, from the law of nature, under the restraints of parental affection for the purposes of nurture, of education, of preparing him to secure and maintain the very rights to which I refer."

This debate is not yet closed. It was not closed by the Civil War. Men still maintain that East Indians and Africans and others ought to be under the restraint and benevolent tutelage of stronger and wiser nations for their own benefit. Well and good. Is the tutelage really benevolent? Then it is training in liberty. Is it training in slavery? Then it is not benevolent. Liberty trains for liberty. Responsibility is the first step in responsibility.

Even the restraints imposed in the training of men and children are restraints that will in the end make greater freedom possible. Is the benevolent expansion of to-day of such a character? Is England trying to see how soon and how effectively the Indians can be trained for self-government or is she willing to exploit them just so long as they can be cajoled or quieted into submission? Is Germany trying to train her Africans to modern citizenship or to modern "work without complaint?" Is the South trying to make the Negroes responsible, self-reliant freemen of a republic, or the dumb driven cattle of a great industrial machine?

No sooner is the question put this way than the defenders of modern caste retire behind a more defensible breastwork. They say: "Yes, we exploit nations for our own advantage purposely—even at times brutally. But only in that way can the high efficiency of the modern industrial process be maintained, and in the long run it benefits the oppressed even more than the oppressor." This doctrine is as widespread as it is false and mischievous. It is true that the bribe of greed will artificially hasten economic development, but it does so at fearful cost, as America itself can testify. We have here a wonderful industrial machine, but a machine quickly rather than carefully built, formed of forcing rather than of growth, involving sinful and unnecessary expense. Better smaller production and more equitable distribution; better fewer miles of railway and more honor, truth, and liberty; better fewer millionaires and more contentment. So it is the world over, where force and fraud and graft have extorted rich reward from writhing millions. Moreover, it is historically unprovable that the advance of undeveloped peoples has been helped by wholesale exploitation at the hands of their richer, stronger, and more unscrupulous neighbors. This idea is a legend of the long exploded doctrine of inevitable economic harmonies in all business life. True it is that adversity and difficulties make for character, but the real and inevitable difficulties of life are numerous enough for genuine development without the aid of artificial hindrances. The inherent and natural difficulties of raising a people from ignorant unmoral slavishness to self-reliant modern manhood are great enough for purposes of character-building without the aid of murder, theft, caste, and degradation. Not because of but in spite of these latter hindrances has the Negro-American pressed forward.

This, then, is the truth: the cost of liberty is less than the price of repression, even though that cost be blood. Freedom of development and equality of opportunity is the demand of Darwinism and this calls for the abolition of hard and fast lines between races, just as it called for the breaking down of barriers between classes. Only in this way can the best in humanity be discovered and conserved, and only thus can mankind live in peace and progress. The present attempt to force all whites above all darker peoples is a sure method of human degeneration. The cost of liberty is thus a decreasing cost, while the cost of repression ever tends to increase to the danger point of war and revolution. Revolution is not a test of capacity; it is always a loss and a lowering of ideals.

But if it is a true revolution it repays all losses and results in the uplift of the human race. One could wish that John Brown could see today the results of the great revolution in Russia; that he could see the new world of Socialism and Communism expanding until it already comprises the majority of mankind; until it has conquered the problem of poverty, made vast inroads on the problem of ignorance and even begun to put to flight the problem of avoidable disease. It has abolished unemployment and is approaching the great day when all men will do for the world what they are best suited to do and will receive in return from the world not all that they want but everything that each man needs.

The greatest source of human rejoicing today is the phenomenal rise of the people of Russia. From an ignorant, despised, suppressed peasantry they have in less than a century become in many respects the leading nation of the world. They have abolished poverty and from the masses have risen an extraordinary number of gifted men. Their system of education surpasses that of any other part of the world and their scientific contribution during the Twentieth Century is among the wonders of mankind.

To this must be added the resurrection of China. This largest nation in the world is rushing forward with unexampled speed and efficiency. Despite the effort of the United States to dismember it, lie about it, and keep it out of the United Nations, it is becoming one of the greatest modern nations.

These are the dates whose events conditioned John Brown and his acts. Beginning with the Battle of Plassy in 1757 the loot of India began to pour into England. In 1769 the steam engine was invented and in 1793, the cotton gin. Between 1784 and 1804 the Sugar Empire in the West Indies began to disintegrate and former slaves and free Negroes controlled Haiti. For this reason and because of the revolt of the British conscience against the cruelties of the trade, in 1808 the British made the African slave trade illegal and other nations including the United States slowly followed. In 1820 the Cotton Kingdom in the United States began to rise, reaching its zenith in 1860. The cotton crop increased from a half million bales in 1822 to five million bales in 1860. All this meant a world change in the production and distribution of goods. Capital increased immensely in the hands of private owners and their subsequent control of labor in industry became almost complete.

The French Revolution had demanded freedom for the individual—the liberty to do as he pleased for what he considered his own good and the consequent good of mankind. But in the Nineteenth Century this freedom rapidly became license for private owners of capital to control industry and income and thus rule mankind. In the first half of the Nineteenth Century, in 1848, Karl Marx and Frederick Engels called attention to this state of affairs in their Communist Manifesto which later Marx further developed in his great work on capital.

In the United States where John Brown lived the demand for "freedom" was still paramount and could be widely realized because land was free and there was an abundance of labor. John Brown never read the Communist Manifesto and knew little of the rise of Socialism. But he did realize that a suppressed and exploited part of the laboring class in America—the Negroes— had been deprived by capitalists and land monopolists of the freedom to earn *a living and to direct their lives which was vital in John Brown's mind to a human being. He espoused therefore the freedom of the slave knowing well that freedom alone was not the settlement of the Negro problem; that this must be followed by education, the right to vote, and treatment as human beings. But all this he assumed was inherent in the American system and would follow the freedom of the slaves. Then in the year that he was crucified came Darwin's* Origin of Species *and gradually a changed attitude of science toward human beings. At the same time many assumed that the doctrine of race superiority was a logical deduction from the doctrine of evolution, but Karl Marx would easily prove the contrary. The Industrial Revolution had taken place in the Nineteenth Century which increased the amount of capital in private hands and this coupled with an extraordinary technical advance and new widely desired materials like sugar and cotton made great increase of wealth under private control possible. It was this itch for larger private capital in Britain and France together with the sugar monopoly in the West Indies and the Cotton Kingdom in the United States that made West Europe and North America seek scientific justification for despising the mass of mankind and refusing to admit them to the new democracy. Those who desired large incomes through ownership of capital used Darwin's doctrine to excuse the growing reduction of the majority of the world's laborers to the cheap use of their toil and land for the increasing profit of capitalism. The result was colonial imperialism built on the new technique of Western industry, fed by free land and raw materials in Asia and Africa and especially capped by the cheapest of labor.*

The state impelled by the capitalists seized control of colonies using the labor in Asia and Africa and the islands of the seas instead of transporting it to America. By the use of this capital in far-off colonies the absentee landlord was replaced by the absentee investor so that the owners of capital knew less and less how their capital was used and were rewarded for this ignorance by increase of profit. This is characteristic of the capitalist system in this day. Owners do not know and gradually begin not to care how their capital is used so long as their income is assured and increases. The Western world consciously or unconsciously depends for its civilization, comfort and luxury on the low wage of colonial labor and the seizure of colonial land and materials. As a result of this we have war to force new divisions in the ownership of colonies and war between colonies and imperial powers.

All this John Brown did not know and could not foresee, but nevertheless he left a clear legacy: First, the right of the enslaved to repel oppression. Then beyond this a new attitude toward human beings and belief in the abilities and character of the great mass of mankind. Even then as Lenin has shown must come a plan of life and work which will ensure the best interests of the masses and a discipline and dictation which shall through education and force compel the workers to follow and activate these plans. Out of this will arise a new interpretation of the word freedom. There must be left a wide individualism and yet no individual must be allowed to infringe upon another's freedom. In other words, the future world will not be free in the sense that anyone can do what he pleases, but freedom in the larger sense of having his acts work for the best interests of the peoples of the world.

All this John Brown did not know and yet his life's work was in consonance with it. He believed in the abilities and worth of the souls of black folk. He believed in the gifts that they would be able to furnish America and he regarded them as equals to all Americans of any color. He believed that men should labor for what they earned and should not get their income by chance or inheritance. He believed in the freedom of the land and its fruits to be distributed in accord with the labor which was put upon it. Thus be was a pioneer in the fight for human equality and in the uplift of the masses of men.

There can be no doubt that the progress of the emancipated slave in the United States since 1863 has been phenomenal. He has touched every phase of American development. He has furnished subjects for American writers and thinkers and himself contributed to American art, music, and literature. He has given the nation invaluable labor and service, has taken notable part in the advance of science and discovery and without his own work, American industry could never have reached the heights which it has. The American Department of State in its desperate effort to fight Socialism and Communism has sought to emphasize Negro progress and has paid out considerable sums of money to bribe Negroes and induce them to travel and praise America in various parts of the world. Despite this, however, it is perfectly clear that while Negro progress has been great, it has not been nearly as rapid as it might have been had the Negro received decent treatment. He has been deliberately paid a lower wage than whites doing the same work or than immigrants from abroad. He has been denied preferment and promotion in industry; kept out of scientific laboratories; discriminated against in scholarships and often actually beaten to submission to superior force and impudent assumption. If American Negroes had been given the chance that the Russian peasant has had since 1917 his contribution to the uplift of the world might easily have been startling. The repression and discrimination which he has met has held back the progress of the United States and the world and is a thing of which this country must always be ashamed.

In murder and unjust punishment America has made a disgraceful record against the Negro race. Between 1882 and 1900, the whites lynched without trial four thousand Negroes besides killing more than ten thousand by mobs. When public opinion stopped lynching, injustice in the courts succeeded.

A Negro had only to be arrested, to be found guilty and convicted in most Southern courts and many Northern. Three times as many Negroes in proportion to population go to prison as whites. Among children twice as many Negroes are arrested as delinquent. Half the prisoners serving life sentences and half those executed in the nation are Negroes who form but a tenth of our population. There is certainly crime among Negroes but it does not exceed that of the whites in anything like this proportion. The chief crime of Negro prisoners is the color of their skin. Not all America has approved or encouraged this injustice. Many have helped and defended the Negro, but the majority have permitted injustice without protest.

John Brown taught us that the cheapest price to pay for liberty is its cost to-day. The building of barriers against the advance of Negro-Americans hinders but in the end cannot altogether stop their progress. The excuse of benevolent tutelage cannot be urged, for that tutelage is not benevolent that does not prepare for free responsible manhood. Nor can the efficiency of greed as an economic developer be proven—it may hasten development but it does so at the expense of solidity of structure, smoothness of motion, and real efficiency. Nor does selfish exploitation help the undeveloped; rather it hinders and weakens them.

It is now a *full century* since this white-haired old man lay weltering in the blood which he spilled for broken and despised humanity. Let the nation which he loved and the South to which he spoke, reverently listen again to-day to those words, as prophetic now as then:

"You had better—all you people of the South—prepare yourselves for a settlement of this question. It must come up for settlement sooner than you are prepared for it, and the sooner you commence that preparation, the better for you. You may dispose of me very easily—I am nearly disposed of now; but this question is still to be settled—this Negro question, I mean. The end of that is not yet."